FOOD LOVERS'
GUIDE TO
SONOMA

Help Us Keep This Guide Up to Date

We would love to hear from you concerning your experiences with this guide and how you feel it could be improved and kept up to date. Please send your comments and suggestions to:

editorial@GlobePequot.com

Thanks for your input, and happy travels!

FOOD LOVERS' SERIES

FOOD LOVERS'
GUIDE TO
SONOMA

The Best Restaurants, Markets & Local Culinary Offerings

1st Edition

Jean Saylor Doppenberg

gpp

Guilford, Connecticut

Editor: Amy Lyons
Project Editor: Lynn Zelem
Layout Artist: Mary Ballachino
Text Design: Sheryl Kober
Illustrations by Jill Butler with additional art by Carleen Moira Powell and MaryAnn Dubé
Map: Melissa Baker © Morris Book Publishing, LLC

ISBN 978-0-7627-7947-5

Printed in the United States of America
10 9 8 7 6 5 4 3 2 1

All the information in this guidebook is subject to change. We recommend that you call ahead to obtain current information before traveling.

Contents

Recipes, 263

About the Author

Raised on an acreage with thousands of chickens and an enormous vegetable garden, Jean Saylor Doppenberg dined on farm-fresh food from an early age. As a child she enjoyed many stolen moments in the garden devouring peas right out of the pod when she was supposed to be pulling weeds. A Sonoma County resident for more than 20 years, she is also the author of the *Food Lovers' Guide to Napa Valley* and the *Insiders' Guide to California's Wine Country*. She's also written about food for the *Napa Valley Register*.

Acknowledgments

One of the most difficult tasks for an author is thanking the people who helped to bring a first-edition book to market. It's not the thanking that's hard, it's remembering all the chefs, farmers, shopkeepers, and insiders who played a role in making the book a reality. My heartfelt thanks go out to the following, in no particular order: Tina Luster, Sarah Tracey, Duskie Estes and John Stewart, Carrie Brown, Trevor Swallow, Michael Collins, Lisa Hemenway, Elaine Bell, Rachel Krieger, Sheana Davis, Renzo Veronese, Sharon Bice, Colleen McGlynn, Gail Dutton, Jennifer Kennedy, and Shannon Wesley.

Thanks also to my husband, Loren, and my sister, Jan Blanchard, who went on road trips with me around Sonoma County, revisiting familiar places and experiencing others for the first time. And to the friends who offered laughs and encouragement, and weighed in with their own opinions of the best places to find great vittles, you have my sincere gratitude: Jan, Mariann, Donna, Julia, Mary Jo, Pat, Cathy, Kathy K., Lynn, Kathy M., Linda, Karen, Doris, Sandy, Phyllis, Michele, Ed, Riki, Nancy, Sue, and Mary.

And finally, thanks to my mom and dad, who first introduced me to "farm-to-table" dining.

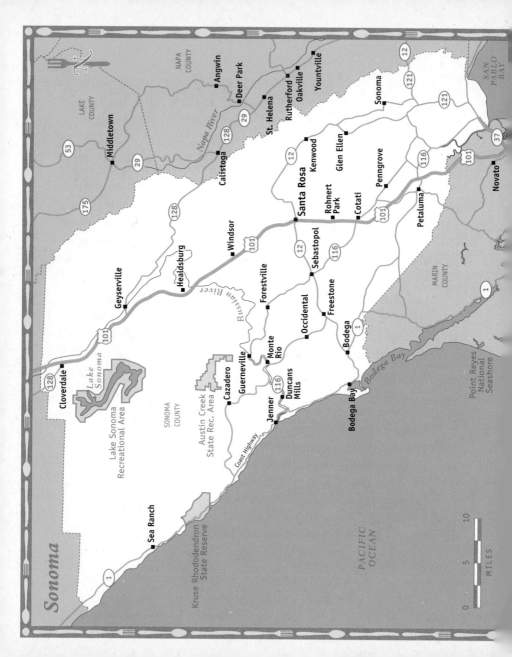

Introduction

In California, introducing yourself by the county you hail from usually says more about you than naming a city or town. State your address as "Sonoma" or "Sonoma County" and most people know immediately that it's Wine Country. But Sonoma is also famous for delicious dining and diverse agriculture, from a scrappy heritage apple known as the Gravenstein to artisan goat cheese and Dungeness crab. Combine a bit of each on a Cowgirl Creamery sea-salt-and-olive-oil organic cracker and you're eating like a true locavore.

Sonoma County has the best of everything: historic and lively small towns, a couple of good-size cities, mile after mile of beautiful ranches and farms, and a pristine coastline where the largest ocean in the world has been offering up its seafood since the first settlers arrived. Much of the farmland is devoted to the growing of wine grapes, but there are huge expanses in the west portion of the county that are better suited for raising dairy cows and lambs, growing vegetables, and tending olive and apple orchards. The Pacific Ocean is also a sustainable source of rockfish, abalone, and oysters, just to name a few species.

Sonoma County, and more precisely the Sonoma Valley, is where the wine industry in California began, thanks to a bold Hungarian known as Count Agoston Haraszthy. He was the first to visualize the potential for growing fine wine grapes here, though some earlier settlers had lesser-quality vineyards already in place. Haraszthy went back to Europe and returned with a few hundred varieties of grape cuttings, and then set about planting 6,000 acres to vineyards.

Today there are approximately 70,000 acres of ultra-premium wine-grape varietals planted throughout Sonoma County, so the count knew what he was doing. It's a shame he pulled up stakes and went off to seek new fortunes in Central America. Legend has it he vanished in the jungle, possibly the victim of a hungry crocodile, never to be heard from again.

Sonoma County has also gained accolades for its new-agey "biodynamic" organic farming methods practiced by many wineries and produce farmers, and the restaurants that source these ultra-fresh ingredients for their menus. It's one more example of how the region is on the cutting edge of practicing sustainable agriculture.

Restaurants, gift shops, and other industries throughout the nation and even overseas have traded on the "Sonoma" name for years, and sometimes in odd ways: a line of clothing, bubble bath and bath salts, and even bathroom linens. One of the strangest was naming a Chevrolet pickup truck in our honor, a model that's since been discontinued. Yet when I find myself on a rural lane behind a dusty tailgate that reads SONOMA, I have to smile.

How to Use This Book

Organized into five chapters, this guide begins with an overview of the Sonoma Valley and the culinary attractions in the city of Sonoma and the towns of Glen Ellen and Kenwood. That's followed by chapters about Petaluma and Penngrove; the city of Santa Rosa and its environs; Healdsburg and the nearby communities of Geyserville and Cloverdale; and the West Sonoma County and coastal region. Each chapter features some or all of the following categories:

Landmark Eateries

Restaurants that have gained some fame—locally or globally—for their longevity or great food and service are profiled. This includes a few establishments that have earned Michelin stars or Bib Gourmand status.

Foodie Faves

From simple taquerias to white-tablecloth bistros to seafood shacks, these eateries are popular with locals and visitors, too.

Restaurant Price Key

So you have some idea how to budget for your meal, Landmark Eateries and Foodie Faves follow this pricing guide:

$	inexpensive; most entrees under $10
$$	moderate; most entrees $10 to $20
$$$	expensive; most entrees $20 to $30
$$$$	very expensive; most entrees more than $30, including prix-fixe menus (not including wine pairings)

Specialty Stores & Shops

The diversity of agriculture in Sonoma is reflected in the diversity of its stores that cater to people who love food. This category includes merchants selling all manner of cooking devices and equipment, as well as bakeries, chocolate and ice cream shops, specialty grocers, well-loved local markets, and even a purveyor of rare heirloom seeds.

Made or Grown Here

Upon settling in Santa Rosa in 1875, famed horti-culturalist Luther Burbank proclaimed that Sonoma County was "the chosen spot of all this earth as far as Nature is concerned." That's a mighty big state-ment for a place to live up to, but Luther went on to prove he could grow almost anything here. (Read more about Luther Burbank on p. 146.)

Global warming aside, this region of northern California has ideal conditions for almost any seed or seedling you want to stick in the ground. Sonoma County may be most widely known for cul-tivating wine grapes and producing award-winning red and white wines, but we grow a multitude of other tasty treats. During the harvest season, many of these freshly picked treasures can be found spilling over the tables at numerous farmers' markets and at-the-source stands.

Sonoma County is big, as are most of California's 58 counties—by comparison, the state of Iowa has 99 counties in an area roughly one-third that of California. At 1-million-plus acres, or 1,768 square miles, the county is larger than the state of Rhode Island, and most of it is rural in nature. While cruising through these rolling hills, you don't have to search long to spy a bucolic farmstead, a pasture dotted with dairy cows or lambs, and orchards of apples and olives—sometimes in close proximity to each other.

Also big are some of the numbers associated with our agriculture and the seafood pulled from the Pacific Ocean. According to the 2010 crop report prepared by the Sonoma County Agricultural Commissioner, our premium wine grapes are far and away the most valuable commodity, in the vicinity of $400 million. Milk and dairy products follow, at nearly $78 million. Other multimillion-dollar commodities are poultry and poultry products ($64 million), vegetables ($8.2 million), and several varieties of apples, including the distinctive Gravenstein ($5.9 million). Crustaceans and other fish caught off the coast were valued at roughly $1.6 million in 2009, with Dungeness crab the primary delicacy being hauled in. Lingcod, rockfish, and sturgeon are also in abundance for recreational anglers.

Olive oil? We're positively dripping in it. Thousands of olive trees are scattered throughout the county, most grown for gourmet oil production. Numerous wineries bottle their own oils and vinegars, too, selling them in their gift shops and offering free tastes.

Artisan cheese? Wheel after wheel. No disrespect to Wisconsin, but the clever national advertising campaign for our cheese says it all: "Great cheese comes from happy cows—happy cows come from California." Sonoma County cheesemakers are also famous for making exceptional goat cheese from, well, happy goats.

Each chapter gives an overview of the many farmers' markets, growers, and food producers and purveyors that can be found here. Though it doesn't include all the countless farmers cultivating produce, making cheese, and raising animals, it's a starting point in your search. Some of the farms and farm stands are seasonal, so it's always best to call ahead to find out what they harvested just that morning.

This category also includes **community-supported agriculture (CSA) programs.** CSA is a way to subsidize local farmers at the beginning of their growing season by typically paying in advance for boxes of fresh produce that are delivered weekly or on another schedule throughout summer and fall to designated drop-off points. Each farm listed as offering a CSA program sets its own prices and policies, and the produce can be quite varied between farms. Many "add-ins" (fresh eggs, flowers, cheese, or other goodies) can also be packed into the box for an extra charge. Most CSA customers find that receiving regular deliveries of farm-fresh produce is a more affordable and tastier way to incorporate healthful ingredients into their meals.

Food & Wine Pairings/Landmark Wineries

"Sonoma" is synonymous with great wine and great food, so it was only natural for winery tasting rooms to combine the two to offer a special treat for visitors. Food-and-wine pairings that match exceptional bites with world-class wines generally require advance reservations. During high season these popular attractions fill quickly, so it's always best to plan ahead. Included in this category are also many historic and noteworthy wineries, large and small, open regular hours or by appointment. (Take note: The type of permit held by a winery dictates whether it can operate a tasting room open to the public for walk-in visitors, or if it's by appointment only. Making an appointment is sometimes as simple as calling the winery five minutes ahead of time and asking if you can stop in.)

Be aware, too, that while you picnic at one of our wineries, the wine you sip with your munchies must be a product of that particular winery. It's not the wineries being difficult—it's mandated by the permits they hold. So as you sit in the shady grove at Simi Winery in Healdsburg, don't pull the cork on the Ferrari-Carano Bella Luce you purchased at your last stop. Please go into the tasting room and buy a bottle of Simi wine.

Brewpubs & Microbreweries

Wine is the drink we may be famous for, but northern California—and Sonoma County in particular—is also microbrewery territory. Each chapter lists at least one popular establishment where the suds are brewed and poured, usually along with tasty pub fare.

Learn to Cook

The local junior college in Santa Rosa offers a full culinary curriculum for serious students of gastronomy. But if you're seeking one specific class to master the baking of pies or the secrets to crafting savory sauces, there's a stovetop and an oven waiting for you. Hands-on instruction and classroom-style options in demonstration kitchens helmed by experienced chefs are numerous.

Getting Around

A woman I know at the Sonoma Valley Visitors Bureau, who greets the tourists and answers their questions about the region, recently told me that first-time visitors are always amazed by the size of Sonoma County, and the long distances—and occasionally long travel times—between its cities, towns, farms, wineries, and the Pacific Ocean. Newbies learn quickly that they must pace themselves and slow down to take in all the good stuff—the abundance of agricultural products for sale, farm animals grazing on hillsides, world-class wines that can be tasted at the source, and destination restaurants.

Traversing this large area takes planning, particularly if you have an ambitious itinerary. Maybe you want to hit a farmers' market on Saturday morning in the city of Sonoma and have dinner that night in Jenner, on the Pacific coast. In between you hope to drop by a couple of farm stands, eat a sit-down lunch at a small bistro, tour an olive orchard, and stop for wine tasting, too. Whoa! It might be possible to accomplish all that in one day, but it's not recommended. The farther you drive away from the only multilane freeway in Sonoma County (US Highway 101), the more twisty and narrow the roads become. Many are two lanes wide (although in some places calling them "two lanes" is a stretch) and almost always scenic. Ask the world-champion cyclists who train on some of these challenging roads—two wheels can be more nimble than four.

Fortunately, we do have some two-lane highways where the traffic moves along at a reasonable pace. Many of the attractions in this book can be found along these roads or not far off. This list starts with descriptions of the highways in the southern tip of Sonoma County, followed by the highways that run west, north, and northwest in the region.

Highway 121

Beginning at Sears Point, site of the Infineon Raceway, Highway 121 is generally referred to as "Arnold Drive" in addresses. It travels through the Carneros grape-growing region, and south of the city of Sonoma it makes a sharp right to join Highway 12 on its way to Napa Valley. It also connects with Highway 116, a road that will take you west to Petaluma.

Highway 12

Highway 12 is the major artery through the Sonoma Valley, originating south of the city of Sonoma. It's designated as a scenic route as it passes through the towns of Glen Ellen and Kenwood, and referred to as "Sonoma Highway" in many entries in this book. It morphs into a four-lane, stop-and-go thoroughfare in Santa Rosa, and for a short distance is freeway-like through the city. West of Santa Rosa, on the way to Sebastopol, Highway 12 again narrows to two lanes and then meanders nearly all the way to the coastline, taking on the alternate name of "Bodega Highway." It intersects with Highway 1 on the far side of the tiny town of Bodega.

US Highway 101

Also known as the Redwood Highway, US Highway 101 serves commuters and commerce. It's a significant road in the state of California, running all the way from Hollywood to the south and up to Oregon to the north. US 101 enters Sonoma County about 5 miles south of Petaluma and continues on to Rohnert Park, Santa Rosa, Windsor, Healdsburg, Geyserville, Cloverdale, and into Mendocino County. In Santa Rosa and the surrounding towns, US 101 is mostly six lanes wide, with "diamond" or "HOV" (high occupancy vehicle) lanes for cars carrying two or more people during regular commute hours. Even with the major widening projects nearly finished throughout the county, traffic slow-downs can still occur at any time.

Highway 1

This is a legendary highway, with stunning coastal scenery in most places, and the twists and turns that go with it. Highway 1 snakes through Marin County to the south and meets the coastline at Bodega Bay. From Bodega Bay to the Mendocino County border, this approximately 50-mile stretch of pavement requires patience. There are many places to pull over and take out your camera to capture the beauty, and to give your backseat passengers a break from the bobbing and weaving. This is not a road for texting or talking on the phone while you drive. First, it's against the law. Second, it's unsafe. Keep both hands on the wheel—you'll be glad you did. (Highway 1 is also often called "Coast Highway 1.")

Highway 116

After connecting Sonoma and Petaluma in southern Sonoma County, Highway 116 joins with US 101 north to Cotati, then splits off and heads northwest through Sebastopol and Forestville. It follows the Russian River and winds through redwood forests for a good part of its length, intersecting with Highway 1 at the coastal town of Jenner.

Highway 128

Best known as the path through the Alexander Valley wine region, Highway 128 is a rambling roadway that can also take you south-easterly toward Napa Valley. Highway 128 meets US 101 just north of Geyserville and follows it to Cloverdale before breaking away again and heading northwest into Mendocino County.

Keeping Up with Food News

Sonoma County's food scene is actively covered in print, including free magazines and brochures found in winery tasting rooms, visitors' centers, lodgings, and other places where visitors spend their time.

Online sites with restaurant reviews (such as Yelp .com) and food news are helpful resources, as long as you take some of the participants' surly criticisms or gushing praise with a grain of salt. It's usually easy to spot anonymous professional posters who find fault with everything about a dining experience, or go to extremes in the other direction, perhaps with a personal agenda.

With social networking now so prevalent, many restaurants, wineries, stores, farmers, mobile food vendors, and seasonal food producers rely on it to keep their customers instantly updated. Though these businesses may also have dedicated websites, the proprietors like the immediacy of posting their latest news on Facebook and Twitter.

The information about Sonoma County maintained by the following print publications and websites is generally unbiased:

www.BiteClubEats.com: Compiled by the *Santa Rosa Press Democrat,* this comprehensive site is devoted to the Sonoma County food scene. Up-to-date and sometimes gossipy, it covers the latest high-profile changes in chefs, cuisine, and restaurant closings and openings.

Edible Marin and Wine Country, in print and online at www .ediblemarinandwinecountry.com: Part of the *Edible* magazine franchise, this regional edition, published quarterly, features articles about growers, farmers, and chefs within Sonoma, Napa, and Marin counties. Expect recipes, profiles, recent news, and green-leaning information.

http://InsideScoopsf.sfgate.com: The *San Francisco Chronicle's* foodie site is generally dedicated to the restaurant goings-on in the city of San Francisco. But the newspaper's restaurant critic also blogs about major changes in Sonoma County's culinary landscape.

www.Inside-Sonoma.com: Different correspondents weigh in with the latest on deals to be found in Sonoma County, dining advice, new developments in area restaurants, and wine-tasting recommendations.

www.SonomaCounty.com: As the official site for Sonoma County tourism, it offers comprehensive information, with lists of dining, shopping, and lodging options, as well as wineries.

Sonoma Magazine, in print and online at www.sonomanews.com: Click on the "Food & Wine" link on this site to find winery events, local food and restaurant news, and interesting features on people with food or wine connections. Published by the *Sonoma Index-Tribune* newspaper in Sonoma, the print edition of the magazine is available by subscription, and single copies are for sale in various stores and hotels in Sonoma.

www.SonomaUncorked.com: Extensive information about restaurants, cooking classes, and events related to food are included on this site. Slide shows of dining establishments, videos from festivals, and winemaker interviews add an extra dimension.

Wine Country This Week, in print and online at www.wine countrythisweek.com: Published since 1981, this glossy magazine squeezes a lot of information into its 80-some pages each week: winery maps, articles about wineries, a list of wineries, and a calendar of events. It also covers a huge territory in northern California. Besides Sonoma County, the magazine has information on wineries and attractions in the wine-growing areas of Mendocino and Lake counties to the north, Napa Valley and Suisun Valley to the east, the Livermore-Lodi-Woodbridge area to the southeast, and even the Sierra Foothills wine scene.

Food Events & Happenings

During certain summer weekends, there is simply too much to do in Sonoma County. Special events and festivals—most of them with food as a major attraction—are so numerous it's impossible to choose between them. You can't be everywhere at once, so you have to pick one good time over another.

We celebrate the bounty of the county practically year-round, thanks to the mildness of our Mediterranean-like climate. Special wine-tasting events in winter take the edge off rainy, cool weather, while the budbreak on the grapevines in spring gives us hope for an exceptional vintage to come. Summer and fall are busy with salutes to the harvest and the "crush" taking place in the vineyards. Throughout the year, chefs are busy cooking up new ways to spotlight fresh produce, artisan cheese, and locally raised meats as they cater one event after another.

The following list gives you a taste of the type of foodie fun you can find in Sonoma County—some of them family-friendly.

A few words about the "passport"-style weekend wine-tasting events: Tickets are usually purchased well before the event, and you are given further instructions at that time. Be advised, also, that many of these events sell out in advance, and no tickets can be sold "at the door," as it were. In most cases you check in at the first participating winery on your list, where you are issued a special wristband and a souvenir tasting glass. From there you can visit as many participating wineries as you wish within the time constraints of the event. Take care with your souvenir glass—it has to survive whatever rough treatment you heap upon it while driving from one tasting room to the next, as well as through multiple pours and possibly a few robust toasts.

The designated driver in your group is not to be pitied—on the contrary, wineries typically shower this person with extra goodies, so it can be a pretty nice gig. These tasting weekends are for adults of legal drinking age, so infants and children cannot be admitted. If you bring a child, you will most certainly be turned away. It sounds harsh, but the wineries must adhere to strictly enforced regulations that are beyond their control while at the same time ensuring that all wristband-wearers enjoy a relaxing, educational experience. Bear in mind, too, that if you reek of the latest fragrance from Justin Timberlake or Jennifer Lopez, be prepared for dirty looks and possible snarky comments. The wearing of personal fragrances is strongly, passionately discouraged at these events, and in tasting rooms at any time, for that matter. Lavishly applied perfume, cologne, and after-shave can ruin not only your palate—the sensory experience of tasting the wine—but also spoil it for everyone around you. Don't be that person.

December to February

Olive Festival, Sonoma Valley Visitors Bureau, 453 First St. East, Sonoma, CA 95476; (707) 996-1090 or (866) 996-1090; www.sonomavalley.com/olivefestival. With so many olive trees being grown in Sonoma County, the Sonoma Valley Visitors Bureau decided in 2001 that it was time to make hay with it. The Olive Festival was conceived to celebrate these lovely trees and their little orbs of fruit with an assortment of activities and events over several weeks, which was also a great way to attract visitors for special discounts on dining and lodgings during the slower winter months. Some of the fun includes watching olives being turned into oil at The Olive Press, a blessing of the olives at Mission Solano de Sonoma on East Spain Street in Sonoma, oil and vinegar tastings, the Feast of the Olive dinner, food-and-wine pairings, a Martini Madness event, art exhibits, and live music. The activities take place in different venues, and many are free or low cost.

January

Russian River Winter Wineland, 498 Moore Ln., Healdsburg, CA 95448; (800) 723-6336 or (707) 433-4335; www.wineroad.com/events. Travel at your own pace from one winery to another (about 140 of them participate) to meet winemakers, enjoy small bites of food, and sample limited production wines and new releases. Each winery offers something different but all are united in providing wine education, showcasing fine art, and guaranteeing a good time, rain or shine. In 2012, this popular event celebrated its 20th anniversary. Tickets are $45 per person for the mid-January Saturday and Sunday (or $35 for Sunday only). Your designated driver pays only $5.

February

Cloverdale Citrus Fair, Fairgrounds at 1 Citrus Fair Dr., Cloverdale, CA 95425; (707) 894-3992; www.cloverdalecitrusfair.org.

Cloverdale goes all out to put on this small fair that takes place over four days in mid-February, regardless of the weather. Most of the citrus you see is oranges used in large exhibits that reflect a particular theme. In addition to some carnival rides, there are usually chef's demonstrations, poultry judging, daily orange-juicing contests, wine tasting for mom and dad, a family "fun zone" for the kids, plenty of fair food, an art show, a hypnotist, and live music in an auditorium. Admission is $6 for adults, $4 for seniors and children 6 to 12, and free for children 5 and under.

Vin Olivo, The Lodge at Sonoma, 1325 Broadway, Sonoma, CA 95476; (707) 935-0803; www.sonomavalleywine.com. Vin Olivo is a major gala, the wrap-up event of Sonoma Valley's 3-month-long Olive Festival. Count on lots of food from the region's restaurants and food artisans, an olive bar, a sparkling wine bar, music and dancing, and schmoozing with many of the Sonoma Valley's wine-makers and chefs. Tickets are $75 in advance, or $85 at the door.

Wine & Chocolate Fantasy, 1455 Old Redwood Hwy., Healdsburg, CA 95448; (800) 678-4762; www.rodneystrong.com. Just in time for Valentine's Day, Rodney Strong Vineyards invites anyone who loves love into the barrel tasting room on a Saturday afternoon to try an assortment of gourmet chocolates and learn how they pair with the wines. This event has been going on for more than 20 years and has gained a wide following. Get your tickets early—$65 per person (includes a commemorative wine glass) or $50 for wine club members.

March

Artisan Cheese Festival, Sheraton Sonoma County Hotel, 745 Baywood Dr., Petaluma, CA 94954; (707) 283-2888; www.artisan cheesefestival.com. With so many artisan cheesemakers in California, I knew it wouldn't be long before there was a festival to bring them together in a celebration of curds and whey. This event began in 2007 and has become bigger with each passing year. On a weekend in late March, curious cheese lovers get to meet the makers of many small-production cheeses—along with various experts, chefs, and *fromagiers*—to learn how to taste, buy, and serve it. The festival spotlights not only cheese but other handcrafted foods, wines, and beer that are made in the state. Check the website for the latest ticket information.

Battle of the Brews, Sonoma County Fairgrounds, 1350 Bennett Valley Rd., Santa Rosa, CA 95404; www.battleofthebrews.com. At this event, you can get Stoopid (Hop Stoopid, that is—one of the brews made by Petaluma's Lagunitas Brewing Company). The "battle" is a fund-raiser for several organizations that help needy children in Sonoma County, presented by the Active 20-30 Club of Santa Rosa. The 2011 bash was the 14th annual, and more than $1 million has been raised over the years to benefit the children. As many as 30 breweries pour their suds and 20 or more food vendors dish up the grub. Be prepared for uptempo live music, too. General admission is $40 per person.

Savor Sonoma Valley Annual Barrel Tasting and Culinary Experience, (866) 794-9463; www.heartofsonomavalley.com. Much smaller in scale than the Wine Road Barrel Tasting (below), this barrel tasting is limited to the Glen Ellen and Kenwood area and includes about 20 wineries. The winemakers' latest vintages are tasted straight from the barrels and paired with food samples prepared by local chefs. Expect live music and art exhibits, too. Tickets are $55 per person for the 2-day weekend.

Wine Road Barrel Tasting, 498 Moore Ln., Healdsburg, CA 95448; (800) 723-6336 or (707) 433-4335; www.wineroad.com/events. Well into its third decade, the annual barrel tasting is all about wine, not food or "themes." Unlike some weekend wine-tasting events, this one is for trying wines right out of the barrel. That generally means they are not yet ready to be bottled and sold, because they are still aging. However, those who attend and like what they taste can purchase "futures" of the wine, so when it is finally ready for market in a year or two, they are guaranteed the end product. In some cases, the wine is so limited in production that buying futures is the only way to purchase it. More than 100 wineries in Alexander Valley, Dry Creek Valley, and the Russian River Valley participate. Tickets can be purchased in advance ($30 per person), and that gets you into all of the wineries you can make time for. Because of its enormous popularity, the barrel tasting takes place over two weekends.

April

Apple Blossom Festival, Ives Park (Jewell Ave. and Willow St.) and the Veterans Memorial Building (282 High St.), Sebastopol, CA 95472; (707) 823-3032 or (877) 828-4748; www.sebasto pol.org. Entering its 66th year, this festival is an excuse to celebrate that the apple trees around Sebastopol are finally in bloom and the juicy fruits will soon follow, necessitating another festival (see the Gravenstein Apple Fair under August events). It begins with a hometown parade on Saturday morning, followed by lots of music (on several stages), food vendors, beer and wine, and an art exhibit, too. General admission per day is $10 for adults, $5 for seniors and children 11 to 17, and free for kids 10 and younger.

April in Carneros, (800) 909-4352; www.carneroswineries.org. Proceeds from this event help to fund scholarships to Santa Rosa Junior College and Napa Valley College (the Carneros wine region, or "appellation" as we call it here, straddles the county lines between Sonoma and Napa). It's one weekend in mid-April, when 20-some wineries open their doors to visitors with food-and-wine pairings, art shows, entertainment, and discounts on wine. A few of the wineries are not usually open for visitors, so this is a rare opportunity to see them up close and taste their products. Tickets are $35 per person.

Butter & Egg Days, downtown Petaluma, CA 94952; (707) 762-9348; www.petalumadowntown.com. When you read the chapter about Petaluma in this book, you'll understand how this event came to be. During the last complete weekend in April, Petaluma remembers its history (and celebrates its thriving current status as an agricultural region) by throwing a parade with marching bands, floats, and goofy costumes with dairy and poultry themes. Join

in a cow-chip tossing contest, and dress up your toddler for the Cutest Little Chick in Town competition. Expect food booths, an antiques fair, and live entertainment, too.

Fisherman's Festival, Westside Park, Bodega Bay, CA 94923; www.bbfishfest.org. Approaching its 40th year, this festival is memorable for the Blessing of the Fleet and the wreath that is thrown into the bay to pay homage to local fishermen who have perished along this coast pursuing their dangerous occupation. Count on numerous food vendors, wine-tasting opportunities, live music by such Bay Area–based bands as the Unauthorized Rolling Stones (including a dead-on Mick Jagger act-alike), a search-and-rescue demonstration by the US Coast Guard, and a pet parade that might include llamas. Admission is $10 for adults, $8 for seniors, and free for kids under 12.

Passport to Dry Creek Valley, (707) 433-3031; www.wdcv .com/passport. Sonoma County is so large, with many wineries and appellations, that most regions have their own version of a "passport"-type weekend (see previous listings under January and March). This Dry Creek Valley weekend is a hot ticket that's much in demand, with a maximum purchase of four tickets at $120 each. Thousands of disappointed wine lovers around the nation—and the world, I gather—go on a waiting list, hoping a ticket holder will be forced to cancel (including my cousin and her daughter in the Midwest, who weren't able to score tickets but had paid for their airfare already, and so went wine tasting in a less hectic appellation that weekend). In its 23rd year in 2012, this passport weekend offers great wine and food, music and performances, and intimate tours of some 45 participating wineries in Dry Creek Valley. The live entertainment can range from circus acts to belly dancers.

May

Passport to Sonoma Valley, (707) 935-0803; www.sonomvalley wine.com. More than 50 wineries sign on to host thousands of visitors during one weekend mid-month. At least 300 different wines are poured, along with food pairings. There might be a traditional Mexican food tasting at Robledo Family Winery (see the listing in the City of Sonoma & the Sonoma Valley chapter) and another winery creating a French bistro theme. Part of the fun is being surprised at what the next winery has in store for you. This passport event includes wineries that are already popular with visitors and some not usually

open to the public. Tickets are $60 per person for two days, or $55 for one day.

Petaluma's Salute to *American Graffiti*, (707) 762-3394; www.americangraffiti.net. In 1972, filmmaker George Lucas came to Petaluma to shoot his movie *American Graffiti,* starring a then-unknown Harrison Ford. The historic downtown had the perfect look for George's coming-of-age film set in 1962, which included lengthy scenes of "cruising" up and down Petaluma Boulevard. The movie didn't make much of a splash when it was first released, but after George made another low-budget film called *Star Wars* a few years later, his earlier work suddenly was cool, and Petaluma became a movie star. This annual celebration during a weekend in mid-May (the 8th year in 2012) is an all-volunteer event that benefits the community with a focus on helping schools and promoting health and safety. A cruise of classic cars takes place in the Plaza North Shopping Center, and the salute to the movie is along the same boulevard where it was filmed. Local artists paint hubcaps with nostalgic scenes, and they are later auctioned. Admission is free, with pay-as-you-go food and other activities.

Taste Alexander Valley, (888) 463-0207 or (888) 289-4637; www.alexandervalley.org. The 2011 tasting weekend started off with a dinner party on Friday evening. The scene was Francis Ford Coppola Winery in Geyserville, the wine was poured by area winemakers, and the food was small plates such as pork cheek with exotic mush-rooms and chilled asparagus bisque. (Read more about Francis Ford

Coppola Winery and the Alexander Valley appellation in the Healdsburg, Geyserville & Cloverdale chapter.) Every year on a Saturday and Sunday in mid-May, participants enjoy food-and-wine pairings at more than 30 wineries, many with live music or other forms of entertainment, and discounts on wine purchases. Tickets are limited but coveted, and usually go on sale months before the event ($75 per person for both days, $55 for Sunday only, and $15 for your designated driver). The Friday night gala, such as 2011's Coppola Winery bash, is extra—inquire when ordering your wine-tasting passes. Taste Alexander Valley celebrates its 15th anniversary in 2012.

June

Beerfest, Wells Fargo Center for the Arts, 50 Mark West Springs Rd., Santa Rosa, CA 95403; (707) 546-3600 or (707) 544-1581; www.f2f.org. Microbreweries are everywhere in northern California, and this festival on one afternoon in early June, rain or shine, showcases more than 40 of them. Almost 30 restaurants and food purveyors—with some brewpubs featuring their own food—lay out feasts ranging from fish tacos to plates of fresh veggies to smoky ribs. Nonalcoholic beverages are available if you only want to nosh. The beer and the food are both inside the Wells Fargo Center and outside under an enormous tent. Contests for the Best Brewery and the Best Foodery are held, too. The all-inclusive tickets are $40 per person in advance, $45 at the door, with a souvenir glass thrown in. You must be over 21, of course, to attend (no children will be admitted). Beerfest is a benefit for Face to Face, the Sonoma County AIDS Alliance.

Sonoma Lavender Festival, 8537 Sonoma Hwy. (Hwy. 12), Kenwood, CA 95452; (707) 523-4411; www.sonomalavender.com. In mid-June, when the fleeting blossoms of the perennial shrub are at their peak, a lavender farm near Chateau St. Jean Winery opens their gates to welcome the public over one weekend. It's difficult to name an aroma in the plant world that's more pleasant than that of lavender. Here you can walk among the 7,000-some shrubs over 5 acres, and cut your own fresh bouquets. Count on lots of lavender-based products for sale, along with honey from hives on-site and education about beekeeping and pollination. For me, the best part of this festival is the lavender-infused food and refreshment. Lisa Hemenway of Fresh restaurant and market (see that listing in the Santa Rosa chapter) created the cuisine for this festival in 2011, and past goodies have included lavender sausages, lavender ice cream, and lavender lemonade. Admission is $5 for adults, free for kids 12 and under. Food and other extras are on a pay-as-you-go basis.

July

Catalan Festival of Food, Wine & Music, Gloria Ferrer Caves & Vineyards, 23555 Arnold Dr. (Hwy. 121), Sonoma, CA 95476; (707)

996-7256; www.gloriaferrer.com. Every third weekend in July for 20 years (in 2012), this winery has hosted a festival that honors its Spanish roots. The flamenco dancers and classical guitarists provide the atmosphere, and the food is authentic Spanish cuisine, such as paella whipped up by Bay Area chefs. Traditional Spanish food products of all types are also for sale. Gloria Ferrer's setting in the heart of the Carneros appellation is lovely, with the view from the patio worth sharing a table with strangers, who may not be strangers for long. Tickets are $45 for one day.

Ox Roast, Sonoma Plaza, Sonoma, CA 95476; (707) 938-4626; www.sonomacommunitycenter.org. The barbecue pits are lit before sunrise, around 4:30 a.m., so that the beef (as much as 1,000 pounds) will be extra tender by afternoon. A couple of bands provide the entertainment, and hundreds of townsfolk show up to partake of this tradition that's approaching its 45th year. Two plates of food are offered for adults: one with beef, corn on the cob, salad, and bread for $12; or a gourmet sausage instead of the beef ($10). A kid's size portion is also available ($7). Beer, wine, and soda are for sale to wash down the meal, as are commemorative T-shirts. Proceeds from the event benefit the Sonoma Community Center's arts education programs.

August

Bodega Seafood, Art & Wine Festival, 16855 Bodega Hwy. (Hwy. 12), Bodega, CA 94922; (707) 824-8717; www.winecountry

festivals.com. The emphasis is on seafood at this festival, highlighted by entertainment on three stages and the work of more than 100 artists and craftspeople entered into a juried art show. The food is prepared by local restaurants and caterers, and the selection is varied: barbecued oysters, clam chowder, salmon burgers, cedar plank salmon, crab cakes, seafood gumbo, calamari, and other tasty morsels. Local wineries and breweries pour the refreshments, and humorous performances by such characters as Captain Jack Spareribs keep the mood festive and fun. The locally popular rhythm-and-blues revue Pride & Joy is among the bands that may provide opportunities for dancing. The money raised goes to help fund the work of the Bodega Volunteer Fire Department and the Stewards of the Coast and Redwoods. The 18th annual shindig was in 2012. (Across and down the highway just a bit is the Bodega Potter School, made famous in Alfred Hitchcock's classic thriller *The Birds*.)

Gravenstein Apple Fair, Ragle Ranch Park, 500 Ragle Rd., Sebastopol, CA 95472; (707) 837-8896; www.gravensteinapplefair .com. While the Gravenstein apples are turning ripe in the West County, Sebastopol throws this annual bash, one of the oldest traditions in Sonoma County, dating to 1910. It started small back then but grew to include ¼-scale buildings made from dried apple slices and exhibits by the many apple processing and packing plants that once thrived around Sebastopol. The apples are still celebrated today, but differently. The fair is like an old-fashioned family-oriented event, with live music and cooking demonstrations, arts and crafts booths, hay wagon rides, a hay maze, and local wine and beer for sale. There's always a commemorative poster available for purchase, too. The fair takes place during a mid-August weekend. Tickets are $12 for adults, $10 for seniors, $5 for kids 6 to 12, and free for kids under 6.

Taste of Petaluma, (707) 763-8920; www.tasteofpetaluma.org. For several years, people have been flocking to this annual event on a Saturday afternoon to take their senses on a "culinary journey." You buy a ticket book ($35 per person) and use one ticket for each sampling of food at the participating restaurants. The list of possibilities is long—about 60 eateries and shops—and the point is to get locals (and visitors) to try places they might not have considered before, and have fun doing it. To keep things moving along, numerous live performers are posted here and there, including belly dancers, folkies, and perhaps an Elvis impersonator. The event is a fund-raiser for the Cinnabar Theater, a cherished nearby venue that for 40 years has staged operas, plays, and other live performances. It's a good cause.

September

B.R. Cohn Charity Events Fall Music Festival, B.R. Cohn
Winery, 15000 Sonoma Hwy. (Hwy. 12), Glen Ellen, CA 95442; (707)
931-7924 or (800) 330-4064; www.brcohn.com. I used to attend
this once-intimate bash years ago, before it was "discovered" and
became, well, a whole lot bigger. At one time the festival was a
single day of music, food, and wine, then it grew to two days to
handle the larger crowds and the separate musical lineups. But
regardless, it achieves its purpose: to raise money for charity. In
the 25 years Bruce Cohn has been hosting this event at his winery,
more than $6 million has gone to good causes such as the Redwood
Empire Food Bank, the trauma center at a local hospital, and the
Sonoma Valley Education Foundation. Some people might say the
stars of the shows are getting a bit long in the tooth, but by
booking the Doobie Brothers, Lynyrd Skynyrd, Leon Russell, Little
Feat, Sammy Hagar, and other classic rock headliners who once
packed arenas, Bruce knows that the shows will appeal to his target
demographic and the tickets will sell out quickly. He's the longtime
manager of the Doobies, and as such is well connected in the rock-
n-roll world. He started this winery in 1984 as a sideline to the
music industry, and has done a lot to give back to the community
(read more about B.R. Cohn Winery in the City of Sonoma & Sonoma
Valley chapter). General admission tickets to the music festival are
$100 per person. VIP tickets around the stage—with lots of perks
thrown in—range from $350 to $1,000. A night-before dinner on
Friday costs $150 per person—in 2011 the celebrity chef was Guy

Fieri (read more about Guy in the Santa Rosa chapter). On Monday, after the rocking is over, the event wraps up with a golf tournament at nearby Sonoma Golf Club.

Kendall-Jackson Heirloom Tomato Festival, Kendall-Jackson Wine Center, 5007 Fulton Rd., Fulton, CA 95439; (707) 571-8100 or (866) 287-9818; www.kj.com. Celebrating its 16th year in 2012, this festival showcases more than 120 varieties of the heirloom fruit, whipped up into gourmet dishes and paired with exceptional wines. You'll be amazed at these colorful and sometimes oddly shaped treats (most are grown on-site), and how they differ in taste and texture. On a Saturday afternoon in early September, more than 2,000 tomato lovers descend on Kendall-Jackson's hospitality head-quarters just north of Santa Rosa for a benefit to raise money for the School Garden Network. Count on a lively chef's challenge, when chefs have 30 minutes to prepare a delicious tomato dish, along with a tomato growers' competition. In 2011, the Best of Show tomato was called Pink Berkeley Tie Dye (groovy!). Tickets are $65 per person.

National Heirloom Exposition—The World's Pure Food Fair, (707) 509-5171; www.theheirloomexpo.com. The inaugural exposition took place in 2011, the brainchild of the owners of the Seed Bank (see the Petaluma & Penngrove chapter). Over three days in mid-September at the Sonoma County Fairgrounds (1350 Bennett Valley Rd., Santa Rosa, CA 95404), approximately 3,000 varieties of heirloom vegetables, fruits, beans, nuts, grains, herbs, and flowers are on display from all 50 states in a combination trade show and exhibit. Also featured is a poultry and livestock show spotlighting heritage breeds. Farmers, gardeners, and school groups are encouraged to enter their produce and flowers in competition for prize money, too. More than 50 food and garden experts and local chefs conduct numerous workshops on the importance of collecting, conserving, and sharing heirloom seeds. Notable speakers at the 2011 expo were Alice Waters of Berkeley's Chez Panisse restaurant and Dr. Vandana Shiva, a pure-food expert. Scads of organic food products, art, and garden items are for sale as well. Admission is $10, free for children 17 and under.

Sebastopol Cajun Zydeco Festival, Ives Park (Jewell Ave. and Willow St.), Sebastopol, CA 95472; (707) 823-3631; www.wine countrycajun.com. Dance to live Zydeco music, volunteer for free Cajun-style dance lessons between the acts, and pig out on Cajun food such as gator sausage and gumbo in this cool, shady venue. As many as five bands take the stage during a Saturday afternoon in an event hosted by the Rotary Club of Sebastopol Sunrise. The 2012 festival was the 17th annual bash. Tickets are $20 for adults, free for children under 12.

Sonoma Valley Harvest Wine Auction, Cline Cellars, 24737 Arnold Dr. (Hwy. 121), Sonoma, CA 95476; (800) 939-7666; www .sonomawinecountryweekend.com or www.sonomavalleywine.com. Celebrating its 20th year in 2012, this wine auction strives to raise money for good causes, and the participants have a rip-snorting good time doing it. The auction is the culmination of a weekend of other events, such as the Taste of Sonoma (next listing) and exclusive dinners and lunches with vintners and winemakers. Always good for belly laughs, the auction is known for not taking itself too seriously. Celebrities who live nearby, such as comedian and winery owner Tommy Smothers and the chief creative guru at Pixar Studios and Walt Disney Animation Studios, John Lasseter, get the crowd pumped for bidding by taking the stage to perform goofy bits. Some of the auction lots in 2011 were "Shopping and Eating Your Way Through New York City," and the "Around the World Wine Excursion"—and more than $1.3 million was raised for charity. Tickets for the auction are $500 per person. Information about all of the weekend's events and ticket prices can be found on the websites.

Taste of Sonoma, MacMurray Ranch, 9015 Westside Rd., Healdsburg, CA 95448; (800) 939-7666; www.sonomawinecountry weekend.com. The Taste is the food-centric portion of a full weekend of events over the Labor Day holiday known collectively as Sonoma Wine Country Weekend. Saturday's Taste is located at the historic MacMurray Ranch, where actor Fred MacMurray raised livestock and children when he wasn't in Hollywood making movies and taping TV shows. As many as 50 local chefs and 170 wineries come together in this beautiful setting to offer cooking demonstrations, generous food samples, and pours of fine wine. Don't miss the "Steel Chef" competition and seminars on wine education and blind-tasting that are led by winemakers and winery chefs. The 2012 event was the 33rd annual. Tickets for the Taste of Sonoma are $150 per person and sell out quickly. Extra charges may apply if you opt for additional tours and tastings. See the Sonoma Valley Harvest Wine Auction listing for more about the weekend activities.

Valley of the Moon Vintage Festival, Sonoma Plaza, Sonoma, CA 95476; (707) 996-2109; www.sonomavinfest.org. Perhaps the granddaddy of all Sonoma County festivals is this one, dating back to 1897, and it's believed to be one of the oldest harvest festivals in the nation. The point is to celebrate harvest time, which in this vicinity refers primarily to wine grapes. The event usually takes place during the last weekend of September. An opening night gala ($85 per person) is a huge party with wine, food, live music, and dancing, located in the historic Sonoma Barracks across from the Sonoma Plaza, the heart of the city. The action on Saturday and Sunday is in the Plaza, where approximately 25 local wineries pour their nectars and local restaurants such as Maya, the Swiss Hotel, Mary's Pizza Shack, and Saddles Steakhouse offer tasty bites. On Saturday morning a priest blesses the year's grape harvest, followed by a parade, a lively grape stomp, and local firefighters fumbling around in a vigorous water fight. Prices for the wine tasting begin at $20 per person for a souvenir glass and five tasting tickets. Then pay as you go, buying extra tickets at the special tent set up for that purpose. If all you want is the glass (to add to your growing collection of logo glasses), it's $10.

Weekend Along the Farm Trails, (707) 837-8896; www.farm trails.org. One weekend every summer (usually the last full weekend in September), many of Sonoma County's farms open their gates and barns to visitors who want to see how produce is grown and livestock is raised. The Sonoma County Farm Trails organization dates to 1973, when local farmers came together in a cooperative effort to sell their products directly to consumers on their properties. The goal of the group is to ensure that the county's agricultural heritage remains intact, and the popularity and participation in this event have thrived through the decades. The annual Farm Trails weekend brings thousands of people to Sonoma County from out of the area, along with the local residents who want to see where their vegetables, fruit, meat, poultry, and other products originated. The farms, some not usually open to visitors, go all out to offer tours, tastings, music, and other activities. It's a good idea to have lots of cash in your pocket for purchasing fresh produce, as some farms cannot accept credit cards. Bring along your own bags, baskets, and coolers for storing your goodies, and wear appropriate shoes, in case you get the opportunity to walk through a pasture. Many of the farms and businesses featured in this book are on the Weekend

Along the Farm Trails routes. In addition, the Gravenstein Apple Fair (see August) is the primary fund-raiser for the Sonoma County Farm Trails organization.

October

Festa Italiana, Veterans Hall, 1351 Maple Ave., Santa Rosa, CA 95404; (707) 591-9696; www.nbicf.org. Not Italian? Want to be? On a Saturday afternoon in early October, you can eat, dance, and sing like a child of Italy at this annual festival that celebrates its 22nd year in 2012. Since it's an Italian festival, food is a huge part of the attraction, along with the educational cooking demonstrations, a car show, bocce games, and other activities. A well-loved local group called the Don Giovannis may be providing the authentic music, along with a Frank Sinatra impersonator. The festival is put on by the North Bay Italian Cultural Foundation. Tickets are $6 for adults in advance ($10 at the door), and children under 12 get in free. The parking is free, too, and there's lots of it.

Sonoma County Harvest Fair, Sonoma County Fairgrounds, 1350 Bennett Valley Rd., Santa Rosa, CA 95404; (707) 545-4203; www.harvestfair.org. During the first weekend of October, Sonoma County's bountiful harvest is celebrated with small-town fervor. Scarecrow contests, largest pumpkin weigh-ins, box after box of colorful apples affixed with blue ribbons, sheepdog trials, llama races, oodles of fair-type food vendors, and boisterous and messy grape stomps offer something for everyone. Professional caterers, bakeries, local markets, cheesemakers, chocolatiers, and scores more artisan food producers enter their finest specialties for judging. Best of Show, double-gold and gold, silver, and bronze awards are handed out (you will see references to Harvest Fair winners throughout this book). But the real draw at this fair is the local wine. The Harvest Fair is the largest regional wine competition in the United States, and the only event in California with a professional competition exclusively for the region's wines, judged by approximately 25 experts. The judging takes place a few days prior to the fair, and the wine tasting is your best—and in some cases only—opportunity to try the many award winners and the sweepstakes red wine and white wine winners. The fair's Marketplace is where you can buy many of the winning wines, along with local food products. Admission to the fair is $8 for adults, $3 for children ages 7 to 12, and free for children 6 and under. Wine tasting (adults 21 and older) is an additional $12 for a souvenir glass and four tasting tickets. Buy more tickets to keep the pours flowing. In many cases, the person pouring your wine is the owner or winemaker who made it. They enjoy answering questions (and there are no stupid questions), so don't hesitate to strike up a conversation.

November

A Wine & Food Affair, 498 Moore Ln., Healdsburg, CA 95448; (800) 723-6336 or (707) 433-4335; www.wineroad.com/events.

What sets this weekend of wine-and-food pairing apart from some of the others is the complimentary cookbook, called *Tasting Along the Wine Road,* a compilation of recipes from many of the participating wineries. When checking in at the first participating winery you decide to try, you'll receive a copy of the cookbook along with a souvenir glass and special wristband. Because this event covers a large territory (Alexander, Dry Creek, and the Russian River valleys), be prepared to do a lot of driving to hit all your favorite wineries within these three appellations. It helps to plan ahead so you make time for all the places you want to visit. More than 105 wineries were open to wristband-wearers in 2011. This popular weekend tasting, held without regard for the weather, costs $70 per person for both Saturday and Sunday, or $50 for Sunday only (your designated driver pays $30).

City of Sonoma & the Sonoma Valley

The rich history of the city of Sonoma and the Sonoma Valley sometimes brings it more attention than other areas of Sonoma County. It's touted as the "birthplace of the California wine industry," among other notable distinctions, and many of the state's oldest vineyards and wineries are located here. It has the northernmost Spanish-Mexican mission in the state (there were 21 built in California, beginning in 1769), called San Francisco de Solano, which still stands watch over the lovely, shady, 8-acre Plaza in the middle of town.

The city of Sonoma (today's population is 11,100) was also the chaotic scene of the Bear Flag Revolt in 1846. That's when ownership of California was transferred from Mexico to the United States. Many of the historic adobe and timber structures around the Plaza still echo with the memories of that era, though some now house restaurants, shops, and boutique hotels.

The Sonoma Valley, known as the "Valley of the Moon," may also see more visitors because it's along the quickest route into Sonoma County for most people who drive directly from San Francisco. Consequently, some visitors tend to use all their time to explore this wine appellation that comprises 13,400 vineyard acres and 81 wineries. Who can blame them? The towns are small and inviting, the restaurants are excellent, and some of the wineries court visitors with sumptuous food-and-wine pairings.

Heading north out of the city of Sonoma on Highway 12, the first town encountered along this roughly 18-mile stretch of road is Glen Ellen. Despite its small size, Glen Ellen offers several excellent places to eat and a market with lots of takeaway food. Up the hill from the town is Jack London State Historic Park, where the renowned author, once the highest-paid writer in America, lived and worked on the ranch until his death there in 1916.

Next on the map is Kenwood, home to roadside tasting rooms and restaurants, and some of the best views in the valley, with vineyards stretching up the sides of rocky mountains.

The Sonoma Valley wine-growing appellation is renowned for producing excellent Chardonnay, Cabernet Sauvignon, and Zinfandel. The smaller Carneros region is better known as a Chardonnay and Pinot Noir producer, encompassing 5,900 vineyard acres and 22 wineries. By comparison, the tiny Sonoma Mountain appellation has only 730 acres of vineyards, much of it rocky and hilly, yet it produces excellent Cabernet Sauvignon.

Cafe La Haye, 140 E. Napa St., Sonoma, CA 95476; (707) 935-5994; http://cafelahaye.com; $$$. A longtime favorite of visitors and locals, Cafe La Haye is small but mighty. Diners come from far and wide to try the daily fish or risotto selection or the roasted chicken. Start with the mussel-saffron soup with chorizo, move onto the fresh pappardelle with slow-roasted pork, and finish with warm almond cake and honey poached pear. Open for dinner Tues through Sat. Reservations are recommended, but you might score seats on a walk-in basis at the kitchen bar.

Estate, 400 W. Spain St., Sonoma, CA 95476; (707) 933-3663; www.estate-sonoma.com; $$$. Perhaps you want a delicious prix-fixe, family-style dinner for just $26 per person. You're in luck—at Estate, the meal might consist of antipasti, gnocchi, braised duck leg with lentils, brussels sprouts with pancetta, and a pumpkin pie tart for dessert. The regular menu offers osso buco, seared rock cod, house-made ravioli, *bucatini all carbonara,* braised rabbit, house-made *salumi,* and several styles of pizza. Don't miss the grappa bar, with about 20 artisan producers represented. One of three restaurants in the Sonoma Valley owned and operated by Sondra Bernstein (see the next two listings), Estate was once called The General's Daughter. In a beautifully renovated farmhouse a block off the Plaza, Sondra has added edgy artwork inspired by old Italian films. Open nightly for dinner.

The Fig Cafe and Wine Bar, 13690 Arnold Dr., Glen Ellen, CA 95442; (707) 938-2130; www.thefigcafe.com; $$. Owner Sondra Bernstein opened this cafe after the success of her Sonoma restaurant, **The Girl & the Fig** (see listing below). You can get the same delicious fig and arugula salad here as is served at Sondra's other place, along with three or four pizza options, a wonderful burger, a cheese plate, grilled lamb, steelhead trout with spinach pasta, and sweet treats such as pumpkin bread pudding. Order the grilled cheese sandwich, which is elevated to a higher plane here. The open kitchen makes it fun to watch your *croque madame* or corned beef hash being prepared. Open for dinner every night, and brunch on weekends.

The Girl & the Fig, 110 W. Spain St., Sonoma, CA 95476; (707) 938-3634; www.thegirlandthefig.com; $$$. The fig and arugula salad is a trademark, topped with Laura Chenel chèvre, pancetta, toasted pecans, and finished with a fig and port vinaigrette. The duck confit comes in two portions, one or two legs; wild flounder is served with Yukon potato puree and spinach; and the braised pork shank is accompanied by spaghetti squash and broccoli rabe. Find this restaurant, which received a Michelin Bib Gourmand rating in 2011, on the ground floor of the Sonoma Hotel. Open for lunch and dinner daily.

Santé at the Fairmont Sonoma Mission Inn, 100 Boyes Blvd., Sonoma, CA 95476; (707) 938-9000; www.fairmont.com; $$$$. Freshly anointed with a Michelin star for 2012, Santé cements its reputation as a classy place with excellent cuisine. Perhaps you'd like to start your meal with some California white sturgeon caviar, followed by roasted Sonoma duck breast or roasted sirloin *à la bourguignonne*. The 5-course tasting menu ($125) might include local asparagus, local artisan cheese, scallops and escargot, lobster, beef rib eye, "grown-up" mac and cheese, and a choice of two desserts such as pear soufflé. The wine list is one of the longest in the region—more than 500 choices. The restaurant is located within the Fairmont hotel and spa. Open for dinner daily (reservations recommended).

Foodie Faves

Black Bear Diner, 201 W. Napa St., Sonoma, CA 95476; (707) 935-6800; www.blackbeardiner.com; $. Watch out for bears! From the life-sized carved behemoths standing outside the entrance to the bear-claw graphics on nearly everything inside (including the servers' suspenders and the wallpaper accents), the theme is pervasive. The bear motif is hokey and over the top, but it's impossible to deny the popularity of the diner and the big helpings dished up for big appetites. You order from a newspaper-like menu that has some nostalgic articles dating from the "good old days," such as when a new car cost $2,000. Try the biscuits and gravy (the "half" order is huge), with a biscuit the size of a softball. This chain restaurant, one of many locations in the western United States, is headquartered in the mountains of northern California. Open daily for breakfast, lunch, and dinner.

Breakaway Cafe, 19101 Sonoma Hwy. (Hwy. 12), Sonoma, CA 95476; (707) 996-5949; www.breakawaycafe.com; $. Good food, not fancy. Some orders are available in two sizes, such as the *huevos rancheros* and *machaca con huevos*. Breakaway has a $5 cheeseburger most days, or go upscale with a pricier burger made from Beltane Ranch grass-fed beef (p. 67). Dinner entrees include cowboy steaks (flatiron, rib eye, and a filet), fish and pork tacos, and jambalaya. Located in a shopping center, Breakaway serves breakfast, lunch, and dinner daily.

Cafe Citti, 9049 Sonoma Hwy. (Hwy. 12), Kenwood, CA 95452; (707) 833-2690; www.cafecitti.com; $$. Steaming bowls of pasta and great sandwiches are guaranteed at this small Italian trattoria where you order at the counter from a large menu. Everything I've ever had at Citti is good, so I can't recommend one dish over another (but try the crispy polenta with marinara sauce). Make your custom pasta by choosing a type of noodle and matching it with a sauce (eight to pick from). The restaurant has been featured on the Food Network's *Diners, Drive-ins & Dives*. The patio is the place to be on a warm day. Open daily for lunch and dinner.

Della Santina's, 133 E. Napa St., Sonoma, CA 95476; (707) 935-0576; www.dellasantinas.com; $$. Craving authentic Italian food in a pleasant setting? Just steps off the Plaza is a trattoria that's been serving delicious traditional fare since 1990. Rotisserie chicken shares the menu with herb-filled pork loin, prawns and sole, and assorted pasta plates. The gnocchi *della nonna* comes highly recommended, along with the housemade pappardelle with duck *ragù*, the rabbit roasted with fresh herbs, and the tortellini soup in an unforgettably delicious broth. Antipasti and desserts, too, like the rum cake. Lunch and dinner are served daily.

Depot Hotel Restaurant, 241 First St. West, Sonoma, CA 95476; (707) 938-2980; www.depothotel.com; $$$. Across from Depot Park on First Street, two blocks north of the Plaza, is a historic stone building that for more than 25 years has been a restaurant, though what it once was—a hotel—is still reflected in its name. Chef Michael Ghilarducci creates northern Italian–inspired cuisine, with dishes like veal scaloppine, pistachio-crusted Pacific sturgeon, braised quail, and roasted Petaluma chicken. Pastas include cannelloni with meat and ricotta filling, fettuccine, orecchiette with Gulf prawns, and capellini with Roma tomatoes. A long list of desserts is led by tiramisu and lemon *panna cotta*. The restaurant is open Wed through Sun for lunch and dinner. (Read about Chef Ghilarducci's cooking classes in the Learn to Cook category.)

Doce Lunas Restaurant & Antiques, 8910 Sonoma Hwy. (Hwy. 12), Kenwood, CA 95452; (707) 833-4000; www.docelunas restaurant.com; $$$. It's not a typo in the name—this restaurant has antique furniture for sale in the upstairs loft, a pleasant distraction as you dig into Doce Lunas specialties such as short ribs, lamb shank, *kau-kau* (a mixed plate of pork and beef), and broiled steak with Hawaiian salt. The sticky toffee pudding is the way to end the meal. Find the restaurant in the shopping center in Kenwood at the corner of Randolph Street. Open Wed through Sat for breakfast, lunch, and dinner; Sun for brunch and dinner; and closed Mon and Tues.

El Dorado Kitchen at the El Dorado Hotel, 405 First St. West, Sonoma, CA 95476; (707) 996-3030; http://eldoradosonoma.com; $$$. If the weather is agreeable, ask for a table in the courtyard, where a large fig tree provides shade. Emphasizing seasonal produce, the Kitchen serves such entrees as braised lamb on summer bean *ragù*, roasted Petaluma chicken on summer squash, pork on polenta with roasted apples, and halibut in spinach and chanterelle mushrooms. A large communal table inside seats 22, with a view of the open kitchen. A less expensive dining option in the hotel is the Corner Cafe ($$), with more of a European vibe. Try small bites of crispy duck wings or a fried-egg pizza and heavier fare such as fish-and-chips, washed down with premium white or red wine on tap or one of numerous local microbrews on the beer list. The Kitchen serves lunch and dinner daily; the Cafe is open daily from 7 a.m. to 10 p.m.

El Molino Central, 11 Central Ave. (at Hwy. 12), Boyes Hot Springs, CA 95416; (707) 939-1010; www.elmolinocentral.com; $. Boyes Hot Springs is a largely Hispanic community on the north edge of the city of Sonoma, and El Molino Central is in a pretty white building trimmed in aqua. Inside, the tortillas are handmade from stone-ground corn every day (and you can watch it being done at 11 a.m.). The fresh tortillas are integral to the Mexican classics served at this popular spot near the highway, the kind of dishes that are not so familiar to Americans. The menu items are more traditional make-at-home Mexican food—dishes that take more time and creativity to prepare than tacos and burritos. Consider the Swiss chard enchiladas, butternut squash tamales, or the chicken tamales with an 18-ingredient mole sauce in a banana leaf. Bigger appetites can order the spicy beef stew called *puerco con verdolaga,* a "workingman's" lunch served with unlimited tortillas. El Molino Central is open daily from 8 a.m. to 8 p.m.

The Fremont Diner, 2660 Fremont Dr., Sonoma, CA 95476; (707) 938-7370; http://thefremontdiner.com; $. Southeast of the city of Sonoma, along Highway 121 (also called Fremont Drive by the locals) is this old-fashioned diner, something we could use a lot more of around here. Sitting at the corner of S. Central Avenue, the Fremont announces itself with a red DINER sign extolling the cold drinks and "country cookin'" within. It's the sort of place you might find in rural Nebraska or Kansas, looking as if it's been there forever, with homey bric-a-brac and well-worn stools. Yet the diner goes beyond the standard breakfast choices, offering chicken and waffles, ricotta pancakes, a brown sugar–bacon biscuit, shrimp and grits, and beans with eggs and griddled bread. The lunch menu has some of the same breakfast items, along with an oyster po' boy, muffuletta sandwich, smoked pork sandwich, and spicy fried chicken. Save room for a fried fruit pie, too. Need a jar of pickles to go? They have it. Grab one of the brightly colored picnic tables outside to suck on a milk shake or a float or to dig into huckleberry pudding or caramel cake. The Fremont Diner also serves wine and beer. Open daily from 8 a.m. to 3 p.m. (to 4 p.m. on weekends).

Garden Court Cafe & Bakery, 13647 Arnold Dr., Glen Ellen, CA 95442; (707) 935-1565; www.gardencourtcafe.com; $. If you're seeking eggs Benedict or an omelet, here's where to go if you're within shouting distance of Glen Ellen. Available in numerous varieties, the 18 or so egg-based dishes are delicious, and the

Benedicts can be ordered small to large (one, two, or three eggs). The lunch menu features huge sandwiches, hamburgers, and entree-size salads. Garden Court is also dog-friendly, offering a menu for your four-legged friend, along with water bowls and treats. Open Wed thru Sun from 8:30 a.m. to 2 p.m. (7:30 a.m. on weekends); closed Tues.

Harvest Moon Cafe, 487 First St. West, Sonoma, CA 95476; (707) 933-8160; www.harvestmooncafesonoma.com; $$$. Using meat and produce from local and regional farms and ranches, Harvest Moon has a frequently changing menu. It's been a "recommended" restaurant in recent Michelin guides, and serves meals that could be classified as California cuisine with Mediterranean influences. Several salads are offered, such as the arugula with mustard vinaigrette, smoked bacon, and gruyère cheese. A side of *bacalhau* (Portuguese-style baked salt cod on grilled garlic toast) or the pork and pistachio terrine might hit

the spot before you tuck into an entree of grilled pork sausages with *pinquito* beans or sautéed Hawaiian butterfish with basmati rice. Bittersweet chocolate *pot de crème* with cocoa nib cookies is a great way to finish the meal. The lovely outside dining area is large—perfect for hanging out on a warm Sonoma evening. On Wednesday night in summer, the cafe shows classic movies (*Young Frankenstein* and *Giant,* for instance) on the outdoor patio, along with a fixed-price 3-course dinner. Harvest Moon is on the west side of the town Plaza, so after dining you can stroll back to your nearby hotel room. Open for dinner Wed through Mon, and brunch on Sun (closed Tues).

Hot Box Grill, 18350 Sonoma Hwy. (Hwy. 12), Sonoma, CA 95476; (707) 939-8383; www.hotboxgrill.com; $$$. An unexpected gem in the unincorporated section of Sonoma known as Boyes Hot Springs, Hot Box Grill at first glance looks like an average greasy spoon. It's anything but. With only 32 seats, Hot Box is small and compact, but there's an open kitchen where you can watch the food preparation going on. The food is exceptional, inspired by Italian and French influences, yet blended into a mélange best described as "California cuisine." As with all local restaurants, the menu is adapted frequently to incorporate the best of what's growing nearby. So you might encounter the persimmon appetizer made with crisp slices of the fruit mixed with honey in a vinaigrette along with endive and pistachios; or the roasted beet salad with goat cheese mousse; or grilled lamb meatballs. The main course could be marinated grilled hanger steak, or a pan-roasted pork porterhouse, made complete with a side of heavenly brussels sprouts with pancetta, garlic, and some chile flakes for pizzazz. The risotto with squash is topped with arugula and jicama. For dessert, you can't go wrong with the s'mores tart. Hot Box is open for dinner Tues through Sun, and for lunch Thurs though Sun.

Mary's Pizza Shack, 18636 Sonoma Hwy. (Hwy. 12), Sonoma, CA 95476; (707) 938-3600; and 8 W. Spain St., Sonoma, CA 95476; (707) 938-8300; www.maryspizzashack.com; $$. The city of Sonoma is where it all started for the late Mary Fazio, who opened her first pizza "shack" along the highway in 1959. The monthly rent was only $60 then, but as her pizza became wildly popular, she had to build a bigger place. More than 50 years later, 18 Mary's Pizza Shacks are scattered throughout Sonoma County and in other parts of northern California, all serving the same consistently good menu, no matter which shack you visit. The Fazio family continues to operate the restaurants, from in-laws to grandchildren to great-grandchildren. Besides pizza, Mary's has pasta: spaghetti, ravioli, rotini, penne, bow ties, lasagna, gnocchi, linguine, and tortellini. Everything is made from scratch—no frozen dough or canned sauces. One of the best deals going is the $6.75 Pronto lunch: a bowl of thick soup (usually minestrone) with a Mary's Salad (crisp greens with eggs, mozzarella, beets, salami, and three-bean salad on top). The Spain Street location has a full bar. Open daily for lunch and dinner.

Maya Restaurant, 101 E. Napa St., Sonoma, CA 95476; (707) 935-3500; www.mayarestaurant.com; $$. As the name suggests, Mayan-inspired cuisine is the specialty. Menus items include snapper Veracruz, hanger steak with chipotle sauce, sliced pork marinated in orange and spices, and prawn enchiladas. Maya is also a tequila bar, with a mile-long list of available nectar from the blue agave plant. Located on the southeast corner of the Sonoma Plaza, the atmosphere at Maya can be lively. Open daily for lunch and dinner.

Murphy's Irish Pub, 464 First St. East, Sonoma, CA 95476; (707) 935-0660; www.sonomapub.com; $$. Murphy's has been providing an authentic Irish experience in Sonoma since 1993. Irish beers and Harp Lager are on tap, along with Guinness and several regional microbrews. The food is better than average for a pub, though many of the traditional dishes are on the menu: shepherd's pie, bangers and mash, fish-and-chips. You can also choose lighter fare, such as a Caesar salad or pan-seared chicken breast. The summer months are alive with entertainment—music of all sorts Thurs through Sun, and also Tues. Pull up a chair, order a pint, and tap your toe to the bluegrass stylings of Snap Jackson & the Knock on Wood Players. Open for lunch and dinner daily.

The Red Grape, 529 First St. West, Sonoma, CA 95476; (707) 996-4103; www.theredgrape.com; $$. Pizza is the star here, oven-fired on thin and crispy crusts, and you can have it made in countless ways. The menu is divided between about 12 "white" pizzas and 12 "red" pizzas: the whites are olive oil– or pesto-based, and the reds are plum tomato–sauce based. Build your own pie from the crust up—the list of toppings goes on and on. There are plenty of other options on the menu, too: entree-size salads, salmon or short ribs, panini sandwiches, and bowls of pasta. The outside patio is really delightful on a gorgeous afternoon. Open for lunch and dinner every day.

Saddles Steakhouse at MacArthur Place, 29 E. MacArthur St., Sonoma, CA 95476; (707) 933-3191; www.macarthurplace.com; $$$. Saddles is a make-no-excuses steakhouse with a horse and saddle theme that's not as cornball as it sounds—they pull it off pretty tastefully. Red meat is the attraction, with three sizes of prime rib, beefsteaks of all sizes and types, and lamb, too. Lighter appetites will appreciate the salmon and chicken options, sides of fennel-roasted beets or asparagus in Hollandaise sauce, and Gorgonzola fondue. Begin the meal with oyster shooters or the cornmeal-dusted onion rings, served with blue cheese aioli. The martini bar shakes up several combinations of the drink, and there is an extensive wine list. Saddles is open daily for breakfast, lunch, and dinner.

Sonoma-Meritage Martini Oyster Bar & Grille, 165 W. Napa St., Sonoma, CA 95476; (707) 938-9430; www.sonomameritage .com; $$$. Perhaps the only place in town where you can get a large selection of seafood, Meritage specializes in chilled platters from small to huge. There are also plates of oysters and clams, ceviche, live Maine lobsters, Dungeness crab, seafood chowders, and so on. If you can swing it and it's on the menu, go for the *brodetto,* a bouillabaisse-like stew with prawns, mussels, clams, and fish, along with a lobster claw and a generous portion of Dungeness crab, all in a spicy tomato and herb broth. Red meat is on the menu, too, if your date doesn't dig fish. One option might be wild boar baby back ribs, served on grilled polenta and finished with a Cabernet Sauvignon shallot sauce. House-made pasta ranges from ravioli to gnocchi made from locally grown potatoes. Order the black fettuccine, made with squid ink and loaded with prawns and baby zucchini in a saffron-cream sauce. The cuisine is inspired by the tastes of northern Italy and southern France, and much of the fresh produce comes from the restaurant's own kitchen garden and a local farmer. Meritage is decorated with locally made hand-blown glass accents and antique redwood boards rescued from old chicken houses. Dinner is served daily, with the happy hour oyster bar specials starting at 4 p.m. Brunch is also served on weekends from 10:30 a.m. to 3 p.m.

Swiss Hotel, 18 W. Spain St., Sonoma, CA 95476; (707) 938-2884; www.swisshotelsonoma.com; $$$. Take a moment to appreciate the age of this building. It's a well-preserved adobe constructed in the 1830s, and it's part of what makes the city of Sonoma so intriguing to history buffs. The Swiss Hotel has its own historical landmark plaque—read it before entering, then order a brick-oven pizza or a plate of pasta. The food is classic Italian fare, and the bar looks nearly the same as it did more than 100 years ago. Try the steamed clams and mussels to begin, or the calamari with marinara sauce, and follow that with the grilled polenta with mushroom *ragù*. Open daily for lunch and dinner.

Vineyards Inn Bar & Grill, 8445 Sonoma Hwy. (Hwy. 12), Kenwood, CA 95452; (707) 833-4500; www.vineyardsinn.com; $$. Serving Spanish food, Vineyards Inn fills a niche in this area of the Sonoma Valley. The menu is varied, with about 25 small plates of tapas to choose from (I can vouch for the "fries with eyes"—yummy flash-fried smelt). The specialties of the house include pork adobo, Basque lamb shank, paella, main-dish salads, and some lighter fare, too. The restaurant sources meat from nearby ranchers and grows all its own produce. With a full bar, several creative cocktails are available, as well as inventive margaritas. There is virtually no waste generated by this restaurant that isn't reused in some fashion. For instance, if you leave a bit of water in your drinking glass, it doesn't go down the drain. Instead, it goes into a container for irrigating the landscape. All of the paper goods are compostable, and as much refuse as possible is recycled. Vineyards Inn has been called the greenest restaurant in the entire San Francisco Bay Area. Open daily (except Tues) for lunch and dinner.

Wolf House, 13740 Arnold Dr., Glen Ellen, CA 95442; (707) 938-8510; www.jacklondonlodge.com; $$. Wolf House is part of the Jack London Lodge hotel, just down the hill from Jack London State Park. Jack's legacy looms large in Glen Ellen and the Sonoma Valley—the park was his ranch, where he wrote most of his books, dabbled in farming, raised pigs, and died on the porch of his small house. At the ranch, Wolf House was the fabulous stone structure Jack was building as his new home, which mysteriously burned to the ground one night. Despite the sad history behind the name, Wolf House dishes up tasty fare such as roast veal sausage, chicken potpie, double-cut pork chop, roast duck, salmon, calf's liver, and New York steak. Wolf House is open nightly for dinner, lunch Mon through Fri, and brunch on Sat and Sun.

Yeti, 14301 Arnold Dr., Glen Ellen, CA 95442; (707) 996-9930; www.yetirestaurant.com; $$. Yeti is in a peaceful setting in Jack

London Village, an aging, but still charming, shopping area along the shady Sonoma Creek. Park in the main lot and walk over the pedestrian bridge—Yeti is straight ahead. The Indian and Nepalese cuisine runs to chicken tikka masala, curries, biryani, lamb shank, prawn or lobster masala, fish curry, tandoori sizzling entrees, and several vegetable dishes. Don't forget an order of fabulous naan bread. Yeti is open for lunch and dinner every day (closed between 2:30 and 5 p.m.).

What is Biodynamic Farming?

You'll see the term "biodynamic" used frequently in this book as it pertains to growing wine grapes and other crops in Sonoma County. If you don't live in an agricultural region, you may not be familiar with the word.

Biodynamic farming is not a new concept—in fact, it's a throwback to how farming once was, before chemicals were used, but with some celestial twists developed about a hundred years ago. Biodynamic methods are now more widely practiced by farmers who wish to go beyond "organic" to raise their crops. Organic farming is growing plants without synthetic pesticides, fungicides, and fertilizers. Biodynamic farming takes organic to a higher level—all natural and in balance with the earth's natural cycles.

On a biodynamic farm, the land becomes a self-sustaining system that maintains its health without any external or unnatural additions. The farm is a living organism with its own ecosystem, the

Specialty Stores & Markets

Barking Dog Coffee Roasters, 201 W. Napa St., Sonoma, CA 95476; (707) 996-7446; and 18133 Sonoma Hwy. (Hwy. 12), Sonoma, CA 95476; (707) 939-1905; www.barkingdogcoffee.com. Barking Dog is a hometown owned and operated coffee business with two locations in the city of Sonoma. The owner's barking dog supplied the name when he was putting the enterprise together in

exact opposite of how "factory" farms have operated for years by using fertilizers and other chemicals to boost per-acre output.

Biodynamic farming involves the mixing of "preparations" or homeopathic "teas" (a combination of herbs, animal manures, and minerals) that are then made into sprays and composts. These are carefully prepared and applied to the soil at specific times. Biodynamic farming respects the lunar cycles and also follows the astronomical calendar when pruning, cultivating, harvesting, and when spraying the preparations.

The idea is to promote the development of desirable microorganisms that will stimulate root growth. Sheep or other grazing animals are frequently brought into the mix to nibble on the grasses and cover crops between rows of vines (without disturbing the grapes) and adding to the ecosystem by leaving their natural fertilizer behind.

Benziger Family Winery in Glen Ellen was one of the first in this region to farm many of their vineyards biodynamically, and they have the official certification to prove it.

1995. The stores host music and poetry readings, and a happy hour takes place every day at both locations, when a 12-ounce cuppa joe is just a buck. The Dog sells the beans, too—its bean-of-the-month specials are a great deal: buy two pounds and get another pound free.

Basque Cafe Boulangerie, 460 First St. East, Sonoma, CA 95476; (707) 935-7687; http://basqueboulangerie.com. There are always satisfied customers sitting at the outdoor tables at this bakery. French-style breads, including an award-winning sourdough, are the specialty. The place does a large wholesale business, too, supplying bread to a long list of local grocery stores, hotels, and restaurants. The cafe side of the store serves light breakfasts, along with generously sized sandwiches and main-meal salads. Try a piece of beehive cake, too. For a special vineyard picnic, the "Vintners' Box Lunch" can be arranged with 24-hours' notice, offering a choice between three sandwiches, three salads, and a cookie. The bakery and cafe are open daily from 7 a.m. to 6 p.m.

The Chocolate Cow, 452 First St. East, Sonoma, CA 95476; (707) 935-3564. The Holstein cow motif leaves no doubt that you're in an ice cream shop. Yogurt is also dished up, along with monster snow cones. Or go directly to mainlining chocolate—choose from the handmade candies in the case and fresh fudge, too. On a hot summer day in Sonoma, a common occurrence, one of those big snow cones really hits the spot.

The Epicurean Connection, 112 W. Napa St., Sonoma, CA 95476; (707) 935-7960; www.theepicureanconnection.com. Sheana Davis's store is a neighborhood gathering spot, a cheese-centric shop that also serves food. Sheana's own cheese, Delice de la Vallee, is here, as are cheeses from other local producers. And, I can't believe it's a—butter bar. Browse through the many choices of cow and goat butter for sale. Daily lunch specials are offered, and there are typically 4 or 5 soups to choose from, 10 to 12 sandwich options, cheese plates, maple-bacon waffles on weekends, and craft beer tastings, too. Local organic meats are for sale, along with fresh breads, local olive oils, jams and preserves, artisan pasta, and much more. The wine list is also extensive. (Read more about Sheana Davis and The Epicurean Connection on p. 66). See The Epicurean Connection's recipe for **Honey Blackberry Flan** on p. 265.

Jacob's Kitchen Culinary Tools, 20350 Eighth St. East, Sonoma, CA 95476; (866) 784-8962 or (707) 933-0807; www.jacobs-kitchen.com. Tucked away in a light industrial park on the eastern edge of the city of Sonoma is a paradise for professional chefs and home cooks, stocked with some the best equipment made for food preparation. Jacob's Kitchen is primarily an online business selling the exceptional and pricey Ruffoni copper cookware direct from Italy, among hundreds of other kitchen items. Most of the online inventory can also be found at this retail location: all manner of kitchen gadgetry, cutlery, bakeware, tableware, espresso machines, and superior kitchen islands made by fine-furniture craftsmen in New York. Jacob's is open from 9 a.m. to 5 p.m. on weekdays, and 10 a.m. to 4 p.m. on Sat.

Johnny's Appliances and Classic Ranges, 17549 Sonoma Hwy. (Hwy. 12), Sonoma, CA 95476; (707) 996-9730; www.johnnysclassic ranges.com. Johnny is a cool cat—a curmudgeonly retro range specialist who restores and repairs vintage kitchen stoves at this shop at the north end of Sonoma city. The brand names may not be familiar if you were born after John F. Kennedy was president, but they were hot stuff once. Today the names sound more like modern country music acts: O'Keefe & Merritt, Gaffers & Sattler, Wedgewood. Johnny, the proprietor and master repairman, usually has 40 to 50 ranges on the showroom floor at any given time, many of them still missing parts and needing TLC. But if you see one you like and want to make whole again, Johnny is your man. He can get his hands on vintage refrigerators, too. These classic appliances aren't cheap, but they may outlive you. Look for the blue neon sign in the window that burns CLASSIC RANGES. Open Sat from 10 a.m. to 5 p.m. (though it's a good idea to call Johnny to confirm), and on weekdays by appointment.

The Olive Press, 24724 Arnold Dr. (Hwy. 121), Sonoma, CA 95476; (800) 965-4839; www.theolivepress.com. Complimentary olive oil tastings, olive-infused gifts and food products, cookbooks, olive-appreciation accessories—all this, and olive pressing and oil production, too. If it has anything to do with olives and their oil, it can be found here. The Olive Press sells its own label of oils, vinegars, citrus oils, pasta and pasta sauce, tapenades, mustards, whole olives, and even Italian-made airtight stainless steel *fusti* containers for properly storing large quantities of premium olive oil in your kitchen. The store's mill runs nearly nonstop during the olive harvest season (October through January), turning out extra-virgin olive oil for its products and custom-pressing oils for other olive growers. The Olive Press is in the Jacuzzi Winery building—step through the main door and go to the right.

Sign of the Bear Kitchenware, 435 First St. West, Sonoma, CA 95476; (707) 996-3722. Whether cooking, baking, or presenting a meal to guests, you'll find what you need in this well-stocked store along the Plaza. You don't have to be a chef to appreciate Sign of the Bear. Every nook and cranny is filled with aprons, trivets, wine stoppers, linens, cake-decorating supplies, must-haves, wanna-haves, doodads, and odds and ends. The collectible Italian ceramics make wonderful serving pieces (and gifts), and there's a knife for any culinary purpose. Expect to see the practical and the downright weird: goggles, for instance, to deflect the weeping that can happen while slicing onions. The wall of gadgets is worth an hour or two of browsing alone. Follow Sign of the Bear on Facebook.

Sonoma Market, 500 W. Napa St., Sonoma, CA 95476; (707) 996-3411; www.sonoma-glenellenmkt.com. The food-to-go selection at this store is impressive and comprehensive. It's also a regular market, carrying most staples the average cook needs for his or her pantry, as well as a full meat department, fresh produce, bakery, wine department, and dry goods. The deli has sandwiches, a huge salad bar, prepackaged fresh salads, a hot food bar, sushi selections, and a cheese and olive department. Locally owned, the store believes in community involvement and supporting good causes and charities. The market's sister store is located in Glen Ellen at 13751 Arnold Dr., (707) 996-6728.

Sonoma's Best, 1190 E. Napa St., Sonoma, CA 95476; (707) 933-0340; www.sonomas-best.com. On the eastern edge of Sonoma is a renovated historic building housing this combination deli/wine shop/gift shop. The shop bottles its own olive oil, carries products by other Sonoma Valley food purveyors, and also serves a big menu, from breakfast options to dinner entrees. Open daily from 7 a.m. to 6 p.m. (8 a.m. to 5 p.m. Sun).

Wine Country Chocolates, 14301 Arnold Dr., Glen Ellen, CA 95442; (707) 996-1010; and 414 First St. East, Sonoma, CA 95476; www.winecountrychocolates.com. Sinfully rich and satisfying are these handcrafted confections that blend red and sparkling wines into the recipes. The Glen Ellen location is where the chocolates are conceived and created, in a tasting room with a viewable kitchen.

Mother-daughter chocolatiers Betty and Caroline Kelly started the business more than 10 years ago, determined to make the creamiest truffles they could, and wine-infused to boot. The "Vintner's Blend" truffles are their best sellers, and the Kellys also make flavors such as cappuccino-tiramisu, orange Grand Marnier, and *dulce de leche*. The Sonoma location is in the El Paseo shopping area, and features olive oils, vinegars, and mustards for sale in addition to the same great truffles.

Made or Grown Here

Farmers' Markets

Sonoma Valley Farmer's Market at Depot Park, First Street West, Sonoma, CA 95476; (707) 538-7023; www.sonomavalley.com. North of the city's leafy main Plaza, this market borders another leafy space, Depot Park. The weather is warmer in the Sonoma Valley compared to some regions of the county, so nearby farmers can be relied on to have certain produce earlier in the season than other local markets. Besides interesting items such as French break- fast radishes and mustard greens, expect fresh flowers, meat raised near Sebastopol, handcrafted breads (including hot giant pretzels baked on the spot), cheese, butter, honey, and mushrooms. The market takes place year-round on Fri, from 9 a.m. to 1 p.m.

Valley of the Moon Farmers' Market, City Hall Plaza, 2 E. Napa St., Sonoma, CA 95476; (707) 694-3611; www.vomcfm.com. You couldn't ask for a more pleasant setting for a farmers' market: in the shade, for the most part. That makes a difference on hot summer evenings in the Plaza. Fresh produce, packaged foods such as local cheese and pasta, and ready-to-eat options (pizza and Thai cuisine, for instance) are all available. The market is open Tues night from 5:30 p.m. until dusk, from May through Oct.

Farms & Farm Stands

Hardin Gardens, 22656 Broadway, Sonoma, CA 95476; (707) 548-4758; www.hardingardens.net. Fruits, herbs, fresh eggs, and homegrown tomatoes are the specialties at this family farm, which is open July through Sept, Wed and Sun from noon to 5 p.m.

Oak Hill Farm of Sonoma, 15101 Sonoma Hwy. (Hwy. 12), Glen Ellen, CA 95442; (707) 996-6643; www.oakhillfarm.net. Seasonal fruits, vegetables, and herbs mingle with a bounty of fresh flowers in the rustic Red Barn Store, a century-old structure on this 700-acre property. Rounding out the offerings are handcrafted wreaths, gifts, and dried goods. Open from April until Christmas, Wed through Sun, from 10 a.m. to 6 p.m.

The Patch, 250 Second St. East, Sonoma, CA 95476; (707) 849-7384. If you're visiting Vella Cheese (p. 67), you might as well check out The Patch while you're at it, across the street just north of the bike trail. This seasonal stand, generally open 10 a.m. to 5 p.m. daily, is set up on the honor system. You weigh what you bag, figure out the cost, then leave the money in a lockbox. The Patch is convenient for day-trippers to Sonoma, being only two short blocks from the Plaza. Grower Lazaro Calderón's large variety of produce can usually be found at the farmers' markets in Sonoma and Santa Rosa, too. From Walla Walla onions to Romano beans, there's a big assortment to choose from. On a recent Saturday morning at the Farmers' Market at Veterans Hall, Lazaro's Romano beans in particular were a hot seller, as they have a short season in late summer. What makes The Patch exceptional is its backstory. The 6 acres within town, surrounded by homes and businesses, have been farmed more or less continuously since 1870. The forward-thinking owner of the property, who died a few years ago, asked that it remain used for agriculture in some fashion as a condition of his will. It would be prime territory for new homes or a boutique hotel, but for now it will stay rural and productive.

Cheesemakers

The Epicurean Connection, 112 W. Napa St., Sonoma, CA 95476; (707) 935-7960; www.theepicureanconnection.com. Owner Sheana Davis wears many hats in her business, but at heart she's a cheesemaker. She crafts her own cheese, called Delice de la Vallee, which can also be purchased on Friday morning at the **Sonoma Valley Farmers' Market** (p. 63). Yet a stop into her new location on West Napa Street is a treat, with all sorts of artisan cheese for sale, fresh ravioli (including those delectable pillows of pasta stuffed with Sheana's own Delice de la Vallee), olive oils, organic meats, daily lunch specials, a coffee bar, and much more. Sheana also shares her knowledge of cheesemaking, with regularly scheduled classes in how to do it (see Learn to Cook). The store is open daily, usually from 10 a.m. to 8 p.m. See Sheana Davis's recipe for **Honey Blackberry Flan** on p. 265.

Laura Chenel's Chèvre, 22085 Carneros Vineyard Way, Sonoma, CA 95476; (707) 996-4477; www.laurachenel.com. A pioneer in the goat-cheese industry, Laura Chenel began her business on a small farm in Sebastopol before relocating her goats to the Carneros region of Sonoma Valley. Ahead of her time, she blazed the goat-cheese trail throughout the 1970s and 1980s for others to follow. A few years ago Laura sold the company that bears her name to a French artisan cheese corporation that widened its distribution, yet she continues to raise and tend her goats at the Sonoma ranch. In 2011, Laura Chenel's chèvre was voted the best chèvre in the nation at the American Cheese Society's annual judging and competition. Visitors are not permitted at the farm, but the Laura Chenel line of goat cheese is available in all good grocery stores in the area, and beyond.

Vella Cheese of California, 315 Second St. East, Sonoma, CA 95476; (707) 938-3232; www.vellacheese.com. The Vella family has held court in this town since 1931, churning out cheese in a building that survived the huge 1906 earthquake that ravaged San Francisco (it shook mightily in Sonoma, too). Vella is most famous for its dry Jack cheese, and there are several versions of the Jack with added flavors and spices (pepper Jack, and so on). The company makes other varieties, too, and hands out samples while offering education about, perhaps, why cheddar cheese is orange.

Meats & Butchers

Beltane Ranch, 11775 Sonoma Hwy. (Hwy. 12), Glen Ellen, CA 95442; http://beltaneranch.com. Rotated through different pastures along this rural stretch of the highway, the ranch's beef cattle are never confined nor fed grain. The result is a beef product with more nutrition than commercially raised feedlot cattle, which is also more delicious and takes less time to cook. The ranch sells its beef to individuals by the quarter, and the butchering and processing takes place at a nearby USDA-inspected facility. The finished beef is then delivered to a drop-off point in Sonoma. Beltane Ranch is also an olive grower, and the olives are cold-pressed at **The Olive Press** (see p. 60).

Olive Grower

B.R. Cohn Winery & Olive Oil Co., 15000 Sonoma Hwy. (Hwy. 12), Glen Ellen, CA 95442; (707) 931-7931; www.brcohn.com. Olive trees have always dotted this parcel of land, primarily the picholine variety imported from France. About a century ago, production of olive oil in this part of California went into decline and stayed that way for many decades. But in the early 1990s Bruce Cohn was among many growers who saw the potential of again squeezing superior oil from the olives. B.R. Cohn Olive Oil Company won the Best of Show award for olive oil at the 2011 Sonoma County Harvest Fair, and the limited-production oil he bottles called Sonoma Estate Picholine Extra-Virgin Olive Oil earned a double-gold award. The company produces several other oils and flavored vinegars, too, that are available at the winery's retail shop and in many local stores. (Read more about B.R. Cohn Winery in the next category.) See B.R. Cohn's recipe for **Blue Cheese Stuffed Figs Wrapped in Prosciutto** on p. 266.

Food & Wine Pairings/
Landmark Wineries

Benziger Family Winery, 1883 Jack London Rd., Glen Ellen, CA 95442; (707) 935-3000; www.benziger.com. This winery encourages you to relax and soak up the scenery, learn a bit about biodynamic farming, and sit a spell to enjoy the wines. Biodynamic is the highest level of organic farming a grower can achieve. That means they use cover crops, animals, and natural composting to maintain the healthy balance in the soil (see the feature on p. 56 for more information). Benziger is located on the side of Sonoma Mountain, above the valley floor, with terraced vineyards and a tram that takes you on an educational tour of the fermentation facility and caves. Picnicking is popular in a grove with many tables and chairs. Benziger bottles Cabernet Sauvignon, Pinot Noir, Sauvignon Blanc, Chardonnay, Merlot, and Syrah, plus a few others. The winery also bottles olive oil, and in 2011 received a gold medal from the Sonoma County Harvest Fair for its estate reserve extra-virgin oil. Open daily from 10 a.m. to 5 p.m.

B.R. Cohn Winery & Olive Oil Co., 15000 Sonoma Hwy. (Hwy. 12), Glen Ellen, CA 95442; (707) 931-7931; www.brcohn.com. The wine came first, the olive oil a bit later. Owner Bruce Cohn has been in the music business for decades, primarily as manager for the Doobie Brothers since 1969. In the 1980s he also entered the wine business, and has enjoyed great success in both fields. The winery produces excellent Chardonnay, Zinfandel, Pinot Noir,

Malbec, a red blend called SyrZin, a Primitivo (similar to Zinfandel), and its signature Olive Hill Estate Cabernet Sauvignon. The white farmhouse set back from the highway is where the wine tasting goes on (check out the collection of gold records on the walls), and the gourmet shop is only steps away. The many olive oils and related products B.R. Cohn bottles and jars can be found here, with lots of sampling permitted. The food products include not only the award-winning olive oils but several vinegars, dry rubs for seafood and steak, tapenades, Cabernet fudge sauce, caramel sauce, mustards, stuffed olives, and logo apparel and accessories. The setting is popular as a wedding venue, with beautiful sun-dappled vineyards in the background, and it's also where Bruce's annual Charity Music Festival takes place. Open daily from 10 a.m. to 5 p.m. (Read more about B.R. Cohn Winery in the Food Events & Happenings section.) See B.R. Cohn's recipe for **Blue Cheese Stuffed Figs Wrapped in Prosciutto** on p. 266.

Buena Vista Carneros Winery, 18000 Old Winery Rd., Sonoma, CA 95476; (707) 926-1266 or (800) 926-1266; www.buenavista carneros.com. Founded in 1857, Buena Vista is a landmark winery for being the oldest in California to produce premium wines. Count Agoston Haraszthy was the man with a plan, responsible for planting Buena Vista's first vineyards and deciding where and how the buildings would be constructed. Much of the rock used in the buildings came from the underground tunnels dug by Chinese laborers, and two of the structures are now California Historic Landmarks. The winery offers a private wine tasting that includes lunch and takes place in the historic press house on the property, or in the outdoor courtyard, starting at $45 per person (reservations required). Wines produced by Buena Vista include Chardonnay, Pinot Noir, Syrah, and Merlot. Visit Buena Vista daily between 10 a.m. and 5 p.m.

Chateau St. Jean Winery, 8555 Sonoma Hwy. (Hwy. 12), Kenwood, CA 95452; (800) 543-7572; www.chateaustjean.com. I use the expressions "beautiful setting" and "breathtaking scenery" more than I should. There are only so many appropriate adjectives in my vocabulary. But this winery really is in a gorgeous spot, well off the highway with a backdrop of striking mountains known as the Sugarloaf Ridge. The tasting room is large and sometimes boisterous, and includes a counter where some food-to-go is sold, including a handy four-portion artisan cheese package specifically designed for wine tasting. The winery sells its private label gourmet food products in the tasting room and also online and by mail. These include a mayonnaise made with Sauvignon Blanc, pear and pomegranate vinegars, flavored grapeseed oils, wine-infused fudge and chocolate sauces, and mustards. A private VIP reserve tasting with small bites ($35 per person) is conducted three times daily, and a "box lunch" program includes a guided tour, followed by a reserve tasting and gourmet eats ($50 per person). Call ahead to inquire about reserving these pairings. The chateau on the 250-acre estate was built in 1920, and the winery was established in 1973. Chateau St. Jean bottles an excellent Cabernet Sauvignon (Cinq Cépages Sonoma County), along with Pinot Noir, Malbec, and Merlot. The white wines include Chardonnay, Pinot Blanc, and Viognier. The tasting room is open daily from 10 a.m. to 5 p.m.

Cline Cellars, 24737 Arnold Dr. (Hwy. 121), Sonoma, CA 95476; (707) 940-4030; www.clinecellars.com. Looking more like an inviting country home than a winery, Cline Cellars is notable for its many outdoor tables where you can enjoy picnic goodies with a glass of the Syrah or Red Truck, roam the lovely and sprawling gardens with thousands of rose bushes, and tour its California Missions Museum. Wine tastings are complimentary, and some cheese and other snacks are for sale in the tasting room. Cline Cellars also produces Chardonnay, Zinfandel, Roussanne, Marsanne, and Viognier. The museum on the property features small-scale models of all of California's 21 historic mission buildings that were built during a 50-year period beginning in 1769. Sounds kind of dull, but it's really fun. Open daily from 10 a.m. to 6 p.m.

Gloria Ferrer Caves & Vineyards, 23555 Arnold Dr. (Hwy. 121), Sonoma, CA 95476; (707) 996-7256; www.gloriaferrer.com. This Spanish-style winery owned and operated by the Ferrer family of Barcelona has a great view of estate vineyards and the rolling hills of the Carneros grape-growing appellation from the terrace. Gloria Ferrer is probably best known for sparkling wine, produced using the *méthode champenoise* process of making superior bubbly. Still wines are also available for tasting, including Chardonnay and Pinot Noir. The tasting room has cheese and Spanish-style snacks for sale to pair with the wine. Olive trees grown in view of the terrace are the source of the olive oil sold exclusively in the tasting room. Gloria Ferrer throws an annual bash called the Catalan Festival, with plenty of Spanish food and wine available (see the Food Events & Happenings section). For future reference, here are some foods that pair well with Gloria Ferrer sparkling wine: shrimp satay with peanut sauce, fried calamari, oysters on the half shell, *foie gras,* olives, and ceviche. Open 10 a.m. to 5 p.m. every day.

Gundlach Bundschu Winery, 2000 Denmark St., Sonoma, CA 95476; (707) 938-5277; www.gunbun.com. One of the oldest family-owned wineries in California, Gundlach Bundschu was established in 1858 by Jacob Gundlach. He bought 400 acres east of Sonoma and brought back rootstock from Germany and France to plant vineyards. Charles Bundschu joined Jacob in the business several years later. Over the decades and through six generations of the Bundschu family, more premium wine grapes were planted, caves were dug, and the wines earned praise and awards. Gundlach Bundschu bottles many varietals, including Merlot, Cabernet Sauvignon, Chardonnay, Tempranillo, Pinot Noir, Syrah, Zinfandel, and others. A cave tour is $20 per person, which includes tasting wines right out of the barrels and a seated tasting in the cave's dining room. The cave tours take place after the harvest season,

Thurs through Mon at 2:30 p.m. Spring tours include an excursion into the vineyards in a 12-passenger Pinzgauer vehicle (a Swiss Army troop transport, refitted for comfort as it scales steep hills), followed by a tasting in the caves ($40 per person). Reservations are required for the tours. The tasting room is open daily from 11 a.m. to 5:30 p.m. (closing at 4:30 p.m. in the off-season).

Kunde Estate Winery & Vineyards, 9825 Sonoma Hwy. (Hwy. 12), Kenwood, CA 95452; (707) 833-5501; www.kunde.com. The Kunde name has been associated with farming and agriculture in Sonoma County for more than 100 years. The family grows wine grapes on approximately 1,850 acres in the Sonoma Valley, many of them surrounding the visitors' center and tasting room on the ranch. The location is serene, with rows of vineyards rising to the east, and the wine cave dug into the hillside. To really get a feel for the lay of the land here, make a reservation for a mountaintop tasting ($30 per person), a private tour that whisks you by van to a scenic spot 1,400 feet above the valley floor to sip wine. Guided hikes through the vineyards are also offered about once a month. Kunde bottles many red and white varietals: Sauvignon Blanc, Viognier, Merlot, Syrah, Zinfandel, Cabernet Sauvignon, and Sangiovese. In addition to great wines, Kunde also makes its own Zinfandel chocolate sauce and a Chardonnay caramel sauce—all available for sale in the tasting room. Open from 10:30 a.m. to 5 p.m. daily.

Mayo Reserve Room, 9200 Sonoma Hwy. (Hwy. 12), Kenwood, CA 95452; (707) 833-5504; www.mayofamilywinery.com. The Mayo family founded their winery in 1993 to make small lots of single-vineyard wines, including reds such as Malbec, Merlot, Cabernet Sauvignon, and Pinot Noir, and whites such as Chardonnay and Viognier. The wine-and-food pairings offered at Mayo are outstanding—the tasting room is set up more like a dining room with tables and chairs. A 7-course menu is presented ($35 per person), pairing Mayo's whites and reds with generous portions of food. Examples: Petit Verdot served with Wagyu flat iron steak, Viognier paired with curried squash soup, Cabernet Sauvignon with soba noodles and shiitake mushrooms, and Zinfandel with pork loin and plum sauce. Reservations are requested in advance for the 90-minute experience. Mayo also has a tasting room in Glen Ellen at 13101 Arnold Dr., (707) 938-9401. Both locations are open daily from 10:30 a.m. to 6:30 p.m.

Ram's Gate Winery & Estate Vineyards, 28700 Arnold Dr., Sonoma, CA 95476; (707) 721-8700; www.ramsgatewinery.com. A new entry into the Sonoma Valley wine scene in 2011 is this showplace winery in the Carneros region. Floor-to-ceiling windows make for a spacious, light-filled environment—fans of beautiful architecture will enjoy studying this place as they lounge on plush seating. Small bottlings of Pinot Noir and Chardonnay are produced, as well as Cabernet Sauvignon, Syrah, and three sparkling wines. The owners believe in offering visitors a relaxing experience that includes pairing food with the wine, and the on-site chef creates small plates for this purpose: lamb meatballs, heirloom tomato gazpacho, sea bass with roasted peppers—some made with ingredients from the winery's culinary garden. Special picnic baskets can also be arranged, filled with, perhaps, fried Petaluma chicken. For now the wines are available exclusively at the winery and through its wine club. Open Thurs through Sun from 10 a.m. to 6 p.m. Call ahead for prices of the food-and-wine pairings, wine tasting, and the picnic baskets.

Ravenswood Winery, 18701 Gehricke Rd., Sonoma, CA 95476; (707) 933-2332; www.ravenswood.com. The Ravenswood motto is "No Wimpy Wines," and that pretty well sets the tone for your wine-tasting experience. The tasting room is more intimate than some, which makes for a better time, in most cases. The winery excels at producing Zinfandel, and they call the place "Zinfomania Central." A plate of local cheese is usually available during the busy season ($15 per person), to pair with your glass of Zin at the outdoor patio. Ravenswood also holds wine-blending seminars on Friday and Saturday ($50) with advance reservations. Tours and barrel tastings are offered, too. Open daily 10 a.m. to 4:30 p.m.

Robledo Family Winery, 21901 Bonness Rd., Sonoma, CA 95476; (707) 939-6903; www.robledofamilywinery.com. Reynaldo Robledo was a teenager in the 1960s when he first came to America from Mexico. He found work in the vineyards and steadily progressed up the ladder of responsibility to become a vineyard manager. In the culmination of his dream, Reynaldo and the Robledo family opened their namesake winery in 2004. The tasting room is a little bit of Mexico, walled in by the oak barrels used for aging the wine. In whites, Robledo bottles Chardonnay, Sauvignon Blanc, a Cuvee Brut sparkler, Pinot Blanc and Pinot Grigio. The "Seven Brothers" Sauvignon Blanc, in particular, is excellent. The reds include Pinot Noir, Merlot, and a Syrah. With prior reservations, a private wine-and-cheese pairing can be arranged for $30 per person. A larger 3-course dinner paired with Robledo wines is also offered for a party of up to 12 people ($80 per person). Several times a year during special events, the winery cooks up great Mexican cuisine to sample with the wines. Ask to taste their award-winning extra-virgin olive oil, too—it won a double-gold award at the 2011 Sonoma County Harvest Fair. Open by appointment only—just call ahead.

Sebastiani Vineyards & Winery, 3889 Fourth St. East, Sonoma, CA 95476; (707) 933-3230; www.sebastiani.com. History is everywhere here, the legacy of a longtime winemaking family, and the largest redwood tank in the world, too (take a stroll back from the tasting room to see it). Founder Samuele Sebastiani learned how to make wine from monks in his native Italy before coming to America in 1895. He began this winery several years later, and during Prohibition was able to continue operations by legally producing sacramental wines and wine for medicinal purposes. Sebastiani is best known for its Cherryblock Cabernet Sauvignon, but it also bottles other reds such as Pinot Noir and Merlot, and whites, too—Chardonnay and Roussanne. With prior reservations, a lengthy tour, tasting, and lunch can be arranged ($30 per person) in a private setting, or a wine-and-cheese seminar ($30) for pairing local *fromage* with the wine. The tasting room is open from 11 a.m. to 5 p.m. daily.

Viansa Winery & Marketplace, 25200 Arnold Dr. (Hwy. 121), Sonoma, CA 95476; (707) 935-4700 or (800) 995-4740; www.viansa .com. This is frequently the first stop for newcomers to the Sonoma Valley if they drive from San Francisco by way of Highway 121. It's a good way to start off your wine-tasting experience, primarily because of the views, the brick-oven pizzas offered on weekends to wine tasters, and the wide assortment of food available. Some people are actually here more for the food than the wine, if you want to know the truth. Viansa has its own line of food products—pizza and pasta sauces, honey, tapenades, marinades, olive oils, and vinegars—and all of them can be sampled. Freshly made sandwiches, soups, salads, and more can also be purchased and taken outside to the patio, which overlooks a wildlife preserve. Viansa bottles many wine varietals, both red and white. The signature series includes Barbera, Primitivo, Cabernet Sauvignon, Pinot Noir, Zinfandel, and others. By-appointment-only wine-and-food pairings can also be arranged, from $25 to $45 per person. These are limited to small groups of six to eight. Viansa is open every day from 10 a.m. to 5 p.m.

Brewpubs & Microbreweries

Hopmonk Tavern, 691 Broadway, Sonoma, CA 95476; (707) 935-9100; www.hopmonk.com/sonoma. The original tavern in Sebastopol was such a success that owner Dean Biersch opened this pub on the other side of Sonoma County. The number of draft brews on tap is enough to satisfy even the pickiest beer drinker, including this producer's namesake unfiltered pilsner—a California-style pale ale—and a dark Bavarian wheat. Hopmonk also pours beers from other northern California microbreweries, and offers more than 100 choices in bottled beer. The food is above average for a brewpub: try the calamari or mussels to start, a grilled cheese-and-ham sandwich, sweet potato fries, fontina chicken, pulled pork sliders, chopped salads, cider-braised salmon, and jambalaya, too. Desserts lean to apple crumble and Death by Chocolate—devil's food cake with raspberry filling, topped with chocolate sauce. Food is served daily from 11 a.m. to 9 p.m. weekdays (to 10 p.m. weekends); the bar stays open a bit later.

Sonoma Springs Brewing Co., 750 W. Napa St., Sonoma, CA 95476; (707) 938-7422; www.sonomaspringsbrewery.com. In a small building along one of the main streets in Sonoma is a boutique brewery producing German-style and California-influenced beers. The founder of the business wanted to start a brewery for the beer drinkers in town—the people who don't drink wine. The brewing equipment is in the back, and the taproom in the front. Five different beers are on tap at any one time, including the Estate

Fresh Hop Ale, Roggenbier, Hefeweizen, Noma Coma India Pale Ale, and Volkbier. Pick a favorite, then take away a 64-ounce growler for $20 (refillable for $14). Open Thurs to Sat 1 to 8 p.m., Sun 1 to 6 p.m., and Mon 3 to 8 p.m.

Learn to Cook

Depot Hotel Cooking School, 241 First St. West, Sonoma, CA 95476; (707) 938-2980; www.depothotel.com. On Monday and Tuesday nights, when this restaurant is closed to the public, it becomes Scuola Rustica, the scene of private cooking classes for small groups. Want to improve your skills in the kitchen or just have fun with friends? Either way, Chef Michael Ghilarducci, his wife Gia, and their son Antonio team up to instruct demonstration classes that last more than 2 hours and include a full dinner. More involved, hands-on master classes last 4 to 5 hours and end with a 5-course dinner served by waitstaff. Classes to help you grill like a pro are offered in summer. Recent classes included instruction in making pasta, and how to put together a Sardinian family-style dinner. Fees run about $85 per person for the 4-course dinner, wine pairings, and recipes. These popular classes with Chef Ghilarducci can sell out if you don't act quickly—check the restaurant's website to see the latest schedule.

The Epicurean Connection, 112 W. Napa St., Sonoma, CA 95476; (707) 935-7960; www.theepicureanconnection.com. Cheesemaker Sheana Davis conducts regular 2-hour cheese classes to teach others the art, usually the second Saturday or Sunday of the month. At $45 per person, these are a good bargain for the expert instruction you'll receive in the creation of crème de ricotta, crème fraîche, *fromage blanc,* and paneer. Students get cheese cultures to take home for making even more *fromage*. The classes take place at Sonoma Valley Inn near Sheana's retail store, and students from out of town usually get a room discount if they stay at the inn. Ask about Sheana's other classes, too. (Read more about The Epicurean Connection in the Specialty Stores & Markets category.)

Ramekins Culinary School, 450 W. Spain St., Sonoma, CA 95476; (707) 933-0450; www.ramekins.com. The possibilities at Ramekins will have your mouth watering. Two teaching kitchens are on-site, one equipped with 36 seats and TV monitors so you don't miss any of the action. The list of classes is broad, encompassing cooking and baking basics to more advanced instruction. Prices are affordable, too: an evening class with legendary local chef John Ash to learn the ins and outs of tapas costs $110. Many other classes cost less. Intensive 4-day culinary camps are centered on a guest chef who takes students to local wineries and farms, where fresh ingredients are selected for the dishes to be prepared. The tariff for these camps includes the price of lodgings (Ramekins is also an inn), 4 days of meals, a spa treatment, and other cool goodies.

Petaluma & Penngrove

Petaluma has always been identified with farming and agriculture, more so than any other region in Sonoma County. This city of approximately 58,000—the second largest in the county—was known for decades as "The World's Egg Basket" and the "Egg Capital of the World." But Petaluma wasn't founded on eggs.

In the mid-1800s, with growth in nearby San Francisco increasing rapidly, large expanses of farmland around Petaluma became important for raising the grains, meat, and dairy products necessary to feed the hungry city. Suddenly Petaluma became a boomtown. Its location along a river made it possible to quickly move the commodities the short distance south into the San Francisco Bay to the waiting markets.

With growth came more industry. During the late 1800s, Petaluma manufactured buggies that were used throughout the western United States, along with shoes. Grain was milled, beer was brewed, and the shipyards hummed with constant activity, as both produce and people came and went on the river barges.

With the invention of a practical portable chicken incubator in Petaluma, the town realized a new opportunity to further its wealth: raising chickens and processing eggs. In the early 1900s, a public relations wizard was hired by the town to market and promote its egg industry. He was so successful that Petaluma's eggs became a must-have delicacy in demand around the world, featured on restaurant menus in New York City and served to passengers aboard luxury ocean liners.

Years later the wizard cooked up other ideas to sell Petaluma's eggs, lobbying for a National Egg Day and mounting a Depression-era campaign to encourage consumers to eat more eggs. People came to Petaluma from all over to seek their fortunes as chicken ranchers. Large egg processing buildings were constructed, and a chicken pharmacy—apparently the only one in the world at that time—did a brisk trade. By the 1950s, demand for the eggs began to fizzle, and the construction of a superhighway (US 101) about that same time changed Petaluma from a town to a city.

Today, Petaluma's downtown core is lined with historic buildings—proud survivors of the 1906 San Francisco earthquake, which caused extensive damage in other parts of Sonoma County. Downtown Petaluma was added to the National Register of Historic Places in 1995, and has been used as a backdrop in feature films several times. These buildings are now occupied by restaurants, some with delightful riverside patios and decks, and boutiques of all types.

Along with dairy, eggs are still an important industry in Petaluma, though not in the huge numbers seen during the chicken-and-eggs heyday. A drive through the surrounding countryside provides numerous postcard scenes of herds of Jersey cattle and pretty ranches and barns.

Foodie Faves

Cafe Zazzle, 121 Kentucky St., Petaluma, CA 94952; (707) 762-1700; www.zazzlecafe.com; $. Zazzle puts the pizzazz in food. The influences circle the globe: Thai, Japanese, Mediterranean, Mexican. The apricot curry wrap, filled with grilled chicken and greens, is loaded with apricot curry aioli. Other popular dishes are fish tacos, several types of noodles in broth, and bowls of pasta. Order a side of the house slaw, too, made of red and green cabbage, carrots, scallions, and jicama. Open daily for lunch and dinner.

Central Market, 42 Petaluma Blvd. North, Petaluma, CA 94952; (707) 778-9900; www.centralmarketpetaluma.com; $$$. The chef, Tony Najiola, is so committed to using fresh ingredients in his cuisine that he purchased a 3-acre farm planted in vegetables and other crops. He also sources produce and meat from nearby farmers such as **Green String Farm** (p. 94). Menus change with the seasons, but might include honey-glazed duck breast with kale and peppers, pork confit, seared scallops over fall vegetable hash, chicken breast with pumpkin hummus, and pizza, polenta, and pasta. Central Market earned a "recommended" rating in the 2011 Michelin guide. Open daily for dinner.

Cucina Paradiso, 114 Petaluma Blvd. North, Petaluma, CA 94952; (707) 782-1130; http://cucinaparadisopetaluma.com; $$. In business for many years, this hometown favorite began in a strip mall before moving to this location in the historic section of downtown Petaluma. Many Italian classics are on the menu, as well as panini sandwiches for the lunch crowd. Start with the calamari salad and an antipasto plate with prosciutto, melon, and prawns. Entrees include grilled pork tenderloin, polenta with mushrooms, and beef medallions sautéed in truffle sauce. The bread is baked fresh daily, and the pasta is all made from scratch every day. Cucina Paradiso is open daily for lunch and dinner, except Sun.

Graziano's Ristorante, 170 Petaluma Blvd. North, Petaluma, CA 94952; (707) 762-5997; www.grazianositalianfood.com; $$$. Housed in one of downtown Petaluma's historic structures dating to the mid-1850s, Graziano's is a traditional Italian restaurant serving many pasta combinations, along with entrees such as veal marsala and veal piccata, sweetbreads sautéed with mushrooms, grilled lamb chops, and steaks. Owner Graziano Perozzi was born in Italy and worked in restaurant kitchens in Europe and the Caribbean before coming to America in 1969. Graziano's also features a first for Petaluma—and most of northern California, I would imagine: the Vodika Lounge, maintained at a chilly 28 degrees for the enjoyment of trying more than 70 premium vodkas. The lounge supplies the coats (faux fur) you'll need to stay warm as you sip the elixir, best served cold. Open Tues through Sun for dinner.

Hallie's Diner, 125 Keller St., Petaluma, CA 94952; (707) 773-1143; $. Why can't there be more places like Hallie's? Steaming plates of eggs and country potatoes, generous strips of bacon, biscuits and gravy, and old-fashioned french toast and waffles are necessities in some diets. Hallie's is generally regarded as the place for breakfast in Petaluma, and it also serves hot and cold sandwiches, soups, salads, and desserts. Open daily from 7 a.m. to 3 p.m.

McNear's Saloon & Dining House, 23 Petaluma Blvd. North, Petaluma, CA 94952; (707) 765-2121; www.mcnears.com; $. Eventually everyone in Petaluma ends up at McNear's, for the beer, a meal, or to have a snack before a live show at the Mystic Theater next door. McNear's is an Irish-inspired institution with a big menu, including at least 10 different hamburgers, plus sandwiches, soups, salads, and big plates of beef, chicken, barbecued ribs, and pasta—with half-orders available, too. The sidewalk tables are truly the way to experience downtown Petaluma, ideal for people-watching and having a brew before heading into the Mystic to see a performance by Joan Osborne, the Young Dubliners, or Junior Brown. Open daily from 11 a.m. to midnight (Sunday brunch begins at 9 a.m.).

Real Doner Turkish Food, 307 F St., Petaluma, CA 94952; (707) 765-9555; www.realdoner.com; $. Right off Petaluma Boulevard, a couple of blocks from the newer cluster of buildings called the Theater District, Real Doner is a local favorite. Come in for lamb and beef *doners,* chicken *doners,* wraps and kebabs, baba ghanoush, and fresh-baked breads and pastries (there's always melt-in-your-mouth baklava). Order at the counter and grab a table outside, if the weather is fine. On Saturday night a belly dancer entertains to live music, which coaxes diners up on their feet, too. Imported packaged foods are also for sale, including tins of Turkish coffee, jars of hot chile paste, bags of olives, and other nibbles. Open daily for lunch and dinner.

Risibisi, 154 Petaluma Blvd. North, Petaluma, CA 94952; (707) 766-7600; http://risibisirestaurant.com; $$$. With a 2011 Michelin Bib Gourmand rating for good value and terrace dining overlooking the Petaluma River, this rustic Italian restaurant has a lot going for it. Risibisi means "rice and peas," a traditional Italian dish. The chef uses local poultry and lamb, and sources organic products whenever possible to prepare veal scalloppini with roasted potatoes, vegetable soufflé, seared salmon over pearl pasta, and heavenly desserts. The intent is to make diners feel as if they are entering an eatery in Italy, not

Petaluma, with the type of fare served in an Italian family's home. Open for lunch and dinner daily.

Water Street Bistro, 100 Petaluma Blvd. North, Petaluma, CA 94952; (707) 763-9563; www.waterstreetbistro.net; $. French-inspired cuisine, a variety of baked goods, sandwiches, soups, salads, quiches, fig tarts—it's all good at this small eatery that overlooks the Petaluma River and the pedestrian bridge over the water. Order a luscious dessert and an espresso or glass of wine, then take a seat on the patio, where you might see kayakers gliding through the water. Open weekdays from 7:30 a.m. to 3:30 p.m., Sat from 8 a.m. to 4 p.m., and Sun from 8:30 a.m. to 2:30 p.m.

Wild Goat Bistro, 6 Petaluma Blvd. North, Petaluma, CA 94952; (707) 658-1156; www.wildgoatbistro .com; $$. This is a charming spot along the Petaluma River, known for its thin-crust pizzas and dinner entrees such as cider-poached salmon, calamari, a daily risotto, beef short ribs, and stuffed chicken breast. Wrap up the meal with a slice of ginger fig cake. Wild Goat can accommodate the wishes of any diner who needs a gluten-free meal—just ask. Open daily for lunch and dinner.

Bovine Bakery, 23 Kentucky St., Petaluma, CA 94952; (707) 789-9556; www.thebovinebakery.com. The name says "bakery" but the menu includes savory items, too. But really, it's the place for Petalumans to score their morning sticky bun, orange chocolate chip scone, chocolate croissant, or poppy-seed bear claw. The bakery's longtime original location, in Point Reyes Station near the coast, is at 11315 Hwy. 1. Petalumans kept asking for an outpost closer to home, so this shop was opened in 2010.

Della Fattoria Bakery, 141 Petaluma Blvd. North, Petaluma, CA 94952; (707) 763-0161; www.dellafattoria.com. Recently, *Bon Appétit* magazine named this bakery one of the 10 best bread bakeries in America. Breadmaking is an art form at Della Fattoria, using all organic ingredients and sea salt. All brick-oven baked, the bread varieties include ciabatta, walnut, semolina, seeded wheat, pumpkinseed, and kalamata. Della Fattoria is a family-owned enterprise with a booming wholesale business, so the breads are available at many grocery outlets, too. The cafe serves breakfast and lunch on weekdays, dinner on Fri evenings, and brunch on weekends.

Full Circle Bakery, 10151 Main St., Penngrove, CA 94954; (707) 794-9445. You can find Full Circle's breads at area farmers' markets and grocers such as Oliver's Markets and Andy's Produce, but it's fun to check out the bakery's retail location in Penngrove, north of Petaluma. Pick up a loaf of rosemary ciabatta, kalamata olive, cranberry semolina, or a multigrain called "Penngrove."

Lala's Creamery, 134 Petaluma Blvd. North, Petaluma, CA 94952; (707) 763-5252; www.lalascreamery.com. Ice cream and everything you can make with it— that's what they do at Lala's, an old-fashioned fountain and parlor. Tea and honey ice cream? Yes, please! Perhaps a Brown Cow (a Coke float with chocolate syrup and vanilla) sounds more decadent. Retro advertising signs are sprinkled throughout, and there's also a pleasant outdoor seating area. Count on many traditional and nontraditional ice cream flavors, plus cookies and coffee.

Powell's Sweet Shoppe, 151 Petaluma Blvd. South, Petaluma, CA 94952; (707) 765-9866; www.powellssweetshoppe.com. Powell's is a Sonoma County–based franchise, with three locations in the county and several elsewhere in California. Powell's sells nostalgia made with sugar—candies you may have forgotten but will remember as soon as you see them: Teaberry Gum, Dum Dum Pops, Pixy Stix, Whistle Pops, Atomic Fireballs, Gobstoppers. Many types are available in bulk quantities, too. If you prefer to rot your teeth in another way, try a gelato flavor such as Bavarian mint. The classic film *Willy Wonka and the Chocolate Factory* is always on the monitor. Other Powell's locations are in Windsor (720 McClelland Dr.), and in Healdsburg (322 Center St.).

The Seed Bank, 199 Petaluma Blvd. North, Petaluma, CA 94952; (707) 509-5171; www.rareseeds.com. "Grow your own" takes on a whole new meaning at this retail store of the Baker Creek Heirloom Seed Company, which is based in the Midwest. Walking into the Seed Bank in downtown Petaluma, you're struck by the earthy aroma, as this former bank building is now the repository of something more valuable than money: 1,400-some varieties of precious heirloom seeds. The choices will make your head spin—I counted more than 100 varieties of tomato seeds alone. Pick out a few possibilities, grab a book or two on farming and gardening, ask for a few planting tips from the staff, and you're all set. Sprinkled among the easy-to-browse seed displays are locally made beeswax candles, gardening tools, handcrafted soaps, and organic herbs and spices. The store holds regular—sometimes weekly—educational workshops, too, covering many subjects related to gardening and growing your own food.

Viva Cocolat, 110 Petaluma Blvd. North, Petaluma, CA 94952; (707) 778-9888; www.vivacocolat.com. This is more like a chocolate lounge, with comfortable seating and loads of gift items to browse through—a chocolate-scented sleep mask for you today? As you savor a cup of rich European sipping chocolate, check out the display cases of delicious confections made on-site, crafted by other chocolatiers around the nation, and some imported from France. On weekends the store has sit-down chocolate

Amy's Kitchen Began in a Petaluma Dairy Barn

Conceived as a way to save for the college education of their new baby girl, Amy, Andy and Rachel Berliner of Petaluma decided to start their own frozen foods company in 1987. Andy had eaten a particularly dreadful frozen meal, and was convinced that he and Rachel could make a better vegetarian product from all-natural and organic ingredients. They called the company "Amy's Kitchen" because they didn't want to use a "green" or "veggie" sounding name. The venture was financed by a loan written against Rachel's car, along with some dollars Andy pocketed from selling a gold watch.

In a small converted dairy barn in Petaluma, the Berliners' first vegetarian frozen product, a potpie, was developed and produced. After attending a national trade show, they received a few orders for the potpie, and other products soon followed. Andy even called the people at the giant Swanson corporation to ask for tips on manufacturing frozen foods. Apparently sensing no threat from Andy's fledgling, homespun business, Swanson cooperated.

The Berliners adapted some of Swanson's techniques, but have essentially kept the production of the Amy's Kitchen line of frozen foods as handmade as possible, preferring the gentle touch of humans to automated machinery. Amy's Kitchen now employs approximately 1,500 people in two plants (one in Santa Rosa) that produce 128 different frozen products and 600,000 units daily, which are shipped nationwide and around the world.

Rachel reads all comments left on the company's website and its Facebook page, and she responds accordingly to customers' suggestions. You can reach Amy's Kitchen's headquarters in Petaluma at (707) 568-4500, or visit www.amys.com.

fondue tastings—stop in to see what they are dipping into the luscious sauce.

Made or Grown Here

Farmers' Markets

Petaluma Farmers' Market, (707) 762-3044; www.petaluma farmersmarket.com. This market celebrated its 25th anniversary in 2011, and it's one of the few held in the afternoon—on Sat from 2 to 5:30 p.m., May through Nov, in Walnut Park at the corner of Petaluma Boulevard and D Street. The afternoon slot is beneficial for farmers with plenty of produce, who can then participate in a Saturday morning market elsewhere. Most vendors are local, growing their vegetables or raising their meat within a few miles of the city. Besides fresh food for sale, count on several vendors with prepared foods, crafts, and live music. (In summer, an additional event called the Petaluma Evening Farmer's Market takes place Wed from 4:30 to 9 p.m., from early June to late Aug, on Second Street between B and D Streets.)

Andersen/Canvas Ranch Vegetable Stand and Pumpkin Patch, 4588 Bodega Ave., Petaluma, CA 94952; (707) 529-1270 or (707) 766-7171; www.canvasranch.com. Besides offering sustainably grown vegetables and fruit from July through October, the place is buzzing in autumn with hayrides, a hay pyramid, and a hay maze, along with a picnic area. Giant pumpkins, too. Open Thurs through Sun from noon to 6 p.m.

Green String Farm, 3571 Old Adobe Rd., Petaluma, CA 94954; (707) 778-7500; www.greenstringfarm.com. Lettuce, squash, tomatoes, beets—this farm grows a cornucopia of produce and it's open year-round, too. From 50 to 60 acres of the 140-acre farm are in cultivation, and some of the produce is grown for area restaurants. Open daily from 10 a.m. to 6 p.m. (5 p.m. in winter).

Apples

Olympia's Apple Orchard at Two Rock Ranch, 1051 Walker Rd., Petaluma, CA 94952; (707) 762-7952; www.tworockranch .com. The Tresch family operates both a dairy (certified organic) and a thriving apple orchard with 500-some trees. More than 50 apple varieties grow on the ranch's 2,000 acres, including Gravenstein, Kidds Orange Red, Jonathan, Wickson, Fuji, and Honeycrisp. The apples are available from August through November at area farmers' markets and also at the ranch's farm stand during daylight hours.

Cheesemakers

Bellwether Farms, 9999 Valley Ford Rd., Petaluma, CA 94952; (707) 763-0993; www.bellwetherfarms.com. Bellwether is one of only a few sheep dairies found in the United States, and they also make cheese from cow's milk. The dairy produces sheep-milk yogurt in five flavors, as well as ricotta, *fromage blanc,* and several other options. Its crème fraîche (French-style cultured cream) is out of this world. On the website you can buy entire wheels of cheese, or just quarters and halves. Bellwether cheeses are sold in most area grocery stores, too. The dairy can't accommodate visitors at this time, but they have plans to eventually open a tasting room to showcase the products.

Cowgirl Creamery, 80 Fourth St., Point Reyes Station, CA 94956; (415) 663-9335; www.cowgirlcreamery.com. This artisan cheesemaker is based just over the Sonoma County line in Marin County, and that's where the store is located, but Cowgirl also has a wholesale and production facility in Petaluma (open to the public only for summer tours). Cowgirl Creamery was established in 1997, and started with only a few varieties of cheese. Today the company produces approximately 3,000 pounds of *fromage* each week. Its most famous signature cheese is Mt. Tam, a triple cream and consistent award-winner made with organic cow's milk. The other cheeses include Red

Take the Guesswork Out of Choosing Cheese

As you approach the cheese department in an upscale grocery store, are you bewildered by the huge selection staring back at you? If your experience with cheese has been limited to peeling sheets of clear cellophane from thin slices of yellow goo, the choices may seem overwhelming.

You are lured by the exotic and tasty possibilities, yet you have many questions. How do I choose a quality artisan cheese that will taste great with a certain wine? How is cheese supposed to be served? How do I store the cheese at home? Each question can bring forth another.

A good cheese department or store will be staffed by at least one expert who can help you sort through these questions, offer samples, and make recommendations. At Oliver's Markets, a homegrown three-store chain in Sonoma County, cheese maven Colette Hatch is an excellent source of information about local cheeses and the many types that Oliver's stocks from around the world (read more about Oliver's Markets in the Santa Rosa chapter).

Hawk, Devil's Gulch (so named for the spicy red pepper flakes within), Inverness, and Wagon Wheel (what they call an "everyday" cheese for cooking and snacking). The creamery also produces cottage cheese, *fromage blanc,* and crème fraîche. The Point Reyes Station retail store is open daily, except Tues, from 10 a.m. to 6 p.m.

Colette recommends that cheese novices ask lots of questions. She says it's not too bold to inquire if a cheese is pasteurized or raw, where it is made, how fresh it is, if it's a seasonal variety, if your guests will love it or hate it (and why), and so forth. She generously dispenses tips for selecting and serving cheese and pairing cheese with wine.

Calling herself Madame de Fromage, Colette worked in the hospitality industry in France, Corsica, and England before moving to the United States and eventually settling in Sonoma County. A cheese educator and specialty food consultant for local restaurants and wineries, Colette has also conducted cheese appreciation classes in San Francisco and at Napa Valley's Culinary Institute of America.

When you bring home good cheese, Colette says to repackage it right away. Don't place plastic directly on the cheese. Instead, wrap it first in parchment paper or wax paper, then add an outer wrap of plastic or place in a lidded plastic container to protect it from drying out and absorbing other aromas in the refrigerator.

Lactose intolerant? Try goat cheese. Research shows that goat milk and the cheese it's made from can be kinder on the human digestive system and is usually lower in calories, fat, and cholesterol, too.

Marin French Cheese Company, 7500 Red Hill Rd., Petaluma, CA 94952; (800) 292-6001; www.marinfrenchcheese.com. The sign on the road says "The Cheese Factory," but it's also known as Rouge et Noir. This is the Marin French Cheese Company, founded in 1865 and the oldest cheese manufacturer in the United States (sorry,

Wisconsin!). The company is famous for Brie and Camembert, and all of its artisan cheese is handmade using European cultures. Besides the first-of-its-kind history, what sets the Cheese Factory apart from others is the location and the lush grounds, an ideal spot for a picnic. Technically the factory is just over the county line in Marin, but we Sonomans embrace it as our own, and the US Postal Service places it in Petaluma. It's open daily from 8:30 a.m. to 5 p.m.

Spring Hill Jersey Cheese and Petaluma Creamery, 711 Western Ave., Petaluma, CA 94952; (707) 762-3446; www.spring hillcheese.com. Approximately 400 pasture-grazed Jersey dairy cows give up their milk west of Petaluma for the award-winning organic farmstead cheeses made by this producer. Numerous local stores carry Spring Hill cheeses and butter, and they can also be purchased at some area farmers' markets. In 2011, the company's salted butter won a double-gold award at the Sonoma County Harvest Fair; the unsalted butter earned a silver award. The retail store at 711 Western Avenue is open from 6 a.m. to 7 p.m. Mon through Fri, and 8 a.m. to 8 p.m. weekends. Tours of the production facility nearby are available for $20, and reservations are preferred. But if you happen to be driving by and want to see how cheese is made, the friendly folks here can usually accommodate your wishes.

Dairies

Clover-Stornetta Farms, Petaluma, CA 94975; (800) 237-3315; cloverstornetta.com. This dairy doesn't give plant tours, but you will see its clever billboards and products everywhere in this region (with the exception of Safeway stores). Many small, family-operated dairy farms supply the moo-juice for the Clover line, which includes a separate organic line. Clo the Cow is the official mascot of the dairy and the star of its advertising that relies on witty puns—many of them contributed by customers—such as "Tip Clo Through Your Two Lips" and "Amazing Graze."

McClelland's Dairy, 6475 Bodega Ave., Petaluma, CA 94952; (707) 664-0452; www.mcclellandsdairy.com. Tumble-churning is the old-fashioned way to make creamy, European-style butter, and McClelland's is known for its organic artisan butter, packaged in nifty brown crocks. The dairy won a double-gold award at the Sonoma County Harvest Fair in 2011, and also holds a third-place national prize. McClelland's 90-minute tours (by appointment) include the opportunity to hand-milk a grass-fed cow (you know you want to). The dairy was founded many decades ago by an Irishman, Bob McClelland, and it continues to be operated by his descendants. The McClelland family milks 800 cows on approximately 600 acres in the hills west of Petaluma.

Poultry & Egg Producers

Petaluma Egg Farm, Petaluma, CA 94952; (707) 763-0921; www.petalumaeggfarm.com. "Local Eggs for Local People" is the motto of this longtime egg producer near Petaluma, the last of its kind in the county to raise hens and eggs commercially on a large scale. If you spend much time shopping for eggs in Sonoma County stores, you will eventually see the colorful cartons produced by the Petaluma Egg Farm. Several versions of the chicken eggs are marketed: Judy's Family Farm Organic Eggs, Uncle Eddie's Wild Hen Eggs, Rock Island Fertile Brown Eggs, and more. The hens are raised cage-free and antibiotic-free, and fed an all-vegetarian diet. The company operates its own store where the eggs are also available (see Skippy's listing in this category).

Petaluma Poultry, Petaluma, CA 94955; (800) 556-6789; www .petalumapoultry.com. Once upon a time, Petaluma was known as the Egg Basket of the World, and there were so many chickens around the countryside that 600 million eggs were shipped away every year. Much of the commercial poultry business declined decades ago, but this company has been going strong since 1969. It introduced the first commercially available free-range chicken, Rocky the Range, in 1986, followed two years later by Rocky, Jr., a smaller version. The Rosie Organic chicken was added soon after, and the popularity of these fresh and flavorful fowl took off. Rocky and Rosie chickens are widely available in local markets and around the West Coast. Now hooked on the fresh taste of the Rockys, I rarely bring home any other brand.

Skippy's Egg Store and More, 951 Transport Way, Petaluma, CA 94952; (707) 763-2924; www.petalumaeggfarm.com. When I was a teenager, my parents constructed and operated a huge chicken-egg processing building, with something like 5,000 hens mingling with 500 roosters, to ensure fertilization of the eggs. I collected, sorted, and stacked hundreds of flats of eggs in my youth, so I'm familiar with small cracks in the shells (called "checks" in the egg biz), double yolks (jackpot!), and other slight blemishes that make fresh eggs less than perfect by government inspection standards, but still incredibly delicious if used promptly. Skippy's is the in-town retail store owned by Petaluma Egg Farm (see listing opposite), where the chickens are raised and the eggs are processed. Skippy's gets daily shipments from the farm and sells the fresh but imperfect checked eggs for as little as $3 per flat (that's 30 great eggs at about the price of a regular dozen). Unblemished eggs from the farm are available, too, along with bulk spices and herbs, baking and restaurant supplies, local dairy products, pasta, and much more. Skippy's is open weekdays from 8 a.m. to 4:30 p.m. and Sat from 8 a.m. to noon.

Split Rail Family Farms, 110 Goodwin Ln., Penngrove, CA 94951; (707) 664-8103; www.splitrailfamilyfarms.com. Seasonal vegetables and fruit, along with lamb and rabbit meat, are available at Split Rail in a restored red barn. Eggs, dairy goats, and sheep are all raised here, so wool, yarn, and soft lambskins are sold as well. The farm is open year-round by appointment, while the barn store is generally open Sun from 10 a.m. to 4 p.m.

Meat & Butchers

Angelo's Meat and Sausage, 2700 Adobe Rd., Petaluma, CA 94954; (707) 763-9586; www.angelossmokehouse.com. Angelo Ibleto is well-loved for his 18 varieties of sausage, 8 types of beef jerky, his Italian barbecue-spice dry rub, and other condiments that can jazz up the fresh Grand Champion tri-tip and steaks he sells at this store. If beef isn't your thing, try smoked hams, bacon, salami, jar after jar of stuffed olives, bottled sauces, and deli items to go. (Angelo also runs Angelo's Wine Country Deli, south of Sonoma at 23400 Arnold Dr.) His brother Arturo is famous around here as the Pasta King, supplying great pasta in marinara sauce or pesto sauce at local fairs, festivals, and farmers' markets. Angelo's butcher shop is open weekdays from 9 a.m. to 5 p.m. and Sat 9 a.m. to 4 p.m.

Bud's Custom Meats, 7750 Petaluma Hill Rd., Penngrove, CA 94951; (707) 795-8402; www.budscustommeats.com. The many cuts of dry-aged all-natural beef are from cattle raised on the premises. Bud's is a meat lover's paradise, with smoked sausages, marinated tri-tips, hams, bacon, beef jerky, and salmon, too. The company's smoked pork loin earned a Best of Show award in 2011 from the California Association of Meat Producers. Craving pheasant, elk, ostrich, quail, wild boar, or other exotic meats? Bud's might have those in stock, too. Bud's is in Penngrove, a small town northeast of Petaluma—look for the brown building. Bud's is open Mon through Sat from 8 a.m. to 5 p.m.

Tara Firma Farms, 3796 I St. Ext., Petaluma, CA 95452; (707) 765-1202; www.tarafirmafarms.com. Tara Firma grows a wide assortment of seasonal vegetables, but they are most noted for pasture-raised chickens, turkeys, pigs, and grass-fed beef. It's not only steaks and roasts, but also the feet, bones, snouts, and whatever other nasty bits you want to purchase. This is truly hoof-to-curly-tail culinary shopping. Stop by the farm Sat and Sun, between 10 a.m. and 3 p.m., for free tours given on the hour. Tara Firma Farms, named for farmer Tara Smith, also operates a CSA with a meat focus—see that later category for more details.

Olive Grower

McEvoy Ranch, 5935 Red Hill Rd., Petaluma, CA 94952; (707) 778-2307; www.mcevoyranch.com. One of the premier olive oil producers in this area is McEvoy, known for its certified organic extra-virgin oil made in the traditional Tuscan style from 80 acres of olive trees on-site. They also sell the olive trees in 1-, 5-, and 15-gallon pots, if you want to try growing olives yourself. The oils are all small-batch products, and the entire process—growing, harvesting, milling, blending, and bottling—takes place at the ranch. McEvoy also sells jars of olives, apple butter, honey, and Meyer lemon marmalade from its own trees and hives. Wine grapes are also grown on the ranch, with nine varietals planted. The wines are not yet ready for public consumption, so check the website for updates. When you've had your fill of the food products, luxuriate in the olive oil–infused body care line called "80 Acres"—lotions, lip balms, soaps, bath salts, and candles. All visits, tours, and sales at McEvoy Ranch are by appointment only—call or go to the website for the latest information. McEvoy's olive oils are widely distributed throughout the region, so look on the shelf of a nearby grocery store.

Honey Producer

Lavender Bee Farm, 764 Chapman Ln., Petaluma, CA 94952; (707) 789-0554; www.lavenderbeefarm.com. More than 5,000 lavender shrubs and numerous hives make for a sweet, fragrant combination. The lavender honey is a gold-ribbon-winning nectar, great for drizzling over semisoft cheese or blue cheese. The farm's culinary lavender is pristine and grown without chemicals, then dried naturally—superb for mixing up your own interpretation of *herbes de Provence* seasoning (three versions with sea salt added are also available). Scads of lavender- and honey-based gifts are sold, too. Open by appointment—call the farm for more information.

Community Supported Agriculture Programs (CSAs)

Canvas Ranch, 755 Tomales Rd., Petaluma, CA 94952; (707) 766-7171; www.canvasranch.com. Deborah Walton left a high-powered advertising career many years ago to get back to the land, or as she puts it so succinctly: ". . . giving up my suits and heels for overalls and muck boots." I once interviewed for a job with Deborah in her high-heels days, and she was one cool lady then. She's even more amazing now. Depending on the season, Deborah gathers together a full box of vegetables for her CSA customers, with add-ins available such as eggs, flowers, organic bread, and artisan cheese. Try her soap, too.

Tara Firma Farms, 3796 I St. Ext., Petaluma, CA 95452; (707) 765-1202; www.tarafirmafarms.com. The specific choices are up to you, of course, but this CSA's weekly, biweekly, or monthly boxes combine cuts of chicken, beef, and pork along with seasonal vegetables and fruits. Extra options might be eggs, butter, honey, mushrooms, and even herb salts. Prices vary widely, depending on your needs and wishes, so check the website for the latest information.

Kastania Vineyards, 4415 Kastania Rd., Petaluma, CA 94952; (707) 763-6348; www.kastaniavineyards.com. Bottling only 800 to 1,000 cases each year, Kastania is a boutique winery offering Pinot Noir and a proprietor's blend of Cabernet Franc and Cabernet Sauvignon. By Sonoma County standards, Kastania is one of the newer wineries in the region, established in the 1990s, with its first grapes harvested in 1997. Kastania is open to the public for tastings on weekends from 11 a.m. to 4 p.m. and by appointment on weekdays.

Keller Estate, 5875 Lakeville Hwy., Petaluma, CA 94954; (707) 765-2117; www.kellerestate.com. Keller was the first winery established in the Petaluma Valley, beginning with the planting of Chardonnay and Pinot Noir vineyards. After selling their grapes to other wineries, the Kellers started their own label. The micro-climate in this region is affected by what's known around here as the "Petaluma gap," which gets marine influences from the San Pablo Bay to the south and an opening in the coastal hills to the northwest that funnels in the fog banks. Pinot Noir grapes love these conditions, and the result is superior premium wine. Keller also bottles Pinot Gris and Syrah. A special food-and-wine pairing is offered that also includes an in-depth tour of the estate ($100 per person). Tastings are available Thurs through Sun from 11 a.m. to 4:30 p.m.—call ahead for an appointment.

Sonoma Valley Portworks, 613 Second St., Petaluma, CA 94952; (707) 769-5203; http://.portworks.com. Made from Petite Sirah and Petit Verdot, Aris is one of this award-winning producer's three ports. The others are Deco (a blend of California grapes and port from Australia) and Maduro (three Australian ports made from Shiraz and Grenache grapes, blended together). A cream sherry called Duet, a fortified muscat called A3, and a grappa named Spirit of the Harvest are all available for tasting. Sometimes the Portworks holds special pairings of its port and sherry with desserts. The Portworks, located in the Foundry Wharf building along the Petaluma River, is open daily from noon to 5 p.m. (Another tasting room for Sonoma Valley Portworks is in Glen Ellen at Jack London Village, 14301 Arnold Dr.)

Brewpubs & Microbreweries

Dempsey's Restaurant & Brewery, 50 E. Washington St., Petaluma, CA 94952; (707) 765-9694; www.dempseys.com. There are few pastimes in Petaluma more pleasant than sitting on the riverside patio table at Dempsey's while sipping the Ugly Dog Stout, so named because the World's Ugliest Dog Contest takes place annually in town. The brewery is also known for Red Rooster Ale, Petaluma Strong Ale, Galaxy IPA, and others. Yet the food is what brings locals in again and again. Dempsey's is well-loved for its thin-crust pizzas, a pizzetta (a smaller version), pork adobo sandwich, pork chop marinated in hoisin sauce, and flatiron steak. Produce for the salads and other dishes is grown locally in biodynamically farmed gardens. Open daily for lunch and dinner.

Lagunitas Brewing Company, 1280 N. McDowell Blvd., Petaluma, CA 94954; (707) 769-4495; www.lagunitas.com. The Lagunitas India Pale Ale is probably the best-selling IPA in the state of California. The brewery also makes Dogtown Pale Ale, Censored Ale (all about malt, with low hops), Maximus (a slightly darker IPA), Imperial Stout (thick, dark, and smoky—sort of dessertlike), and Hop Stoopid, for those who like lots of hops in their beer. Lagunitas also makes a Czech-style pilsner. Take a tour to see how the beer is bottled, labeled, and packaged, followed by free samples. The food in the "Taproom and Beer Sanctuary" is no-frills, just good eats: panini sandwiches, a few appetizers, and a salad or two. The brewery sells a slew of logo merchandise, too. The taproom is open 2 to 9 p.m. Wed through Fri, and 11:30 a.m. to 8 p.m. Sat and Sun.

Learn to Cook

Bauman College of Holistic Nutrition and Culinary Arts, 10151 Main St., Penngrove, CA 94951; (707) 795-1284 or (800) 987-7530; www.baumancollege.com. Located in the small town of Penngrove north of Petaluma, this outpost of Bauman College is one of four in the United States that offer holistic nutrition and culinary arts programs. The 5-month natural chef's training course teaches students how to use plant-based organic and natural foods to prepare healthful meals for therapeutic purposes or for personal fulfillment. The course is intensive, covering basic kitchen skills, global cuisine, farm-to-table food preparation (including a field trip to a local organic farm), business skills, and more. Another program teaches nutrition consulting based on whole organic foods and herbs.

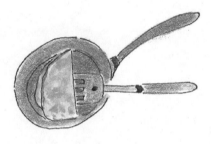

Santa Rosa, Rohnert Park, Cotati & Windsor

Santa Rosa is the "big city" in Sonoma County, home to approximately 168,000 people and the center of county government. Geographically it's situated somewhat in the middle of the region, with all the other cities, towns, and wine-growing areas profiled in this book scattered in nearly all directions, like spokes on a wheel. It's been my home for almost 25 years, yet it still surprises me when I spy a historic building I've never noticed before, discover a new hole-in-the-wall place to grab a sandwich, or pass a pop-up farm stand that might be here today and gone tomorrow.

Santa Rosa has the majority of restaurants in the county, including the many chains and fast-food joints found everywhere. But it has interesting clusters of locally owned eateries in neighborhoods such as Historic Railroad Square, right off the freeway on the west edge of downtown. Bounded by Wilson and Davis Streets and between the numbered streets of 3rd and 5th, Historic Railroad Square has seen many good restaurants come and go. It's also lined with boutiques and antiques shops, too. At the corner of 4th and Wilson is the former Northwestern Pacific Railroad depot, now an official California Welcome Center and the Santa Rosa Convention & Visitors Bureau. The depot had a starring role in the Alfred Hitchcock film *Shadow of a Doubt* back in the 1940s, and it looks about the same now as it did then.

Still on the drawing board for the area west of the depot is a huge food and wine center, where local wine and cheese would be sampled and farm-fresh produce purchased, and several restaurants would offer an eclectic mix of cuisine.

On the other side of the freeway downtown, 4th Street is the main restaurant row, which includes a brewpub among the eateries (plus another a block away), and an assortment of boutiques. Fourth Street is the site of the annual Downtown Market, a Wednesday evening event in summer that lines the entire street with fresh produce and local artisan food vendors.

Farther east in Santa Rosa is the Montgomery Village shopping center, where several good restaurants and stores cater to foodies.

South of Santa Rosa, the planned community of Rohnert Park is home to Sonoma State University, part of the California State University system. With a population of approximately 41,000, it's family oriented with many recreational opportunities, city parks, and one of the last bowling centers still thriving north of San

Francisco. It's generally considered to be the "big box" community of Sonoma County, with large discount stores, chain restaurants and motels, and cookie-cutter businesses lining both sides of US Highway 101 through the city. Yet because it's a university town, excellent locally owned restaurants do a brisk business, and at least two exceptional live music venues (one at the university) are located here.

Next door to Rohnert Park is Cotati, a community of 7,300 that is fiercely protective of its local businesses, occasionally embroiled in fights to keep out corporate restaurants and coffee shops. The town was developed around a hexagonal plaza in the 1890s, said to be one of only two such plazas in America. Cotati has a small but lively farmers' market that takes place on Thursday evening in summer.

Once considered a bedroom community for Santa Rosa, Windsor is along US 101 as you drive north toward Healdsburg. With a population of approximately 27,000, its formerly crumbling downtown was completely rebuilt a few years ago, replaced by brightly painted, vintage-style buildings that are occupied by retail stores and restaurants at ground level and living spaces above. The Town Green is where families come for picnics, the twice-weekly farmers' market in summer, and to watch free movies by moonlight.

John Ash & Co., 4330 Barnes Rd., Santa Rosa, CA 95403; (707) 527-7687; www.vintnersinn.com; $$$$. It's still named for the Sonoma County chef who opened it 30-some years ago—and who still works locally as a consultant, author, and culinary instructor. John Ash & Co. still creates "wine country" cuisine that reflects his influences. That's appropriate, because there are more than 90 acres of vineyards just outside. Start your unforgettable meal with a poached farm-fresh egg with prawns, Black Pig Meat Co. bacon, and grits; or roasted pear and brie soup with pecans. Main dishes include brick chicken with creamed sweet corn, leeks, fingerling potatoes, and smoked bacon; or a bone-in pork chop with polenta. The restaurant has one of the best wine lists around, with approximately 600 selections from Sonoma County and beyond. For a lighter meal that's less expensive, try the Front Room Bar and Lounge ($$). The menu choices range from oysters on the half shell to *calamari fritti* to a pizza of the week. The eateries are located at the Vintners Inn, a French-inspired hotel with balconies overlooking the vineyards, and relaxing courtyards with fountains. A conference center was added to the property recently. John Ash & Co. is open for dinner daily; The Front Room is open daily from 4 to 10 p.m. (3 to 11 p.m. weekends).

Zazu Restaurant + Farm, 3535 Guerneville Rd., Santa Rosa, CA 95401; (707) 523-4814; www.zazurestaurant.com; $$$. Perhaps more than any other cooking couple in recent local history, chef Duskie Estes and her *salumi*-making husband John Stewart thoroughly embrace the farm-to-table approach to fine dining, and have done so for many years. Much of the produce used in their dishes comes from the gardens on-site, while their chickens supply the fresh eggs used in many recipes. What Duskie and John don't raise or source themselves comes from producers with a 30-minute radius of the kitchen. "Support Local Food" is their mantra, seen on the T-shirts they frequently wear while cheffing. Since it opened in 2001, Zazu has been heaped with praise in the media, from the *Los Angeles Times* to *Bon Appétit* and *Food & Wine* magazines. The restaurant is consistently on many "best of" lists, too. In 2010, Duskie gained TV reality-show fame as one of 10 chefs fighting for the title of "the Next Iron Chef" on the Food Network. In 2011, she and John competed in a regional chef's competition that focused on heritage pork, which led to their win at the Grand Cochon (pig) national finals in Aspen. (John and Duskie also run their own company called **Black Pig Meat,** see p. 188). So what's on the menu at Zazu? Depends on the season and what's growing out back. Both small and big plates are offered. An autumn soup option might be spicy tomato, paired with a grilled Carmody cheese sandwich; a main dish could be saffron and green olive braised lamb shank smothered in yogurt, eggplant tagine, and spicy cucumbers. Finish with the sweet gingerbread and persimmon bread pudding with nutmeg crème anglaise. "Pizza and Pinot Nights" are Wednesday and Thursday, when a special pizza is prepared to pair well with local

Pinot Noirs. Zazu is open for dinner Wed through Sun, and brunch on Sun from 9 a.m. to 2 p.m. See the recipe for **Zazu Chicken, Cherry, Chocolate & Chile Tostada** on p. 267.

Foodie Faves

Ca'Bianca Ristorante Italiano, 835 Second St., Santa Rosa, CA 95401; (707) 542-5800; www.cabianca.com; $$$. The beautifully restored white house just east of the main downtown core (Ca' Bianca is Italian for "white house") is where classic regional Italian cuisine is served. The building dates to 1876, the setting is romantic (a table on the patio may be the perfect place to pop the question), and the restaurant is the scene of many wedding receptions and celebratory dinners. Try the salad with poached pears, polenta and mushrooms, prosciutto-stuffed chicken, roasted pork, or butternut squash ravioli. Open for dinner every day and lunch on weekdays.

Chloé's French Cafe, 3883 Airway Dr., Santa Rosa, CA 95403; (707) 528-3095; www.chloesco.com; $. Ooh-la-la! It's worth seeking out this place for the pastries alone. Chloé's is located on the first floor of a medical office building just off Highway 101, an unlikely spot to find a much-loved cafe, but it's been a popular draw here for years. Make the turn into the large parking lot, where you will see the restaurant's vintage French "truckette"—christened

Chloé by the owners' parents. This vehicle saw a lot of action in France as the delivery truck for the Pisan family, who operated a patisserie in Saint-Tropez. The current owners of the cafe had these sweet wheels shipped to America and restored. Park and walk to the back of the building, where shady trees surround the cafe's patio. The Pisans use enduring family recipes in much of their baking and cafe menu. For breakfast, score a couple of *pains au chocolat, palmiers,* or the buttery croissants. Many traditional French cafe items are offered, such as quiche lorraine, *croque monsieur,* and crepes. Select a cold or grilled sandwich, or one of the huge salads. Save room for an éclair or lemon curd tart. Chloé's is open Mon through Fri from 8 a.m. to 5 p.m.

El Coqui, 400 Mendocino Ave., Santa Rosa, CA 95404; (707) 542-8868; www.elcoqui2eat.com; $$. If you like a place with energy and good Puerto Rican food, look no farther than El Coqui. Many of the recipes were prepared for decades by the current owner's grandmother, so the food is as genuine as you will find within many, many miles. El Coqui is small, and usually has a line on busy weekend nights. It's fun to eat at the bar if the tables are all occupied. (Expect high-octane Latin and salsa music concerts by crooners such as Marc Anthony on the TV monitors.) The restaurant's most popular entrees may be the *chicharron de pollo* (fried chicken with rice and beans, sweet plantains, and avocado salad), *jibarito* (seasoned ground beef, tomatoes, and Jack cheese between two layers of fried green plantains), and *chuletas* (thin pan-fried pork chops with the same sides as the fried chicken). A Cubano sandwich is offered, too, along with main-dish salads. El Coqui is open for lunch and dinner daily.

Flavor Bistro, 96 Old Courthouse Sq., Santa Rosa, CA 95401; (707) 573-9600; www.flavorbistro.com; $$. Sitting just inside the patio, in the small lounge area, is my favorite spot in this restaurant. I've enjoyed many plates of great pasta, excellent soups, and even the *croque madame* a few times. The basket of focaccia bread gets you off to a good start. Try the pear bruschetta, pork and shrimp wontons, prawn salad, risotto, lasagna, chicken breast and sausage with white beans, burgers of all types, house-made sausage pizza, and house-made gelato, too—the variety is wide and everything is delicious. Flavor is open daily for lunch and dinner, and open for breakfast at 8 a.m. on weekends.

Fresh, 5755 Mountain Hawk, Santa Rosa, CA 95409; (707) 595-1048; www.freshbylisahemenway.com; $$. Considered one of the pioneers of "California cuisine," Chef Lisa Hemenway has had a long and successful career in the restaurant and catering business in Sonoma County, and beyond. She was the original sous chef and pastry chef at John Ash & Co., then went on to run her own namesake restaurant in Santa Rosa for many years. She also opened restaurants in Vietnam and Singapore. Fresh is her newest venture. Besides being a restaurant and wine bar, Fresh is a market with a cheese department, gourmet deli and take-out counter, beverages of all types (including beer and wine), jars and bottles of locally produced food, fresh produce, and old-fashioned candies. Lisa can usually be found walking the circuit around her restaurant and market, checking to make certain all departments are running smoothly, diners are happy, and the various displays are perfectly arranged. Fresh's menu includes many sandwiches and great pizza from the brick wood-fired oven. The pancetta and onion quiche is killer, along with curry chicken salad. Buy a dessert to go from the bakery—cookies, cakes, and chocolates from **Sonoma Chocolatiers** in Sebastopol (see the West Sonoma County & the Coast chapter). The market, deli, and bakery at Fresh are open daily from 8 a.m. to 8:30 p.m.; the restaurant is open daily for lunch from 11 a.m. to 3 p.m., and dinner starts at 5 p.m. Brunch is served Sun from 10 a.m. to 3 p.m. See the recipe for **Lisa Hemenway's Crab Cakes** on p. 279.

Hana Japanese, 101 Golf Course Dr., Rohnert Park, CA 94928; (707) 586-0270; www.hanajapanese.com; $$. Many diners are here for the eight-seat sushi bar, where the selection is first-rate and the menu is immense. Others come for traditional Japanese favorites such as tempuras. The Wagyu beef appetizer is perfectly seared, then sliced and served with a green onion sauce and balsamic reduction. The asparagus and pork tempura roll with poached egg is also delicious. Seaweed salad, maitake mushroom tempura, grilled

Japanese cuttlefish, sea bass, and toro sashimi are all options. The chef also offers a tasting menu ($80 to $100 per person). Located in the Doubletree Hotel complex, Hana is open daily for lunch and dinner.

In-N-Out Burger, 2131 County Center Dr., Santa Rosa, CA 95403; and 5145 Redwood Dr., Rohnert Park, CA 94928; (800) 786-1000; www.in-n-out.com; $. I wouldn't normally include a fast-food chain in a book like this, but In-N-Out is better than most. It's California-based, dating to 1948, and there are more than 200 locations in the Golden State, and a few more in neighboring states. The posted menu keeps it simple: burgers, fries, shakes, and sodas. Yet there are not-so-secret options available to anyone who asks: much larger burgers (with two, three, or even four beef patties and up to four cheese slices on one sandwich), a grilled cheese sandwich, and a burger wrapped in lettuce instead of a bun (messy, but many fewer calories). You may wonder why the palm trees at the Santa Rosa location are crossed to form an X. It's a design gimmick, having to do with the late founder's love for the movie *It's a Mad, Mad, Mad, Mad World*. Open daily for lunch and dinner (to 1:30 a.m. on Fri and Sat).

Italian Affair, 1055 Fourth St., Santa Rosa, CA 95404; (707) 528-3336; www.italianaffair.com; $$$. Serving up Italian-American fare for more than 30 years, the Ghilarducci family—Vince is the executive chef—has a long history in the Bay Area. Vince's dad operated a pub south of San Francisco, and Vince worked at a Palo

Alto restaurant before the family moved to Santa Rosa. Vince's own sons, Joseph and Gregorio, now work alongside their father at Italian Affair. Vince makes his own pizza dough, and the linguine with Manila clams is a house favorite, along with the veal scallopine and veal piccata. Italian Affair is homey (in fact it's housed in a former private residence), and the setting for many special dinners, such as the night my family toasted "bon voyage" to my niece on the eve of her departure for Italy to study abroad. You may have another excuse for a celebration. Italian Affair is open for lunch and dinner Wed through Fri, and for dinner on weekends.

Jackson's Bar and Oven, 135 Fourth St., Santa Rosa, CA 95401; (707) 545-6900; www.jacksonsbarandoven.com; $$. Chef Josh Silver opened his second restaurant in downtown Santa Rosa in 2010, and it was an immediate hit. Named after his son, Jackson's specializes in wood-fired pizza, sandwiches, and entrees such as paella. It's snazzy inside, ultramodern and tastefully decorated, and the noise level can get cranked up a bit high at times, making conversation difficult. Crispy hot fries come in a cone, the hefty salads are delicious, and the black bean chili is presented in bowl set on a platter with square containers of the add-ons: sour cream, chopped onions, and shredded cheese. Try the excellent Buffalo wings, or the smoky shrimp in hot butter sauce cooked in the wood oven. The larger plates include wood-oven-roasted trout with couscous, a pork chop (also roasted over the wood) with risotto and broccolini, and grilled New York steak with parsnips and potatoes. Desserts might be sugar-glazed beignets with raspberry and chocolate sauces on the side, or a Nutella pizza with hazelnuts. Jackson's is at the east end of the concentrated Historic Railroad Square action, with its antiques shops, wine bars, and other eateries. It's open daily for lunch and dinner. (Chef Silver's other downtown Santa Rosa restaurant is **Petite Syrah**—find it in this category.)

Johnny Garlic's, 1460 Farmers Ln., Santa Rosa, CA 95405; (707) 571-1800; www.johnnygarlics.com; $$$. Having earned a degree in hospitality management, Guy Fieri is a natural front-of-the-house type (see the profile of Guy on p. 138). He opened this restaurant in 1996, establishing a fine reputation for its garlicky cuisine. A second location opened 3 years later in Windsor (8988 Brooks Rd. S., 707-836-8300). Flush with success, Guy opened Tex Wasabi's in 2003 (see the listing in this category). Johnny Garlic's has starters such as key lime calamari, a basket of Maui onion straws, French onion soup, and roasted garlic soup. The main-dish salads are excellent, as are the Neapolitan-style pizzas. Guy's Big Bite burger is on the menu, too, along with a meat-loaf sandwich, American Kobe steaks, seafood dishes such as cedar plank salmon and seared ahi tuna, and game meats on a rotating basis: elk, alligator, ostrich, wild boar, and so on. The tequila key lime tart is a refreshing end to the meal. Open daily from 11 a.m. to 10 p.m.

Monti's Rotisserie & Bar, 714 Village Ct. (in the Montgomery Village shopping center), Santa Rosa, CA 95405; (707) 568-4404; http://starkrestaurants.com; $$$. The patio at Monti's is your best bet for an enjoyable meal when the weather is pleasant. It's fun to watch the shoppers strolling past, and can be even more interesting when there's a live band nearby during special afternoon and evening concerts (get there early to grab a table). I've spent several happy hours sitting with friends after noshing on a Monti's cristo sandwich and the superb exotic mushroom pizza. The house-made charcuterie includes wild boar, and other starters might be calamari, or a beet salad. Entrees are usually hanger steak, sirloin burger, lamb shank, and quiche and fish selections of the day. Every night after 5 p.m., a specially prepared meat is available from the rotisserie: Moroccan barbecued goat, baby back ribs, leg of lamb, suckling pig, prime rib, veal, or duck. Monti's has received recent Bib Gourmand recognition in the Michelin guide, too. Open daily for lunch and dinner, and for Sunday brunch from 10:30 a.m. to 2 p.m.

Omelette Express, 112 Fourth St., Santa Rosa, CA 95401; (707) 525-1690; http://omeletteexpress.com; $. One of the things I like most about Omelette Express is the huge piece of delicious griddled bread that comes with the breakfast platters. A big lunch menu is offered, too, but it's breakfast that brings in the locals. At least 40 omelet options are listed, from plain to seafood versions. Even when the place has a line out the door, service is fast and your food is delivered quickly. The restaurant opened in 1977, when Historic Railroad Square was still a dicey part of town to hang out in. (Railroad Square is now *très* chic.) The original owner's son, Don, has been running the place since 1987, and is usually seen greeting customers. Open for breakfast and lunch daily, until 3 p.m. A second Omelette Express is located in Windsor at 150 Windsor River Rd.

Petite Syrah, 205 Fifth St., Santa Rosa, CA 95401; (707) 568-4402; www.petitesyrah.com; $$. Syrah was good—Petite Syrah may be even better. For many years, chef-owner Josh Silvers ran a restaurant at this location called Syrah, a high-end eatery that was always busy. Then he closed the place to give it a new look inside and to revamp the whole menu. The result is the cleverly named Petite Syrah, as the dishes are now small plates, and your final bill is likely to be more petite, too. Start with a mixed salad with endive, hazelnuts, and chopped dates, topped with blue cheese dressing. Several scrumptious vegetable appetizers are on the menu, such as potato gnocchi with fresh peas and carrots, roasted beets with a *panna cotta* flavored with a bit of horseradish sauce, and roasted asparagus with balsamic vinegar and radish shavings. Protein-rich dishes include grilled steelhead trout, California halibut, duck confit, and hanger steak. Chef Silver also owns **Jackson's Bar and Oven** (see the listing in this category). Open Mon through Sat for lunch and dinner.

Rendez Vous Bistro, 614 Fourth St., Santa Rosa, CA 95401; (707) 526-7700; www.rvbistro.com; $$. Courthouse Square in downtown Santa Rosa has seen its share of restaurants come and go. This one, on the corner of Fourth Street, has an inviting patio—comforting on a slightly crisp autumn afternoon with the warm sun at your back. Could this be Paris? The interior is patterned after a 1930s French bistro. As charming as the interior can be, the patio is the place to order the truffled mushroom sandwich or the *périgourdine* crepe (duck confit, sweet onions, béchamel and fontina cheese). Mains at dinnertime include a bacon-wrapped pork tenderloin, pan-seared salmon, and beef bourguignon. Rendez Vous is open every day for lunch and dinner.

Rosso Pizzeria + Wine Bar, 53 Montgomery Dr. (in the Creekside shopping center), Santa Rosa, CA 95404; (707) 544-3221; http:// rossopizzeria.com; $$. Known for its sensational pizza, the Rosso booth is a regular sight at the Santa Rosa and Windsor farmers' markets, selling slices to the hungry shoppers. But if you can manage it, experience Rosso's pizza—and *pia-dine*—at the main source. In an ordinary strip center on the edge of downtown proper, Rosso uses wood-burning ovens to produce authentic Neapolitan-style pies. The *funghi* and Margherita pies are wonderful. Start by trying the mozzarella bar, with a house-made *bur-rata, salumi,* oven-roasted octopus, or meatballs with polenta. The wine list is generous, with plenty of by-the-glass options, reasonably priced and from labels near and far. Open daily from 11:30 a.m. to 10 p.m.

Stark's Steak & Seafood, 521 Adams St., Santa Rosa, CA 95401; (707) 546-5100; http://starkrestaurants.com; $$$. Now the proprietors of four (soon to be five) Sonoma County restaurants, Mark and Terri Stark got their start in the business with **Willi's Wine Bar** (see the listing in this category). After that came **Willi's Seafood and Raw Bar** in Healdsburg (p. 175), **Monti's Rotisserie & Bar** in Santa Rosa (p. 122), and this high-end steak house near Historic Railroad Square in downtown Santa Rosa. Stark's recently enhanced the seafood selections on the menu, and oysters are a great way to ease into a good steak. If Dungeness crab is more to your liking, order the crab "tater tots" with *padron* peppers and a ginger mustard aioli. The steaks are in-house 28-day dry-aged Angus: bone-in New York, bone-in rib eye, porterhouse, and filet mignon. An American Kobe flatiron is also an option. The steaks can be topped with several goodies such as bone marrow, truffle fried egg, and blue cheese butter. Plenty of sides, too, from traditional big baked potatoes to rosemary yam fries. The non-carnivores can order barbecued prawns, ahi tuna steak, butterfish, Arctic char, petrale sole, Maine lobster, or Alaskan halibut. Stark's is open daily for lunch and dinner.

Superburger, 1501 Fourth St., Santa Rosa, CA 95404; (707) 546-4016; $. Burgers, dogs, onion rings, fries, tator tots, shakes, and pie—it's no frills at Superburger. Fans come from all walks of life, whether they cop to it or not: CEOs, police officers, sales reps in high heels, retirees with canes, college students, working stiffs. Around a U-shaped counter we all bump elbows—and knees at times—in the 17 coveted seats inside (there are a couple of tables outside, too). Some of the burgers are named for nearby neighborhoods and streets (McDonald, Montecito, St. Helena), and many get a light brush of sweet and smoky barbecue sauce on the grill. Relish, pickles, peppers, and chopped onions are in help-yourself containers on the counter. Vertical rolls of paper towels act as napkins—tear off as many as you need. Grease gets under your fingernails, and the place gets under your skin. Open daily from 11 a.m. to 8 p.m. (to 9 p.m. Thurs through Sat).

Tex Wasabi's, 515 Fourth St., Santa Rosa, CA 95401; (707) 544-8399; www.texwasabis.com. $$$. When Guy Fieri opened this combination sushi bar and barbecue joint in downtown Santa Rosa, we all thought he'd lost his marbles. Yet Guy made it work, successfully enough to open a second location in Sacramento. Appetizers are numerous (approximately 20 to choose from), so you can craft a whole meal from any combination, but count on most of them being spicy with Asian and Latin influences. Go for the Cabo fish tacos (filled with marinated and grilled cod), the Garden of Good and Evil Lettuce Cups, or the Vegas fries (extra crispy and tossed in Buffalo sauce with a side of bleu-sabi). The sushi is plentiful, the Tokyo Cobb salad turns the traditional bowl of greens and goodies on its ear, and Guy's Big Bite burger is a half-pound meal in a bun with a fat onion ring on top. The house-smoked barbecued meats are chicken, pulled pork, tri-tip, and half and full racks of St. Louis–style ribs. Other entrees are blackened catfish and chicken or shrimp tempura. Wash it all down with one of the 64-ounce cocktails, if you dare. Open weekdays from 11:30 a.m. to 11 p.m., Sat 11 a.m. to 11 p.m., and Sun 11 a.m. to 10 p.m. (the bar is open until 1 a.m. weeknights and Sat).

Willi's Wine Bar, 4404 Old Redwood Hwy., Santa Rosa, CA 95403; (707) 526-3096; http://starkrestaurants.com; $$$. I was first introduced to the "small plates" concept at Willi's. The portions may be small, but you get to try many different flavors and textures, and share them with others, which is part of the fun. I've never been disappointed in any of the plates. Filet mignon sliders, for instance, are exceptional, complete with béarnaise sauce on brioche buns, and with spinach on the side. Curried crab tacos are full of good-sized crab lumps with a curried, creamy dressing packed into crisp and crunchy shells. The organic brick chicken plate is a chicken breast pressed flat on the grill to quickly sear and seal in the juices, accompanied by hot sauce and a small salad topped with fried onions. For more greens, add the little gem lettuce salad, made with romaine lettuce dabbed with mustard vinaigrette, flakes of cheddar, sliced Fuji apples, and candied walnuts. Willi's is also popular for the 2-ounce pours of wine, so you can try one first before committing to a full glass or a bottle. The Michelin guide has given Willi's its Bib Gourmand recognition

Food Vendors Keep on Truckin'

Taking their cue from the popularity of taco trucks that have served hungry Sonomans for years, mobile food vendors rolled around the county in greater numbers more recently to market other ethnic and "fast" cuisines. It's an ever-changing landscape for these mobile kitchens, however, necessitating Twitter feeds and Facebook updates to keep loyal followers alerted to their whereabouts.

Here's a rundown of some Sonoma County–based mobile vendors:

Charlie Bruno's Chuckwagon, the mobile kitchen operated by Bruno's on Fourth Restaurant, 1226 Fourth St., Santa Rosa, CA 95404; (707) 331-3398; http://brunoschuckwagon.com. The menu includes pulled pork sandwiches with coleslaw, potato croquettes with blue cheese dressing, meat-loaf sandwiches, calamari, sweet potato fries, and a chopped salad loaded with avocado and tomatoes.

Chicago Style Hot Dogs, (707) 591-1986. Get your Polish here, at an old-fashioned vendor that's all about dogs—jumbo, chili, and more. Owner Jeff Tyler frequently dispenses his dogs in downtown Santa Rosa near Russian River Brewing Company.

Fork Catering, (707) 494-0960; http://forkcatering.com. Based in Sebastopol, caterer Sarah Piccolo sources many locally grown and raised ingredients for her menu—all prepared in her fully equipped 2001 Ford Grumman truck.

Karma Bistro, (707) 795-5273. Indian food goes mobile with selections such as chicken *tikka masala, samosas, pakoras, masala chai,* chicken *chaat* or mixed vegetable *chaat,* curry plates, and a choice of wraps. Karma's Facebook page has the latest information.

La Texanita, 1667 Sebastopol Rd., Santa Rosa, CA 95407; (707) 527-7331; www.latexanita.com. This restaurant's mobile kitchen and grill is one of the most popular in the area, a mainstay at many public events, serving up tasty Mexican food such as tacos, flautas, and burritos.

Match Box Diner, (707) 318-8667; http://thematchboxdiner.com. This bright red mobile kitchen sells cheeseburger sliders, barbecued pork sliders, pork mini tacos, hot dogs, slaw, and fries.

The Sifter of Sift Cupcake & Dessert Bar, (707) 282-5333; www .siftcupcakes.com. The Sifter is a brightly painted pink van dispensing the over-the-top cupcakes and desserts that Sift became famous for as the 2010 winner of *Cupcake Wars* on the Food Network. The menu includes 10 or 12 cupcake varieties, frosting shots, profiteroles, whoopies, and macaroons.

Street-Eatz, http://street-eatz.com. Count on the celebration meal of Guatemala known as *pepian*. Also on the menu may be New Orleans spicy chicken pasta and Japanese fried tofu. Other options are the pulled pork taco plate, coconut curry vegetables, rosemary fries, carne asada fries, and even fresh steamed broccoli for adding a healthful side dish to your meal.

Ultra Crepes, www.ultracrepes.com. Try delicious light pancakes filled with many sweet and savory stuffings, such as the ham-and-cheese duo (add an egg for extra protein). Dig into the Nutella, strawberry, and banana crepe for dessert. Find Ultra Crepes on Facebook to track them down.

in the past. Open for dinner on Sun and Mon, and lunch and dinner Tues through Sat.

Specialty Stores & Markets

A'Roma Roasters Coffee & Tea, 95 Fifth St., Santa Rosa, CA 95401; (707) 576-7765; www.aromaroasters.com. Promoting itself as the oldest coffee roaster in Santa Rosa, A'Roma celebrated its 20th year in business in 2010. This coffeehouse with live music on weekend evenings is the place in Historic Railroad Square to grab a bag of beans and run, or to sit and sip the large selection of single-variety coffees, coffee blends, and teas of all types—and a bit of ice cream, too. Try the A'Roma Espresso Italiano or Babe's Rocket Fuel for a big kick. Light meals such as soups, salads, and tamales are served throughout the day and night. The coffeehouse attracts a broad spectrum of society, from the theater crowd (there are two community theaters within walking distance), after-dinner diners out strolling for some distinctive decaf, students cramming for finals with caffeine coursing through their veins, and teenagers from a nearby teen center. Open daily at 6 a.m. Mon through Fri (7 a.m. on weekends), until 11 p.m. (to midnight on Fri and Sat).

Community Market, 1899 Mendocino Ave., Santa Rosa, CA 95401; (707) 546-1806; http://srcommunitymarket.com. Founded as a small worker-run organic and vegetarian food market in 1975, Community Market has steadily grown into a good-size store in the Santa Rosa Junior College neighborhood. The market's roots came out of the "Food for People, Not for Profit" movement in the San Francisco Bay Area in the disco decade, leading to the establishment of a local workers' movement from which this business sprouted. The market has strict policies about its inventory. Generally speaking, they won't sell meat or dairy products, any product with artificial additives or ingredients, and any product whose advertising methods they find offensive. Nearly all the food products on the shelves, canned and fresh, are organic—and many are vegan, too. A bulk food section offers several types of rice and dried soup mixes, nuts and candies, dog and cat food, and an organic olive oil dispensing station, as well.

Corrick's, 637 Fourth St., Santa Rosa, CA 95404; (707) 546-2423; www.corricks.com. Corrick's is a Santa Rosa institution, in business since 1915. It's big, a city block deep, with entrances on both 5th Street and 4th Street. It's largely a stationery store with office supplies and so forth (if you enter through the 5th Street door), but the front of the store that faces 4th Street is loaded with fabulous tableware and serving pieces. Customers have been shopping at Corrick's for generations to find wedding gifts, or invest in a good set of china for themselves. The flatware selection alone is worth stopping to see: Reed & Barton, Ralph Lauren, Lenox, and others.

Tableware is by Wedgwood, Waterford, Spode, Franciscan, Noritake, and other major brands. Everyday dinnerware and accessories can also be found at Corrick's. The store is open Mon through Sat from 10 a.m. to 5:30 p.m.

Franco American Bakery, 202 W. 7th St., Santa Rosa, CA 95401; (707) 545-7528; http://francobreads.com. Sourdough bread is probably most associated with San Francisco, but this longtime Santa Rosa bakery makes the delectable staple using the same "mother dough" starter that dates from the company's founding by the Bastoni brothers in 1900. The starter is the secret to the tangy taste, and it's kept going in perpetuity by saving a small amount of dough from a previous batch and adding it to the next batch. Hence, the lactobacillus culture in the dough keeps moving forward. The company has remained in the Bastoni family for more than 100 years, and in the same location where it all began, on 7th Street. Mario and Frank Bastoni started their business by delivering door-to-door and supplying the bread to the farm families working in the vineyards and hop fields. The company now bakes its bread under two labels: Franco American and Mezzaluna, both of which are widely available locally in most supermarkets and specialty stores. Altogether the bakery makes nine different types of bread

(sourdough, white, wheat, rye, rolls, baguettes, *pane lievitato,* and focaccia, among others). Chances are good that the bread in the basket delivered to your table at most area restaurants is a Franco American or Mezzaluna product. The company sells wholesale all over, and you can order the breads online if you don't live here. Fresher still is the bread they sell at the small retail store right at the bakery. It's open weekdays from 8:30 a.m. to 4:30 p.m., and 8 a.m. to 2 p.m. on Sat.

G&G Supermarkets, 1211 W. College Ave., Santa Rosa, CA 95401; (707) 546-6877; www.gandgmarket.com. When I lived not far from this market, it's where I left my weekly (and sometimes twice-weekly) grocery money. Locally owned and operated, G&G was founded in 1963 by the Gong family. The business steadily grew, and by 1981 a bigger store was required. At the time, the new 84,000-square-foot supermarket was one of the largest of its kind in the state of California. The store is huge, I can attest to that, and has everything you could want: meat, dairy, produce, Chinese takeout, deli, cheese shop, wine shop, and even a demonstration kitchen called the **Ginger Grille** (p. 159). G&G's prices are very competitive, and sometimes well below what other markets charge for the same items. They can always be counted on for plenty of Dungeness crab when the annual season for the crustacean begins in mid-November. G&G has a second store in Petaluma at 701 Sonoma Mountain Pkwy. Both stores are open daily from 7 a.m. to 9 p.m.

Hardisty's Housewares, 1513 Farmers Ln. (in the Farmers Lane Plaza shopping center), Santa Rosa, CA 95404; (707) 545-0534; http://hardistys.com. Calling itself a "culinary toy store," Hardisty's has operated since 1924, when it became a spin-off of the Continental Tea & Crockery Company, which did a big business in coffee, tea, and kitchen accessories. From the beginning, founder Lee Hardisty tried to stock whatever new kitchen gadgets and small appliances came on the market. The store expanded in the 1940s and 1950s to include children's toys, stationery supplies, and other non-food-prep merchandise. In the 1960s, the Hardisty family refocused their attention on the kitchen, selling cookware, china, bulk coffees and teas, and much more for meal preparation and food appreciation. Today Hardisty's also stocks major names in small appliances (Cuisinart, Waring, KitchenAid), and many of the replacement parts, too. Count on finding wine accessories, canning supplies, scales, strainers, wooden pizza paddles, apple corers, and marinade injectors.

Lola's Markets, 440 Dutton Ave., Santa Rosa, CA 95407; (707) 577-8846; and 1680 Petaluma Hill Rd., Santa Rosa, CA 95404; (707) 571-7579; www.lolasmarkets.com. What started as a small take-out restaurant in 1992 has grown to become three fully stocked Latino grocery stores. Gringos flock to Lola's for the hot food to go and to buy ingredients they can't find elsewhere to use in their own recipes. The markets' bakeries produce fresh *conchas* and *bolillos* every day, and do custom baking such as *tres leches* cakes, wedding cakes, and *quinceañera* cakes. The meat departments stock chicken, beef, fish, and  cheese, as well as specialty cuts like pig's feet. Dried chiles, seasonal fruits and vegetables, sugar cane, guayabas, and *tejocotes* make up the produce departments. The kitchen at each Lola's has a huge selection of hot traditional Mexican food for taking home, including numerous kinds of salsa. A third Lola's is located in Healdsburg, at 102 Healdsburg Ave. (take the Central Healdsburg exit off Highway 101—it's to your right as you merge onto Healdsburg Avenue).

Oliver's Markets, 560 Montecito Ave., Santa Rosa, CA 95409; (707) 537-7123; and 461 Stony Point Rd., Santa Rosa, CA 95401; (707) 284-3530; www.oliversmarket.com. It all started with Steve Maass selling produce out of the back of his truck at a simple roadside stand. The grocery business that Steve went on to build, Oliver's Markets, is a locally operated three-store chain. More than any other grocer in Sonoma County, Oliver's actively promotes and sells wine, bread, cheese, meats, and other foods and goods that are made by Sonoma County producers. So you can count on extra-fresh food from one end of the store to the other. I'm an Oliver's customer at least twice a week, picking up Rocky Jr. chicken breasts, a local cheese or two, vegetables and fruits, and a deli item that I'm addicted to: John Hooker's Asiago Pasta Salad. If you have a question about local or imported *fromage,* ask for cheese expert Colette Hatch in the stores' cheese departments—she rotates between locations (see Colette's tips for buying artisan cheese on p. 96). Oliver's consistently wins numerous Sonoma County Harvest Fair awards for the innovative recipes it creates in all categories: desserts, cakes, salads, entrees, and appetizers. All of these goodies are available for sale in the stores. Attentive, personal service is also a hallmark of Oliver's. The original Oliver's Market—the first of the three to open, more than 20 years ago—is in Cotati at 546 E. Cotati Ave.

Pacific Market, 1465 Town & Country Dr., Santa Rosa, CA 95404; (707) 546-3663; www.pacificmkt.com. Plopped down in the middle of a residential neighborhood is the Town & Country shopping center, anchored by Pacific Market. This two-store chain has been owned and operated by the same family for generations. The Sebastopol store, at 550 N. Gravenstein Hwy., opened first, followed by the Santa Rosa store. Both stores feature local organic produce, delis with self-serve hot food and salad bars, fresh sushi, wine departments, cheese departments, fresh fish and meats, and freshly pressed Sebastopol apple juice, too.

Santa Rosa Seafood, 946 Santa Rosa Ave., Santa Rosa, CA 95407; (707) 280-2285; http://santarosaseafood.com. Most locals know about Santa Rosa Seafood from the company's year-round presence at the **Farmers' Market at Veterans Hall** (p. 139). Based at this retail store with a commercial kitchen just south of downtown, they sell to individuals while also operating a wholesale business. This is the best and largest selection of seafood you'll find in one place north of San Francisco, and it usually includes locally caught king salmon, petrale sole, flounder, lingcod, sand dabs, and red snapper. Much of the fish is available whole. Other seafood comes from the East Coast, including live Maine lobsters. Also expect rainbow trout, striped bass, swordfish steaks, jumbo scallops, prawns, fresh barbecued oysters, sushi-grade items, and smoked fish. Open Wed through Sat from 11 a.m. to 6:30 p.m., and Sun 11 a.m. to 5 p.m.

Sur la Table, 2323 Magowan Dr. (in the Montgomery Village shopping center), Santa Rosa, CA 95405; (707) 566-9823 or (800) 243-0852; www.surlatable.com. OK, so it's a chain, with 24 stores in California alone. But it's always inspiring to stroll through the enormous selection of baking accessories and supplies (more than 200 cookie-cutter shapes!), the small electrics, the mysterious and sleek Swiss- and Italian-made machines that brew espresso and cappuccino, and the yards and yards of linens for the kitchen and dining room. Always check the "clearance" shelves for great deals on cool stuff. I've shopped at Sur la Table in the past for many birthday and holiday gifts, and the recipients are always delighted. This outpost is one of

GUY FIERI IS EVERYWHERE

When Santa Rosa restaurateur Guy Fieri (pronounced "fee-eddy") made it into the finals on *The Next Food Network Star* competition a few years ago, we Sonomans assumed it was a flash in the pan, one of those "15 minutes of fame" deals. But with a persona that's part surfer dude, part pro wrestler, and part game-show host, Guy won over the network and negotiated his own show, *Guy's Big Bite.* That led to another, *Diners, Drive-ins, and Dives,* with Guy seen interviewing busy grill cooks in hot kitchens around the nation as they prepare their comfort-food specialties.

Easily recognizable by his spiky blond 'do, ubiquitous sunglasses, chunky neck chains, and distinctive chin hair, Guy seems to be everywhere at once. He lives in Sonoma County and is a frequent guest chef at local fund-raising events, or can be seen stalking the food booths at the county fair—including his own—where I literally bumped into him once. He might pop up to address a cooking class at the Culinary Institute of America in neighboring Napa Valley, and be on television the same night, encouraging average Joes and Jills to do something stupid for money on a prime-time NBC show called *Minute to Win It.* (What'd I tell you? Part game-show host.) More recently Guy was paired with Rachael Ray on a Food Network program called *Celebrity Cook-Off.*

At least for now, Guy is still considered a culinary "rock star," though these days he's much more of a character than a cook. He's stretched his 15 minutes of notoriety into a pretty good high-profile career, with several cookbooks on the market, the continuing popularity of his Santa Rosa restaurants (**Johnny Garlic's,** p. 121, and **Tex Wasabi's,** p. 126), and even his own line of gourmet sausages and hot sauce, among other things.

only seven Sur la Table stores in California with a fully equipped culinary classroom for hands-on instruction and demonstrations (p. 160).

Made or Grown Here

Farmers' Markets

Cotati Farmer's Market, in Old Plaza Park at Old Redwood Hwy. and W. Sierra Ave., Cotati, CA 94931; (707) 795-5508; www.cotati .org. Thursday evenings get interesting in Cotati, with this market much like a street fair because of its hours, 4:30 to 7:30 p.m. Get your produce shopping finished first so you can stay for the prepared food (some offered by food trucks), the live tunes, a pint of beer, or to take your kids to frolic in the park's playground.

Farmers' Market at Veterans Hall, 1351 Maple Ave., Santa Rosa, CA 95401; http://thesantarosafarmersmarket.com. Year-round 2 days a week, this is considered the biggest and most varied farmers' market in Sonoma County, particularly during the harvest season. The Wednesday morning market (8:30 a.m. to noon) usually includes some of the merchants and farmers who will also appear at the larger Saturday morning event (8:30 a.m. to 1 p.m.). It's one of the best opportunities to "meet the face that feeds you," with growers from such farms as **The Patch** in Sonoma, **New Family**

Farm in Sebastopol (ask for Adam), **Hector's Honey Farm** in Santa Rosa, and **Bernier Farms** near Healdsburg (all profiled in this book). In the parking lot of the Veterans Hall, 100 or more vendors sell produce, seafood, flowers, cheese, crafts, clothing, jewelry, and ready-to-eat food such as pizza and oysters. There's always live entertainment, too—one crisp autumn morning it was an acoustic guitarist quietly and expertly strumming "Layla." The lot at the Veterans Hall is big, so there's plenty of free parking (and clean restrooms inside the hall).

Rohnert Park Certified Farmers' Market, Rohnert Park Expwy. at State Farm Dr., Rohnert Park, CA 94928; (707) 588-3496; www .rohnertparkfarmersmarket.org. The planned city of Rohnert Park is known mostly for its big-box merchants and chain restaurants along Highway 101, but it promotes fresh food, too. In summer, Party on the Plaza happens on Friday from 5 to 8 p.m., in an open parking lot location that can make for a warm evening. Bring along a cooler for your fresh produce if you want to linger later for a glass of wine or beer while checking out the crafts booths.

Santa Rosa Downtown Market, along Fourth Street, between Mendocino Ave. and E St., Santa Rosa, CA 95401; (707) 524-2123;

www.srdowntownmarket.com. Beginning in mid-May and ending in late August, this Wednesday night event is dominated by restaurant food stands, crafts, political causes, and live music (on three street corners, including a main stage)—in other words, everything that represents the diversity of Sonoma County. The fresh produce can be found primarily on E Street, along with a couple of food trucks. In 2011, a wine-tasting area was added to the mix. The action gets under way about 5 p.m. and wraps up at 8 p.m.

Windsor Farmers' Market, Town Green in downtown Windsor, CA 95492; (707) 838-1320; www.windsorfarmersmarket.com. Windsor is a small town with a jazzy, recently refurbished downtown core where several streets of decaying buildings once stood. Part of the redevelopment included the creation of a large town green, and the locals throw some type of shindig in it as often as possible. That includes a straight-ahead farmers' market on Sunday from 10 a.m. to 1 p.m., May through December. Many of the same local farmers who attend the county's other markets can be found here, too. Between June and August, on Thursday from 5 to 8 p.m., the town green is again transformed into a farmers' market, but it's really more of an excuse to party. A lively rock band, vendors of prepared food such as **Rosso Pizzeria** (p. 124), and the beer and wine booths guarantee you'll have a good time.

Crane Melon Barn, 4935 Petaluma Hill Rd., Santa Rosa, CA 95404; (707) 795-6987; www.cranemelon.com. Almost a century ago, Oliver Crane crossed a Japanese melon with a California cantaloupe and—voilà!—a new melon was born, called the Crane. It's unique to Sonoma County, officially grown only here, though others have tried in other regions. The vine-ripened melons are almost never available in stores, and are picked ripe daily during their regular season—approximately September 1 to October 31. It's a short window of opportunity to enjoy this one-of-a-kind fruit, but well worth it. Round like a soccer ball, the Crane is sweet and juicy, weighing from 4 to 7 pounds. Named for the Crane family that has owned the land for more than 160 years, the fruit is specific to the soil, the climate zone, and the farming techniques. Open seasonally Mon through Fri from 10 a.m. to 5:30 p.m., and Sat 10 a.m. to 5 p.m.

Imwalle Gardens, 685 W. Third St., Santa Rosa, CA 95401; (707) 546-0279. Dating back to 1886, this farm still owned by the Imwalle family has gone from being an out-in-the-boonies property to holding its own as the city has grown up all around it. At one time the Imwalles harvested hops and raised cattle on this site. Generations of loyal customers have been purchasing the fruits and vegetables grown here, along with veggie seedlings, flowers, and herbs. The Imwalles raise most of their own produce, but some products are brought in from warmer California farming regions where the crops are harvested earlier. The store is open daily starting at 8:30 a.m. Mon through Sat, and Sun from 10 a.m. to 4 p.m.

Mike's Truck Garden, 1319 River Rd., Fulton, CA 95439; (707) 528-4081. Mike's is a large seasonal farm stand just west of the intersection of River and Fulton Roads, open approximately from mid-March to mid-November. The fresh produce lures you in, but the yellow and green stand also stocks local cheese and apple juice, snacks, cookies, candy, bread, tortillas, and other staples. Mike's is open from 10 a.m. to 7 p.m. daily.

Redwood Empire Farm, 55 Middle Rincon Rd., Santa Rosa, CA 95409; (707) 953-6150; www.redwoodempirefarm.com. This farm stand has special appeal to me, being less than a mile from my home. It's also an at-the-source stand, so while busy traffic is zipping past, the 8 acres of vegetables, fruit and nut trees, and free-ranging chickens is a pleasant pocket of rural Sonoma County in an otherwise urban setting. It's believed that the fruit trees here are antique varieties originally purchased at Luther Burbank's nursery in the early 1900s (including the Burbank Imperial Prune), while Luther was still alive and overseeing his successful horticulture empire. The farmers, Jeff and Ariel, sell their produce year-round at the Farmers' Market at Veteran's Hall on Saturday morning. A recent display of their bounty included watermelons, beans, eggplants, cucumbers, squash, numerous varieties of tomatoes, and basil. The stand on Middle Rincon Road is open seasonally on Tues and Thurs from 3:30 to 6:30 p.m. Redwood Empire Farm also offers CSA subscriptions—see that category for details.

Tierra Vegetables, 651 Airport Blvd., Santa Rosa, CA 95403; (707) 837-8366; www.tierravegetables.com. The vegetables, beans, and other crops are grown behind the large white barn the owners saved from a nearby farm that was being bulldozed for a new hospital. The large painting of Luther Burbank behind the cash register seems fitting at Tierra. This family farm is now in its third decade, and owners Wayne, his sister Lee, and Wayne's wife Evie run the show (Wayne is easy to spot—he's always barefoot). The trio's vast knowledge of produce and the ways to prepare it bring the regular customers back year after year. Tierra grows many traditional vegetables but also more interesting crops, weather permitting. Try sweet peppers and chile peppers, smoked onions, tepary beans in three varieties, blue and green cornmeal, and several types of kale. (Tierra also operates a CSA; see the listing in that category.) It's helpful to bring your own bags and baskets if you plan to buy an assortment of produce. If the spirit moves you, stroll through the fields, too, when the stand is open: Tues through Fri from 11 a.m. to 6 p.m., and Sat 10 a.m. to 4 p.m. (rain or shine).

Valley End Farm, 6300 Petaluma Hill Rd., Santa Rosa, CA 95404; (707) 585-1123; www.valleyendfarm.com. Growing vegetables since 1996, Sharon and her son Clint claim to have the largest organic produce farm in Sonoma County, on 70 acres east of Rohnert Park. The fertilizer used on the crops is composted recycled food waste, not manure, and the farm is irrigated by an underground aquifer. Valley End Farm is a regular vendor at the seasonal farmers' market in Rohnert Park. Monthly visits to the farm are offered during summer months, and cooking demonstrations are also on the calendar from time to time. Take a peek at the fabulous chicken coop, or as they like to call it "El Hotel de Pollo." See the CSA category, p. 151, for Valley End Farm's offerings.

Cheesemaker

Matos Cheese Factory, 3669 Llano Rd., Santa Rosa, CA 95403; (707) 584-5283. The cheese created on this working farm by owners Joe and Mary Matos has been featured in Williams-Sonoma catalogs and can be found in upscale grocery stores, too. But it's more fun to go directly to the source and pay much less per pound. The single product they create from the raw milk of their own cows is a semihard round called St. George. Joe and Mary grew up in the Portuguese Azores and brought along the recipe for their native cheese when they immigrated here in the 1970s. Their factory is off the beaten path, surrounded by countryside and cows, but well worth the drive. Call before stopping by, or if you need directions.

Burbank's Legacy Continues to Grow

By all accounts, Luther Burbank was a horticultural genius. He spent the early part of his life in Massachusetts, where he developed a curiosity for plants at a young age and went on to create the Burbank potato when he was only 21. He then moved to Santa Rosa in 1875, where he bought a 4-acre parcel and set about propagating other new plant varieties.

The number of now-common fruits, vegetables, and flowers attributed to his experimentations is staggering (estimated at more than 800), and most of the plants are high-yielding and hardy, too. Hundreds of varieties of plums, prunes, berries, strawberries, apples, peaches, pears, nectarines, and nut trees can be traced back to Luther's work in his greenhouse in Santa Rosa and the 18-acre plot he bought in Sebastopol called Gold Ridge Farm. In an attempt to increase the world's food supply through

Meats & Butchers

Carolina Wild, 5280 Aero Dr., Santa Rosa, CA 95403; (707) 526-7038. It's a meat and seafood shop, as well as a place to grab a good sandwich. The display cases hold an array of fresh beef, chicken, and sausages. Shrimp from South Carolina and other his experimentations, he even developed a spineless cactus for feeding to livestock in desert regions.

Luther became famous during his lifetime with the publication of his catalog, called *New Creations in Fruits and Flowers*. He also had a hand in writing several books about his experiments and methods. He was revered by most, yet scorned by the devout, who preached that only God could bring forth a "new" plant. He was prolific in the greenhouse until his death in 1926, with 3,000 plant experiments still in development on his Sonoma County lands. Luther is buried on the Santa Rosa property, now a city park.

You may not realize it, but there is likely something on your dinner plate that is directly descended from Luther's plant propagations: the Russet Burbank potato, the most widely cultivated potato in the United States and the dominant potato used around the world in processed foods.

Luther's legacy is remembered in other ways, too: Many schools throughout California and in other parts of the United States are named for him, though the show-business city of Burbank is not.

seafood from California are available fresh or frozen. The current owners have plans to smoke meats and make their own sausages, too. Order a sandwich at the counter (the roast beef is tender) and enjoy it at one of the tables inside, or outside in warm weather. Carolina Wild is roomy, bright, and clean.

Santa Rosa Meat & Poultry Co., 940 Ludwig Ave., Santa Rosa, CA 95401; (707) 542-6234. Ever wonder where a local chef buys the meat that will be served in his or her restaurant that same night? Chances are, it's from this supplier. Not a typical butcher shop—you don't walk in and select cuts from a refrigerated case—Santa Rosa Meat & Poultry is primarily a wholesaler, yet it's open to the public on weekdays from 7 a.m. to 3 p.m. It works like this: Enter the office, peruse a list of what's available, and tell them what you would like to try. The staff recommends that you start small—order a couple of rib-eye steaks, for instance, take them home, and see how you like them. From a list of various cuts of beef, pork, chicken, lamb, and more, you can call in an order for a few more helpings of this or that and it will be waiting for you. Planning a big barbecue? Phone ahead for one of the 10-pound boxes of freshly-ground hamburger patties. Need a turkey? The company processes its own line of free-range natural turkeys, including big toms. They even carry some specialty meats like quail, rabbit, goose, buffalo, and wild boar. Most items can be purchased in any amount, small or large.

Willie Bird Turkeys, 5350 Sebastopol Rd., Santa Rosa, CA 95407; (707) 545-2832 or (877) 494-5592; www.williebird.com. The history of this business goes all the way back to 1924, when the Benedetti family began raising turkeys in Sonoma County. The free-range turkeys came later, and have been raised that way for more than 40 years. What a long way this family business has come, with their fresh turkey products now served in high-end restaurants such as Spago in Hollywood, and available through the Williams-Sonoma catalog. Those same products can be purchased at this store west of Santa Rosa along the highway. Fresh turkeys, chicken, and duck are seasonal for the holiday market, while the smoked birds can be purchased year-round. The store is open Mon through Fri from 10 a.m. to 5 p.m., and Sat 9 a.m. to 4 p.m. Willie Bird also operates a restaurant south of downtown Santa Rosa at 1150 Santa Rosa Ave. (707-542-0861), untouched by time and trends and still serving the delicious turkey the family is known for. Willie Bird also grills its huge turkey legs at area farmers' markets and fairs—the smell is irresistible.

Willowside Meats & Sausage Factory, 3421 Guerneville Rd., Santa Rosa, CA 95401; (707) 546-8404. House-made sausages, beef jerky, fresh cuts of beef, chicken, pork, smoked bacon, duck, duck fat, and butchering services for area lamb and pig farmers are all provided by this shop. If they don't carry a particular type of meat or a specific cut, they can usually get it for you. Willowside Meats is west of Santa Rosa near Willowside Road. The store is open Mon through Sat from 8 a.m. to 5 p.m.

Honey Producers

Bear Foot Honey Farm, 4372-D Sonoma Hwy. (Hwy. 12), Santa Rosa, CA 95409; (707) 570-2899; www.bearfoothoney.com. Along a busy stretch of highway on the east side of Santa Rosa is an unlikely find: a place to learn about bees, honey, and the three generations of history behind this venture, along with a plethora of honey products. Tours are only $4, though the temperature must be above 60°F to go into the hives. (Naturally, tiny children and anyone with an allergy to bees should steer clear.) The selection for sale is vast—raw honey by the jar, creamed honey, honey sticks, beeswax candles, beauty products, gift baskets, and more. Other hives controlled by this company are installed in various locations throughout Sonoma County, in fields of lavender, clover, wildflowers, and apples, all to give pollination a boost and absorb the surrounding flavors.

Hector's Honey Farm, 2794 Fulton Rd., Fulton, CA 95439; (707) 579-9416. Hector Alvarez and his family are familiar faces at the local farmers' markets, selling unprocessed honey in a multitude of flavors. Other bee products, from pollen to beeswax candles to propolis (a bee by-product with some medicinal benefits), are offered. Hector also markets bee eradication and pollination services. Yet there's much more to Hector's—he grows loads of tomatoes, figs, onions, and other seasonal produce, too. Call for an appointment before stopping by the farm.

She Hasta Bee Honey, 4989 Occidental Rd., Santa Rosa, CA 95401; (707) 575-9761. "She hasta bee a great queen to have a great hive," say the owners, explaining the name given to this producer of raw, natural honey. Their luscious chocolate honey is remarkable right out of the jar, generously plopped by the spoonful into hot tea, spread on toast, or in any other use that suits your fancy. She Hasta Bee is usually found at the Santa Rosa Downtown Market, or visit the farm site directly to learn more and buy the products.

Community Supported Agriculture Programs (CSAs)

Redwood Empire Farm, 55 Middle Rincon Rd., Santa Rosa, CA 95409; (707) 953-6150; www.redwoodempirefarm.com. Bags of seasonal produce are generously filled by this farm between May and November for $25 per week, with the option to add free-range, organically raised chicken eggs. CSA members can pick up their bag at the farm stand, or at another location closer to the center of the city.

Tierra Vegetables, 651 Airport Blvd., Santa Rosa, CA 95403; (707) 837-8366; www.tierravegetables.com. What's in the box? A typical October "menu" might be wax beans, celery, fennel, cauliflower, a lettuce and endive mix, summer squash, and yellow onions. In 2011, the weekly price for a box of fresh produce from this grower was $22. Tierra's CSA season is long, usually from late May through December. Read more about Tierra under Farms & Farm Stands.

Valley End Farm, 6300 Petaluma Hill Rd., Santa Rosa, CA 95404; (707) 585-1123; www.valleyendfarm.com. This CSA offers both a weekly or biweekly box of fresh fruits and vegetables, all certified organic, that varies with the season and weather influences. Lots of add-ons, too: cheese, goat milk, baguettes, eggs, flowers, and even fresh sauerkraut. Prices in 2011 ranged from $60 for a small box delivered four times, to a large box for $100 that feeds five to six people, also delivered four times. Valley End Farm can usually be found selling its produce at the **Rohnert Park Farmers' Market** (see that listing).

Food & Wine Pairings/ Landmark Wineries

DeLoach Vineyards, 1791 Olivet Rd., Santa Rosa, CA 95401; (707) 526-9111 or (800) 441-9298; www.deloachvineyards.com. DeLoach was one of the first wineries to plant Pinot Noir grapes in the Russian River Valley. In the 1970s, Cecil DeLoach, a San Francisco firefighter, founded the winery that still bears his name. It's now owned by Boisset Family Estates, which operate a few other boutique wineries in California. The Boisset family converted the vineyards and the gardens around this property to the "biodynamic" method of farming, and anyone in the tasting room can explain it to you (read more about biodynamic farming on p. 56). DeLoach bottles delicious, soft Pinot Noir, along with Chardonnay, Sauvignon Blanc, Syrah, Zinfandel, and Cabernet Sauvignon. Food plays an integral role at DeLoach, with pairings offered that include cheese plates ($10 per person) and even a fully stocked picnic basket with gourmet goodies, utensils, stemware, and so on ($30 per person)—both options require advance reservations. A tour is also offered that comes with bites of food made from the produce grown in the garden, paired with a few of the wines. Open daily from 10 a.m. to 5 p.m.

Hanna Winery & Vineyards, 5353 Occidental Rd., Santa Rosa, CA 95401; (707) 575-3371; www.hannawinery.com. The winery's flagship vineyard in the Russian River Valley is at the Occidental Road location, where 25 acres are planted to Pinot Noir and Chardonnay. This location is also the production facility. Picnic grounds onsite overlook the vineyards, where you are welcome to bring food and pair it with Hanna wines. The winery's Alexander Valley hospitality center and tasting room (9280 Hwy. 128, Healdsburg, CA 95448, 800-854-3987) is the site of an 88-acre vineyard and where the wine-and-food pairings take place. Hanna matches its wines with Bellwether Farms cheese ($15 per person in advance), and box lunches can also be arranged for adding to the reserve or classic wine tastings ($10 and $20 per person). Hanna bottles Cabernet Sauvignon, Merlot, Malbec, Sauvignon Blanc (always fabulous), a rosé, and a red blend of mostly Zinfandel. Both tasting room locations are open daily from 10 a.m. to 4 p.m.

Kendall-Jackson Wine Center, 5007 Fulton Rd., Fulton, CA 95439; (707) 571-8100; www.kj.com. Jess Jackson was an interesting man, once listed by *Forbes* magazine as one of the 400 wealthiest Americans. Besides founding and running a huge wine empire, he loved raising Thoroughbred race horses, and did pretty well at that, too, with at least one of his beauties winning the Preakness Stakes and the Breeder's Cup Classic in 2008. Jess died in 2011, leaving behind a legacy of 35 wineries worldwide. At the time of his death, Jess owned 14,000 acres of vineyards in Sonoma, Napa, and Mendocino Counties. He built up his wine business on the Chardonnay grape, and later added many other varietals, both white and red. Most of the K-J bottlings can be tasted at this hospitality center located in Fulton, an unincorporated burg on the northwest edge of Santa Rosa. The setting is lovely, surrounded by gardens of culinary herbs, vegetables, and "international" crops such as bok choy and Chinese cabbage and mustards. It's these gardens that supply some of the ingredients used in the food-and-wine pairings. A reserve wine tasting, matching 7 wines with 10 to 12 bites of great nibbles (pork-belly sliders, fennel and tomato soup, tacos, *panna cotta,* and a crepe with prosciutto and cheese) is available by appointment ($30 per person). A less expensive cheese pairing ($25) matches six wines with six local artisan cheeses. For your sweet tooth, opt for the wine-and-dessert pairing, with five wines teamed with macaroons, chocolate, biscotti, and mousse ($20). Open daily from 10 a.m. to 5 p.m.

Ledson Winery & Vineyards, 7335 Sonoma Hwy. (Hwy. 12), Santa Rosa, CA 95409; (707) 537-3810; www.ledson.com. Most visitors are usually taken aback by the sight of this gothic structure, situated off in the distance with rocky mountains rising up behind it. Inside are three tasting rooms, along with one of the best-stocked markets of gourmet food, cheese, and food-related gifts at any winery in Sonoma County. Several deli-style sandwiches are made fresh, with a choice of side salads and sweets, too. The grounds at Ledson are ideal for a picnic, with many tables set out under shady trees, so take your Ledson wine and food outside for the full experience. Ledson bottles many wine varietals in small lots, so there's something for everyone's palate. Whites include Sauvignon Blanc, Chardonnay, and Riesling; reds include Pinot Noir, Merlot, Zinfandel, and more than 10 meritage blends. Production is limited to 40,000 cases per year, and the wines are sold exclusively at the winery. Open from 10 a.m. to 5 p.m. every day.

Paradise Ridge Winery, 4545 Thomas Lake Harris Dr., Santa Rosa, CA 95403; (707) 528-9463; www.prwinery.com. Perched on a hillside overlooking the northwest edge of Santa Rosa, Paradise Ridge is memorable for its sculpture garden, which unfolds as you make the long drive to the top of the hill. It's a world-class art collection, so slow down to look at each carefully chosen piece. Once at the winery, enjoy a wine-and-cheese pairing for $20 per person (reservations requested), which matches local cheeses with toppings such as figs, mango jam, and salami to Chardonnay, Sauvignon Blanc, Zinfandel, and Cabernet Sauvignon. The Byck family opened this winery in 1994 to showcase their amazing white wines. Red wines soon followed: Merlot, Syrah, Pinot Noir, Zinfandel, Cabernet Sauvignon. They also bottle a Blanc de Blancs sparkler. Paradise Ridge is known for its awesome Wednesday-night gatherings to watch the sun setting on the horizon. After the winery officially closes, the murmured oohs and ahhs begin after 6 p.m., May through Oct. Visit Paradise Ridge daily from 11 a.m. to 5 p.m.

St. Francis Winery & Vineyards, 100 Pythian Rd., Santa Rosa, CA 95409; (888) 675-WINE; ww.stfranciswinery.com. There's a culinary garden on-site planted with garlic, onions, broccoli, and more. These ingredients are used to make some of the inspired small plates of food paired with the wines St. Francis is known for—Viognier, Malbec, Cabernet Franc and others. The 4-course food-and-wine tastings ($35 per person) take place two or three times daily (except for Tues and Wed), featuring such goodies as heirloom tomato and nectarine salad and seared duck breast (reservations are recommended). A meat-and-cheese plate on the patio in summer is available twice daily ($25 per person). In winter, a similar plate is served inside near the fireplace ($20). These generally are available without prior reservations. St. Francis also bottles an "Old Vines" Zinfandel and several other varietals. Open every day from 10 a.m. to 5 p.m.

Small "Mexicantessan" Grew into a Big Tortilla Business

Jose Tamayo was already past the age of 50 when he and his wife Mary settled in Sonoma County. Jose had left his native Mexico as a young man, drawn to the Midwest by the promise of railroad work while American soldiers were fighting in World War II. He eventually raised five sons in Nebraska after a career with the Union Pacific Railroad.

In the mid-1970s the Tamayo family came to Santa Rosa seeking to start a business of their own. Drawing on their Mexican heritage, Jose and Mary opened a taqueria-style deli, dubbed a "Mexicantessan," while they developed a way to mass-produce fresh corn and flour tortillas that wouldn't need refrigeration. The Tamayos opened a second taqueria, increased production of the tortillas as more local grocery stores placed orders, and gave their new company a name: **La Tortilla Factory**.

By 1988 Jose and Mary had closed the taquerias and were making tortillas full time in a production facility on the south side of Santa Rosa. Popularity of the products soared, and additional versions of the tortillas came to market. Eventually the company moved to a larger factory near the Sonoma County airport, where all the tortillas are made today. The entire line of tortillas is widely distributed throughout the United States.

Three generations of Tamayos have operated La Tortilla Factory, and it is still family-owned, although Jose died in 2010.

Brewpubs & Microbreweries

Russian River Brewing Company, 725 Fourth St., Santa Rosa, CA 95404; (707) 545-2337; www.russianriverbrewing.com. The year-round featured beers are called Pliny the Elder (a double India Pale Ale), Damnation (a golden ale), and Blind Pig IPA. Russian River also makes barrel-aged beers and Belgian-style ales. You gotta love these names for the other suds: Perdition, Redemption, Supplication, Temptation, and Salvation (in whatever order you desire). Check the chalkboard at the bar: 15 brews are usually on tap, and some in bottles, too. The brewery's Pliny the Younger creates a sensation when it's released on tap once a year: long lines around the block and the 64-ounce Pliny growlers scalped online at hugely inflated prices—that sort of hysteria. The food is pub-style and varied—lots of pizza combos in three sizes, calzones, side salads, sandwiches, a charcuterie plate, and wings. The brewery is open from 11 a.m. to midnight Sun through Thur, and to 1 a.m. on weekends. The kitchen stays open until last call.

Third Street Aleworks, 610 Third St., Santa Rosa, CA 95404; (707) 523-3060; http://thirdstreetaleworks.com. I've never left here disappointed by the food, or the beer. It was the first micro-brewery to open in downtown Santa Rosa in modern times (1996), and it's been popular with locals ever since. The flagship ales, always on tap, are Annadel Pale Ale (named for a nearby state park), Stonefly Oatmeal Ale, and Bodega Head India Pale Ale. On tap a lot of the time are the American Wheat golden ale, Kolsch Bier (a German barley ale), and Blarney Sisters' Irish Stout, a classic Dublin brew. The grub at this pub is evenly divided between appetizers, soups and salads, burgers, pizzas, and sandwiches. Specialties are shepherd's pie, Asian chicken and shrimp skewers, and Cajun pasta with chicken, shrimp, and hot sausage in a creamy marinara sauce. Open daily from 11:30 a.m. to midnight (to 1 a.m. on weekends); the kitchen is open for lunch and dinner until 11 p.m. (11:30 p.m. weekends).

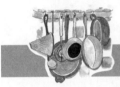

Learn to Cook

Ginger Grille, G&G Supermarket, 1211 W. College Ave., Santa Rosa, CA 95401; (707) 546-6877; www.gandgmarket.com. Inside this supermarket is a roomy, fully equipped demonstration kitchen and classroom where regular instruction is offered to the general public, and where private classes also take place. The Northern California Center for Well-Being conducts classes in such topics as making nutritious baby food and cooking healthful alternatives to high-fat meals. Prices vary, so visit the store's website to see the latest information.

Santa Rosa Junior College Culinary School, 1501 Mendocino Ave., Santa Rosa, CA 95401; (707) 527-4011 or (800) 564-SRJC; www.santarosa.edu. For food enthusiasts seeking individual classes and anyone wishing to enter a certificate program in the culinary arts, Santa Rosa Junior College has a new Culinary Arts building where all the learning takes place. Across the street from the main campus, the building includes five teaching kitchens, several classrooms, a bakery, and a 60-seat cafe open to the public. Students are taught traditional and modern food-prep techniques and restaurant business operations, to earn one of several certificates: Culinary Arts, Bakery and Pastry, Front House Operations, and Restaurant Management. Part of their training involves working in the public cafe in real-world conditions. The certificate programs can generally be completed in one or two semesters. The new building is also where fun and informative evening and afternoon classes take place in food-and-wine pairing, cheesemaking, baking bread, canning produce, making candy or pasta, and many others. Fees for the food-enthusiast classes typically cost from $50 to $100. Reservations to dine at the cafe are recommended.

Sur la Table, 2323 Magowan Dr. (in the Montgomery Village shopping center), Santa Rosa, CA 95405; (707) 566-9823 or (800) 243-0852; www.surlatable.com. The classroom at this retail store (p. 137) offers instruction in such basic topics as essential knife skills, or learning to whip up classic Spanish dishes, chocolates and truffles, gnocchi, risotto, tamales, and other goodies. Prices for the evening and weekend classes range from $59 for a single session to $200 for multiple sessions covering one subject or theme. The resident chef instructor, Les Goodman, is an engaging fellow who does most of the teaching. Classes are usually limited to 16 students for the hands-on instruction, and up to 30 for the demonstrations. An added bonus: After class you get a 10 percent discount on your store purchases.

Worth Our Weight, 1021 Hahman Dr., Santa Rosa, CA 95405; (707) 544-1200; www.worthourweight.org. WOW, as it's called for short, isn't a traditional learn-to-cook school. Instead, it's a culinary apprentice program for young people ages 16 to 24 who have struggled in life. They may have been foster kids or homeless at one time, or are familiar with the inside of a jail cell or juvenile home. At WOW, they get a chance to change their lives through tuition-free culinary and food-service training. As they learn skills to prepare food, they are also being prepared for life. Donations are always welcome, and revenue from the cafe also helps fund the program. Every weekend, WOW opens its doors for brunch, prepared and served by the students. The hours are 9 a.m. to 2 p.m. on Sat, and 9 a.m. to 1 p.m. on Sun—reservations are recommended. Evelyn Cheatham is the visionary behind WOW, and she is also an instructor with the Santa Rosa Junior College Culinary Arts program (see listing above).

Healdsburg, Geyserville & Cloverdale

The Sonoma Valley may be where California's wine industry was born, but for many visitors to Sonoma County, Healdsburg is the quintessential Wine Country town. Its population (11,254) puts it head-to-head in size with the city of Sonoma, yet Healdsburg can boast of being the gateway to three large American viticultural areas (AVAs) or "appellations" (Alexander Valley, Dry Creek Valley, and the Russian River Valley) and a couple of smaller ones (Chalk Hill and Rockpile).

Healdsburg is where people come to relax and enjoy high-end dining, spa treatments, and beautiful sunsets from the balconies of such lodgings as Hotel Healdsburg or the patio at Bear Republic Brewing Company. You might find yourself window-shopping along the Plaza with actress Anne Hathaway one night after dinner, or sharing the sidewalk with a lively group of spandex-clad bicyclists who have just rolled into town after a long ride.

Though it's lately been criticized for pandering to wineries hoping to open even more tasting rooms around or near the central Plaza, Healdsburg still has 100-some wineries out in the rolling vineyards to the east, west, and north of town—most of them less than a 20-minute drive away.

Looking like puzzle pieces on a map, the appellations in this region have distinct growing conditions and numerous microclimates. The Alexander Valley is known for its Cabernet Sauvignon, Chardonnay, and Zinfandel. It encompasses 14,400 vineyard acres, supports 43 wineries, and is largely protected from direct marine influences. Dry Creek Valley has more wineries (63) but fewer vineyard acres (8,600), and morning fog from the ocean burns off early in the day to reveal sunny skies and toasty temperatures. Dry Creek Valley's top varietals are Zinfandel, Cabernet Sauvignon, and Sauvignon Blanc.

The Russian River Valley appellation supports 50 wineries and 16,400 acres of vineyards, many of them planted in Pinot Noir and Chardonnay grapes. Fog from marine and river influences keeps the berries cool at night to prepare them for sunny and warm afternoons. Far to the north, west of Cloverdale, is the tiny appellation called Rockpile, planted with 150 acres of vineyards of Cabernet Sauvignon, Petite Sirah, and Zinfandel.

Geyserville is not quite a "blink or you'll miss it" community, but it is small and compact, with a population of less than 900. Home to a couple of great restaurants and a cool wine-tasting collective, it's also a stopping-off point for the many visitors coming and going from River Rock Casino, perched on the hillside a few miles away. Before wine and gambling, the area was known for its pear and plum (prune) orchards, along with other commodities such as cattle and grain.

Geyserville earned its name by being in close proximity to natural hot springs and steam vents that once were a major spa attraction called The Geysers. Two American presidents and Mark Twain were among the vacationers at The Geysers resort in its heyday. Now, the renewable geothermal energy nearby is harnessed by the Calpine Corporation to produce electricity at the largest complex of geothermal power plants in the world.

The northernmost community in Sonoma County is Cloverdale, which began as a bustling railroad town in the late 1870s and now has 8,600 residents. Cloverdale was once named one of the "Ten Coolest Small Towns in America" by *Budget Travel* magazine, and the "No. 1 Coolest Town in California." I know for a fact it's true. Cloverdale is also known for its annual Citrus Fair, which has been going on every February since 1892 (see the Food Events & Happenings list). A leisurely walk up and down Cloverdale Boulevard offers many diversions for dining, shopping, and appreciating historic buildings.

Cyrus, 29 North St., Healdsburg, CA 95448; (707) 433-3311; www
.cyrusrestaurant.com; $$$$. Often called Sonoma County's answer
to the French Laundry, the world-famous restaurant in nearby Napa
Valley, Cyrus was the only restaurant in the county to receive a
2-star award in the 2012 Michelin guide. The restaurant has been a
consistent Michelin star winner, for good reason. When the caviar
and champagne cart rolls up to your table, your unforgettable
experience is under way. *Gourmet* magazine named Cyrus as one
of the top 50 restaurants in America, and other "best of" praise
has been widely published. Chef Douglas Keane offers an 8-course
tasting menu ($130 per person, with a separate vegetarian menu),
or a 5-course menu ($102). Mouthwatering dishes come out of the
kitchen in elegant fashion, all artfully prepared. The menu changes
frequently with the seasons, but might include such delights
as ginger–bone marrow custard, roasted lobster in cauliflower
cream, crispy chicken thigh with truffled risotto, prime strip loin
with bordelaise sauce, and with a sweet finish like vanilla bean
Fontainebleau with apple ice. Reservations are necessary for the
main dining room, though sometimes you can get a table in the bar
without waiting, and still enjoy many of the
same savory dishes, cheese plates, and desserts a la carte. A private room for up to 12
diners is also available. Cyrus is open
for dinner Thurs through Mon.

Dry Creek Kitchen, 317 Healdsburg Ave., Healdsburg, CA 95448; (707) 431-0330; www.charliepalmer.com; $$$$. On the first floor of Hotel Healdsburg is one of the top-drawer restaurants owned by chef Charlie Palmer—others are in Manhattan, Reno, Dallas, and Las Vegas. Dry Creek Kitchen celebrated its 10th anniversary in 2011, attesting to its popularity and durability. Starters at dinner could be smoked shrimp and mascarpone tortellini, white corn soup, or a platter of house-made charcuterie. Try the Rocky Jr. chicken cassoulet for your main course, or honey-brined pork loin, or brioche-crusted Alaskan halibut. Sides are extra, and can include red quinoa pilaf. For the full experience, choose the 6-course chef's tasting menu ($74 per person, or $143 with paired wines). The first course might be ahi tuna crudo, followed by the corn soup, the aforementioned tortellini, the halibut, a Kobe flatiron steak, and ending with one of several desserts on the cart that night. Lunch might consist of grilled chicken paillard, Kobe mini-burgers, and a smoked flank steak and brie sandwich. The interior is lovely, but ask for a patio table for a more casual feel, and for the best people-watching. Open for dinner nightly and for lunch Fri through Sun.

Madrona Manor, 1001 Westside Rd., Healdsburg, CA 95448; (707) 433-4231; www.madronamanor.com; $$$$. The Madrona Manor inn is the grand dame of Victorian-style inns in these parts (Francis Ford Coppola once tried to buy it), and the restaurant within is a perennial favorite of locals and visitors, and recipient of one star in the 2012 Michelin guide. The setting west of Healdsburg on a hill is beautiful, the grounds a favorite locale for weddings and receptions. The restaurant decor is elegant, to reflect the historic nature of the whole place, but not stuffy. The tasting menus can be 4, 5, or 6 courses (starting at $73 per person), with wine pairings additional. Some of the dishes might be a poached oyster, Yukon Gold potato gnocchi, local king salmon, rabbit or lamb, abalone, veal tenderloin, and cheese courses. Try the ice cream made table-side while you watch—cool. Open for dinner Wed through Sun.

Foodie Faves

Barndiva, 231 Center St., Healdsburg, CA 95448; (707) 431-0100; www.barndiva.com; $$$–$$$$. Extolling "modern country food," Barndiva is a few doors south of the Plaza. The whimsical display of vintage wooden shoe forms will bring a smile to your face when you step through the main doors. In fine weather, the patio is where you want to be. Healdsburg can stay balmier at night than other areas of Sonoma County, so enjoy your dinner outside. Choose from lobster risotto, pork tenderloin, beet and endive salad, an American Kobe burger, or beef tenderloin with creamy morel mushrooms, Yukon Gold tater tots, and carrot puree. A 5-course tasting menu can also be ordered (for the whole table only, please) for $75 per person. Barndiva is open for lunch and dinner Wed through Sun, and brunch on weekends.

Bovolo, 106 Matheson St. (inside Cooperfield's Books), Healdsburg, CA 95448; (707) 431-2962; www.bovolorestaurant.com; $$. The owners of this small, casual eatery like to call it "slow food—fast." Chefs Duskie Estes and John Stewart own **Zazu Restaurant + Farm** in Santa Rosa (p. 113), and also operate **Black Pig Meat Co.** (p. 188). As such, some of the items you order at Bovolo will feature house-cured meats. The menu is always changing, but one of my favorites for breakfast (it's usually offered at lunch, too) is pasta carbonara with John's Black Pig bacon throughout the creamy sauce. The sandwich made with Black Pig bacon, egg and Carmody cheese is also wonderful. Open Mon through Thurs from 9 a.m. to 4 p.m., Fri and Sat from 9 a.m. to 8 p.m., and Sun from 9 a.m. to 6 p.m.

Cafe Gratitude, 206 Healdsburg Ave., Healdsburg, CA 95448; (707) 723-4461; www.cafegratitude.com; $$. Part of a chain based in the San Francisco Bay Area, Cafe Gratitude specializes in vegan and raw dishes. It's a bit new age-y, what the chain's owners refer to as "sacred commerce" in their mission statement. Be prepared to engage in some philosophical Zen and Tao back-and-forth with the person who takes your order at the cash register. For those of  you who remember hippies, this might be classified as "hippie" food. The dishes all have affirmation-type names that begin with "I Am"—I Am Elated is an enchilada in a "live" spinach tortilla. I Am Pure is a seasonal Greek-style salad; I Am Extraordinary is a BLT with maple-coconut bacon. The produce is sourced from an organic farm near Vacaville, northeast of the Bay Area. Be aware that if you have an allergy to tree nuts or seeds, these ingredients are used extensively in the meals. The indoor dining area is small; outside are a few tables in the sun with vintage metal chairs. Open daily from 11 a.m. to 9 p.m.

Catelli's, 21047 Geyserville Ave., Geyserville, CA 95441; (707) 857-3471; www.mycatellis.com; $$. For longevity, you can't beat Catelli's—founded in 1936. This location was occupied by another restaurant for a few years that has since closed, and now Catelli's—once called Catelli's The Rex—is back in the original space, though it's been refreshed and brightened up. Younger generations of the Catelli family now run the place and cook the meals, so it's truly an all-in-the-family enterprise. And it's good for families, too, with kids welcome. Appetizers might be minestrone (the same family recipe served for decades) and lightly battered calamari. Pastas are made on the premises, along with house-made sausage and the family's secret sauces. Meaty main courses include chicken *sauté sec* with polenta, a burger on a ciabatta bun, grilled rib-eye steak, and meatball or chicken sandwiches. There are always some seasonal specials on the menu, too: in autumn, expect grilled rabbit, lasagna with fresh chanterelle mushrooms, and veal osso buco. Open every day but Mon for lunch and dinner.

Diavola Pizzeria & Salumeria, 20121 Geyserville Ave., Geyserville, CA 95441; (707) 814-0111; www.diavolapizzeria.com; $$. *Salumi* and pizza—these are the two words behind the success of Diavola. Pasta, too, like the tagliatelle with pork cheek ragu. But it's the house-cured meats and the blistered, thin pizzas that account for the lines out the door. Order the "cha cha cha" pizza, topped with house-smoked pork belly and roasted red peppers with goat cheese and onion. At lunch you can try a bratwurst panini, beef brisket panini, or salad with oven-roasted sardines and olives. Diavola is open for lunch and dinner daily.

Hamburger Ranch, 31195 N. Redwood Hwy., Cloverdale, CA 95425; (707) 894-5616; www.hamburgerranchandbbq.com; $$. In a red building on the north edge of Cloverdale is this favorite of locals that serves breakfast, lunch, and dinner. Try a huge traditional breakfast, a "burger breakfast" with fried eggs and presented on an English muffin, or lighter egg-and-toast combos. Lunch includes more than 10 hamburger choices (British, Latin, and the Swiss Albert), along with a rib-eye steak sandwich, hot dogs, fish-and-chips, and grilled cheese. The dinner menu is loaded with barbecued rib platters, grilled salmon, oysters, and skewered prawns. Open daily from 7 a.m. to 9 p.m.

Healdsburg Bar & Grill, 245 Healdsburg Ave., Healdsburg, CA 95448; (707) 433-3333; www.healdsburgbarandgrill.com; $$. The less-expensive restaurant in Healdsburg overseen by Chef Douglas Keane (see **Cyrus** under Landmark Eateries, p. 165) is popular for the large outdoor patio on the southwest corner of the Plaza. Keane took over this restaurant in 2008 and rejiggered the menu, making the cuisine more upscale but still reasonably priced and family-friendly, too. The "adult" mac and cheese is a hit, along with the huge, juicy burgers. Enjoy a pulled pork sandwich, ahi tuna salad, sweet potato fries, truffle fries, and a peanut butter cup or pumpkin pie skillet for dessert. The patio is where many visiting wine tasters end their day with a cold craft beer. Open daily for lunch and dinner.

Mateo's Cucina Latina, 214 Healdsburg Ave., Healdsburg, CA 95448; (707) 433-1520; http://mateoscucinalatina.com; $$. After years of selling his Yucatan-inspired food at local farmers' markets, catered events, and the occasional pop-up dinner, Mateo Granados finally opened his own restaurant in 2011. Inside, chunky wood tables and chairs line the walls, with a wine and tequila bar sharing the space. Comfortable outside tables are numerous, offering views of the kitchen staff hard at work on the meals. Mateo is from Yucatan, and his menu reflects the dishes locals have come to love. Starters include the empanada, a tortilla turnover filled with squash blossoms and onions, then topped with feta cheese and seared peppers. The suckling pig tamale, wrapped in a banana leaf instead of a corn husk, is filled with shredded pork. Olive oil is used instead of lard in making the tamales. Main dishes might be *pollo adobado,* a marinated Rocky chicken breast roasted in a banana leaf, or the *bistec yucateco,* thinly sliced slow-cooked beef. Mateo also sells his tamales and handmade tortillas in 6- and 12-packs to go, along with his signature sauces. As a full bar, Mateo's has one-of-a-kind cocktails created by "mixologist" Scott Beattie, who is widely known in the industry for inventing innovative new ways to blend alcohol (see **Spoonbar** in this category, p. 174). Several local wines are also available by the glass or carafe. Mateo's is open for dinner daily, for lunch from 11 a.m. on weekdays, and for brunch on weekends from 10 a.m. to 2 p.m.

Pick's Drive In, 117 S. Cloverdale Blvd., Cloverdale, CA 95448; (707) 894-2962; $. Pick's can be spotted by the vintage sign along the street, and the feeling that the last few decades have passed this place by. Parking is limited, and there are only a few places to sit at the counter and at picnic tables. Hamburgers, fries, onion rings, shakes and floats, and some other sandwich options are offered. It's no frills, to be sure, but it's fast and good. Make sure to add their house-made Famous Red Relish to your burger, and buy a jar to go, if you like what you taste. Open daily from 11:30 a.m. until 6 p.m. (to 7 p.m. on Fri, and to 5 p.m. Mon through Wed).

Rustic—Francis's Favorites, 300 Via Archimedes (at the Independence Lane exit off US Hwy. 101), Geyserville, CA 95441; (707) 857-1485; www.francisfordcoppolawinery.com; $$$. The "Francis" is Francis Ford Coppola, iconic film director and winery owner. Drive into the winery that bears his name, sweep dramatically up the grand staircase outside and come in through the double doors. Turn right at the bright red Tucker automobile, glide down the hallway past more of Coppola's fascinating film memorabilia, and stop at the enormous neon martini glass. You've arrived at the door to Rustic, the restaurant within Coppola's winery. (Read more about the winery on p. 192.) Based on the celebrity aura that surrounds it, Rustic could have coasted on mediocrity and still packed 'em in. Yet the food is excellent. The meats are grilled Argentine-style on a wood-fired *parrilla,* which evolved from primitive barbecues used by gauchos to cook beef. When installed here in 2010, it was the first authentic *parrilla* grill in California. Francis's *parrilla* is used to sear not just meats but also vegetables. Three different kinds of wood heat the *parrilla,* and a team of specially trained grill masters oversees the cooking. Around the restaurant is Francis's collection of 4,000 olive oil tins, to keep you occupied while you wait on short ribs Argentine-style with *chimichurri* sauce, or Mrs. Scorsese's lemon chicken, named for the mother of Francis's moviemaking contemporary Martin Scorsese. Try the patio on a fine weather day—the scenery is stunning. Open for lunch and dinner daily.

Scopa, 109 Plaza St., Healdsburg, CA 95448; (707) 433-5282; www .scopahealdsburg.com; $$. Named for an Italian card game, the small 40-seat Scopa has been quietly luring customers away from other longtime Healdsburg dining establishments based on great reviews from locals. Recommended menu items: grilled romaine loaded with shaved Parmesan, with anchovy-garlic dressing and a white anchovy crostini on top; and Nonna's tomato-braised chicken stew over polenta, which comes to the table in a little black kettle. Several pizza options are available, as well as grilled rib-eye steak for two people, grilled calamari, baked goat cheese salad, and radicchio and pear salad. As with all good restaurants, expect seasonal ingredients to shape the offerings on the menu. One might be a cucumber and heirloom tomato salad, simply presented with a light dabbing of olive oil and balsamic vinegar. Save room for the molten chocolate soufflé (order with your dinner so it will be ready when you are). The space is narrow, so diners are cozy—you might make new friends before the night is over. Open daily for dinner.

Spoonbar, 219 Healdsburg Ave., Healdsburg, CA 95448; (707) 433-7222; www.h2hotel.com/spoonbar; $$. When the h2hotel opened in 2010, I was excited to see its ground-floor restaurant, Spoonbar, was practically alfresco, right along the sidewalk so passersby would be lured in to join the fun on a warm evening. We need more places like this in Sonoma County. Apparently our visitors think so, too. Spoonbar has been a hit from the day it opened, with specialties such as the Moroccan salads; cavatelli; gnocchi; brick chicken; salmon; and the burger with bacon, horseradish sauce, and fries. Add a cocktail to your meal—bartender and cocktail creator Scott Beattie has written books about his experiments over the alcohol cauldron. Some are classics (Manhattans, mojitos), while Scott has tweaked many others. Order a pitcher of Dark n' Stormy, made more interesting with fresh lime juice, oil of ginger, and Angostura bitters. Because Healdsburg's many B&Bs and hotels are within walking distance, it's possible to indulge in Scott's elixirs without having to get behind the wheel afterward. Open daily for dinner, Thurs through Mon for lunch, and brunch on weekends from 11:30 a.m.

Taqueria El Sombrero, 245 Center St., Healdsburg, CA 95448; (707) 433-3818; $. Finding a dining bargain in Healdsburg can be a challenge at times. That's when a really good taqueria comes in handy. Healdsburg has many places to enjoy inexpensive Mexican food, and all of them are commendable. Among the best is El Sombrero, just around the corner from the Plaza, which serves excellent carne asada, fish tacos, and a delicious octopus cocktail. Open daily from 10 a.m. to 9 p.m.

Willi's Seafood and Raw Bar, 403 Healdsburg Ave., Healdsburg, CA 95448; (707) 433-9191; http://starkrestaurants.com; $$$. Willi's recently underwent an expansion to accommodate more diners and the raw bar, with a neon sign that reads EAT OYSTERS, LOVE LONGER. Be that as it may, there are eight kinds of the raw bivalve, some from Tomales Bay off our Pacific coast, and others from Oregon and British Columbia. If oysters give you the willies (sorry, couldn't resist), opt for a lobster roll or the platter of 18 Prince Edward Island mussels, or the barbecued bacon-wrapped scallops. Fried Ipswich clams from New England are also offered, and platters of assorted shellfish and crustaceans in three sizes.

THE FIFTH TASTE: *UMAMI*

Sweet, sour, salty, bitter—these are the four tastes we all experience while eating. There's also a fifth taste called *umami*, isolated almost a century ago by a Japanese food scientist. *Umami* means savory, and refers to the protein taste we enjoy that is based on the amino acid called glutamate.

Naturally occurring glutamate is found in meat and vegetables such as fish and shellfish, cured meats, mushrooms, tomatoes, spinach, and fermented and aged products (soy sauce and cheese). It's complicated science, but it explains why we crave certain foods and textures over others. In short, *umami* makes us salivate.

An important element in balancing food with wine, *umami* brings out the best flavors of both. I'm overgeneralizing a bit, but here are a few guidelines for pairing *umami*-dominant foods with wine:

Light wines (Riesling, Sauvignon Blanc, Chenin Blanc, Viognier, rosé, Pinot Noir, Merlot, and Syrah) are best matched to sweet, spicy, and protein-rich foods: Chinese or spicy Szechuan dishes, pastas with tomato sauce or cream sauce, Thai food, fresh mozzarella and smoked cheeses, and spicy Mexican food.

Try an excellent ceviche, followed by a choice of grilled skewers (chicken, lamb, and hanger steak), and small plates such as salads, calamari, fish tacos, baby back riblets, and a Dungeness crab cake. Steamer pots, too—mussels; oysters; clams; or crab legs in beer, garlic butter, and Old Bay seasoning. Pair your seafood with lots of cold beer or one of several interesting cocktails (like the Melonious

Crisp and fruity wines (Champagne and sparklers, Pinot Grigio, Viognier, Sauvignon Blanc, Riesling, Pinot Noir, Merlot, Sangiovese, and rosé) pair well with salad greens such as arugula, spinach, and radicchio; oily fish like sardines and salmon; shellfish and smoked fish; oysters with lemon or cocktail sauce; asparagus and artichokes; and fresh goat cheeses.

Most red and white wines (Pinot Grigio, Chenin Blanc, Riesling, Sauvignon Blanc, Chardonnay, Pinot Noir, Syrah, Zinfandel, Cabernet Sauvignon, and others) are well matched to seasoned meats, poultry, and seafood; the salt-based ingredients in a dish, such as bacon or pancetta, olives, and capers; acid-based sauces made with wine, mustard, vinegar, or lemon/lime; soups, stews, and casseroles with salt-based ingredients; and cheddar, gruyère, and fontina cheeses.

Sweet dessert wines: This one is easy—Madeira, port, muscat, Riesling, sherry, and Sauternes are easily matched with desserts. Pair these wines with most chocolate goodies, including brownies and truffles; creamy desserts like cheesecake, ice cream, and crème brûlée; nut and caramel desserts such as pecan pie; cakes, cookies, and pastries; strong blue cheeses; and fruits like apples, pears, and berries.

Thunk: vodka, watermelon, basil, and lemon). Willi's is open every day for lunch and dinner.

The Wurst Sausage Grill & Beer Garden, 22 Matheson St., Healdsburg, CA 95448; (707) 395-0124; $. Owner Charles Bell has changed careers so many times that being a sausage slinger is just

one more intriguing bullet point on his resume. From Detroit originally, Charles once played bass guitar with the rollicking rockers
MC5, and his Fender bass is on display here as a reminder. He also
studied cooking in San Francisco, went off to England to enroll in
butler school, worked as a caterer to the royal family, and dashed
around Kensington Palace frequently in the presence of Prince
Charles and the late Princess Diana. Fast-forward to Healdsburg
and those sausages: The eight tube steak choices are spicy to mild,
available with a variety of different toppings. The brats come from
Wisconsin, the Polish from Detroit. Chicken sausages are also on
the menu, along with the SMASH burger, reportedly one of the
best hamburgers in Sonoma County. Ask for a side of Charles's own
Memphis slaw—it's exceptionally tasty. He makes his own mayonnaise, too. Get a milk shake to complete the meal, or sip one of
the many regional craft beers poured here, such as Tiburon Blonde,
Boont Amber Ale, or Scrimshaw. Charles is easy to identify—he's
usually the guy busing tables and greeting you with a warm smile.
Open daily for lunch and dinner.

Zin, 344 Center St., Healdsburg, CA 95448; (707) 473-0946; www
.zinrestaurant.com; $$$. A restaurant that calls itself Zin can be
counted on to provide plenty of Zinfandel choices on its wine list,
and the perfect food pairings for that varietal, too. Consider the
barbecued ribs, which is usually the Blue Plate special on Monday.
Blue Plates on other nights are southern fried chicken, chicken and
dumplings, spaghetti and meatballs, and Yankee pot roast. All pair
well with Zinfandel, yet other red and white wines are available,

too. One of the most popular appetizers at Zin is the green beans dipped in a batter made with Mexican beer, then deep-fried. A charcuterie plate of house-cured pork is also a good starter, or duck tamales with a spicy dipping sauce. Mains can include marinated lamb sirloin, grilled ahi tuna, risotto, a posole with pork shank and butternut squash, grilled hanger steak, and wild mushroom and goat cheese chile rellenos. The chef, Jeff Mall, makes his own andouille sausage, and he adds white-corn grits to the menu in interesting ways. Zin is open nightly for dinner and weekdays for lunch.

Specialty Stores & Markets

Big John's Market, 1345 Healdsburg Ave., Healdsburg, CA 95448; (707) 433-7151; www.bigjohnsmarket.com. They thought of everything to include in this store. There's a huge cheese department with an expert staff, and a deli with hot food options such as eggplant rollatini and chicken Swiss casserole. Serve yourself at the hot food bar with comfort food by the pound such as pork ribs and potatoes au gratin, or dish up fresh salads and greens at the salad bar. Big John's sells what appears to be the entire line of Amy's Kitchen frozen organic meals, cereal and nuts in bulk, shelves filled with local wines, and local Clover Stornetta dairy products. Big John's is a traditional grocery store, too, where you can load your cart with paper towels, toothpaste, and so forth. The store is open daily from 7:30 a.m. to 8 p.m.

Costeaux French Bakery, 417 Healdsburg Ave., Healdsburg, CA 95448; (707) 433-1913; www.costeaux.com. You might think that this bakery came along only after Healdsburg became a major destination for wine and food aficionados. You would be wrong. Originally called the French American Bakery, it began in 1923 next door to the current address, and underwent several name changes and different owners over the decades. It became Costeaux French Bakery in 1972 when it was purchased by a French couple named Costeaux. It changed hands again in 1981 and has been owned by the Seppi family ever since, but the Costeaux name has stuck. The bakery has garnered numerous awards over the years, most recently being named the 2009 Retail Bakery of the Year by *Modern Baking* magazine. Costeaux is a perennial Sonoma County Harvest Fair award-winner, with seven of its specialty breads winning double-gold awards in 2011. It's a cafe, too, with breakfast, along with many lunch items. Choose from omelets, quiche, breakfast sandwiches, *pain perdu* (french toast), and the house-made granola. Lunch fare might include a portobello mushroom or chicken panini, a multigrain turkey sandwich, more quiche, and a Parisian sandwich of ham and cheese. (Legendary crooner Tony Bennett, while in the region recently to perform in concert, reportedly dined at Costeaux three times in the same day—that's how good the food is.) The bakery is open daily at 7 a.m., closing at 4 p.m. Mon through Thurs, at 5 p.m. on Fri and Sat, and at 1 p.m. on Sun.

Downtown Bakery & Creamery, 308-A Center St., Healdsburg, CA 95448; (707) 431-2719; www.downtownbakery.net. Take home some of this bakery's raw dough, cake mixes, and pie shells and you can bake up a storm in your own kitchen without doing the heavy lifting, or the exhausting mixing. The bakery has been serving Healdsburg since 1987, baking bread made from organically grown flour and natural sourdough starters. There are always loaves of sweet French, sourdough French, *pugliese,* and sourdough wheat-rye ready to take away. Additional breads baked weekly include hot dog and hamburger buns, raisin-cinnamon loaves, and multigrain loaves. Breakfast pastries are made fresh every morning: sticky buns, scones, muffins, croissants, and more. The creamery in the name refers to the homemade ice cream and sherbets— the flavors change with the seasons. The bakery's cafe provides breakfast and lunch Fri through Mon from 8 a.m. to 2 p.m. Some selections from the menu are cheesy scrambled eggs, poached eggs and polenta, pizza and cal-zones, and quiche. Open daily from 6 a.m. (later on weekends) to 5:30 p.m. Mon through Fri, to 5 p.m. on Sat, and to 4 p.m. on Sun.

Dry Creek General Store, 3495 Dry Creek Rd., Healdsburg, CA 95448; (707) 433-4171; http://drycreekgeneralstore1881.com. Is it a deli, a gift shop, a market, or a wine shop? It's all of the above, and with a tavern attached. The Dry Creek General Store is an institution, in business more or less since 1881, and a popular diversion along this particular stretch of Dry Creek Road. There's a little bit of everything to do with wine—glasses, books, accessories. A cooler is stocked with butter, eggs, milk, and cheese. Some small supplies of dry goods are also for sale, if you forgot to pack Bisquick or laundry soap. Depending on when you stop by, the deli can be crazy busy with hungry bicyclists or fatigued wine tasters queuing up to order sandwiches. Then it can clear out and be all yours for a short spell, until the next van of visitors rolls up. The store opens early every day (6:30 a.m. weekdays, and 7:30 a.m. weekends) and closes daily at 5:30 p.m. The bar starts pouring beer at 3 p.m. Mon through Thurs, and at noon on Fri and weekends. Closing time is whenever.

Jimtown Store, 6706 Highway 128, Healdsburg, CA 95448; (707) 433-1212; www.jimtown.com. For more than 20 years, Carrie Brown has owned and operated this vintage store, first built in 1895 as a market and post office. The place was in a shambles when Carrie and her late husband snatched it up and set about restoring it. The store has been a destination for locals and visitors ever since. As you wait on a sandwich or coffee drink to be made, poke around among the flotsam and jetsam that is the ever-changing inventory. Few places sell both premium wine and whoopie cushions within a few feet of each other, but that's the charm of this place. You will find the practical (light bulbs and batteries) and the whimsical (toy airplanes and paper dolls). In back is a huge assortment of antiques. But most people are here for the fresh food and the numerous

Jimtown products lining the shelves (wine, sauces, spreads). It's pretty hard to miss this icon along the highway—look for the old red truck and the bright green trim on the building. Seasonal hours are observed, but typically the store is open Thurs through Mon from 7:30 a.m. to 3 p.m. (to 5 p.m. on weekends), and closed Tues and Wed. See the Jimtown Store's recipe for **Pan-Roasted Chicken with Fig Glaze, Olives & Capers** on p. 269.

Moustache Baked Goods, 381 Healdsburg Ave., Healdsburg, CA 95448; (707) 395-4111; http://moustachebakedgoods.com. What happens when two young guys, born and bred in Sonoma County, become full-time bakers? They open a small store without the usual feminine vibe most "bakeries" tend to exude. From the understated wooden sign hanging over the sidewalk (with only a black moustache, no words) to the minimalist decor inside, this store sells "all-American classics with character." That is to say, they do inventive cupcakes, cookies, and other sweet stuff, including custom orders (72 hours' notice, please). The options in the display case may change frequently, but ask for one of the cupcakes with a big piece of bacon sticking out of the frosting, or one with a cute frosting monkey on top. Do not leave without a Moustachi-O, their version of the Oreo cookie that I was assured is "so moist it tastes like you've already dipped it in milk." They were right. Select a couple of sweets and a cup of good java and take a stool by the window to watch shoppers strolling by. Open 10 a.m. to 8 p.m. daily, except Tues.

Oakville Grocery, 124 Matheson St., Healdsburg, CA 95448; (707) 433-3200; www.oakvillegrocery.com. The original Oakville Grocery is in Napa Valley, and this Healdsburg outpost is a more modern version. The inside is stocked with any type of food, fresh or packaged, for eating now on a picnic or using in your own meal preparation later. Peruse shelf after shelf of mustards, olive oils, breads, and many items you never knew existed but sound delicious nonetheless. Sandwiches, hand-tossed pizzas, salads, and desserts can be made to order

and enjoyed out on the patio, overlooking the Plaza and the many pedestrians out window-shopping. Open daily in summer from 8 a.m. to 7 p.m., closing at 6 p.m. in winter.

Plaza Gourmet—The Kitchen Store, 108 Matheson St., Healdsburg, CA 95448; (707) 433-7116. It's narrow and packed to the rafters, a haven for home cooks who want to add more can't-live-without gadgets to their kitchen drawers. Small yet well-stocked, it's also for serious cooks who need a specific Cuisinart or All-Clad saucepan, or a paella pan. Browse through the many cookbooks on specific subjects, and the beautiful kitchen and dining room linens. If you can't find what you're looking for, ask owner Darlene Powell for assistance. Open 10 a.m. to 5:30 p.m. daily.

Made or Grown Here

Farmers' Markets

Cloverdale Farmers Market, Cloverdale Plaza at Broad Street, Cloverdale, CA 95425; (707) 894-4470; www.cloverdaleartsalliance .org. On Friday night from June through September, downtown Cloverdale is humming with activity. The town combines its weekly farmers' market with "Friday Night Live," an Arts Alliance event that supplies the live music while you shop for arugula. The fun gets going around 5 p.m., with the music and dancing starting at 7 p.m.

Healdsburg Farmers' Market, North and Vine Streets, Healdsburg, CA 95448; (707) 431-1956; www.healdsburgfarmers market.org. This is one of the older certified farmers' markets in California, founded in 1978, and it draws farmers who grow their crops and raise their animals nearby, as well as some from out of the area. Cooking demonstrations are a highlight one Saturday each month. The Healdsburg market keeps the early birds from making out like bandits—a cowbell sounds promptly at the starting hour, so no purchases can be transacted before the bell rings. This allows vendors to be better prepared for the onslaught and makes it possible for all shoppers to get a crack at those farm-fresh eggs collected from a chicken coop that morning.

Between May and November, the market is open on Saturday from 9 a.m. to noon.

(A Tuesday evening version, from 4 to 6:30 p.m., takes place from June through October.)

Farms & Farm Stands

Bernier Farms, 3192 Alexander Valley Rd., Healdsburg, CA 95448; (707) 849-7592; http://bernierfarms.com. The Bernier family sells produce at local farmers' markets and to area restaurants, such as Scopa and Catelli's, but they also have a farm stand open weekdays from 10 a.m. to 4 p.m. Known for growing 14 types of garlic (Chinese Purple, China Stripe, Native Creole, and Rose du Lautrec, to name a few), the family also sells lettuces, tomatoes, apples, melons, potatoes, squash, and more. The Berniers got into growing garlic big-time when a neighbor offered them seeds of the Northern Italian Red variety, and they've never looked back.

Dry Creek Peach & Produce, 2179 Yoakim Bridge Rd., Healdsburg, CA 95448; (707) 433-8121; www.drycreekpeach.com. In this valley of what seems like only vineyards is a certified organic farm growing white and yellow peaches, nectarines, and plums. The Sullivan family jars their own peach jam, too, and they sell many other interesting items at the stand. The season for the fruit is short, so the stand is open usually only on Fri, Sat, and Sun between July and mid-Sept, from noon to 5 p.m. If you love peaches, you won't want to miss this farm.

Preston Vineyards, 9282 Westside Rd., Healdsburg, CA 95448; (707) 433-3372; www.prestonvineyards.com. Among winery owners, Lou Preston was ahead of his time, growing vegetables, olives, and strawberries, and raising pigs, chickens, and sheep on his winery property long before many others jumped on the "sustainable farming" bandwagon. Lou's produce is so bountiful that a couple of years ago he decided to open a store on the property where the tomatoes, onions, zucchini, carrots, peppers, eggs, and more are sold on the honor system. Open daily from 11 a.m. to 4:30 p.m., the store is next to the wine-tasting room, past a small picnic area. Lou bakes his own bread, too—be sure to ask if any loaves are still available on the day you visit. The winery is accessed down a long lane off a narrow, sharp corner of Westside Road. (Read more about **Preston Vineyards** on p. 198.)

Verdure Farm, 2476 Westside Rd., Healdsburg, CA 95448; (707) 433-1403. Home cooks, top chefs, and everyone else who loves heirloom tomatoes swear by the juicy fruits grown on this farm by Tamara Scalera. She cultivates approximately 200 tomato varieties, both early- and late-season types, and Italian varieties of basil, squash, peppers, eggplant, and cipollini onions. Look for heirloom melons and culinary pumpkins, too, in season. The stand is open daily from 11 a.m. to 6 p.m. between Aug and Nov.

Meats & Butchers

Black Pig Meat Company, 106 Matheson St., Healdsburg, CA 95448; (707) 523-4814; www.blackpigmeatco.com. John Stewart, along with his wife, Duskie Estes, make outstanding bacon and *salumi* from heritage-breed pigs that are raised free of hormones and antibiotics and allowed to roam free. John studied the art of *salumi* with Chef Mario Batali and also at the University of Iowa Meat Lab. The slow process involved in making John's salty, smoky, and sweet bacon is dry-curing it in brown sugar, followed by a long applewood smoking. This bacon is tossed generously into the pasta carbonara that John and Duskie serve at their restaurant **Bovolo** in Healdsburg (p. 168); it also shows up in other dishes at their Santa Rosa restaurant, **Zazu** (p. 113). The bacon is sold in several local grocery stores and other outlets in the San Francisco Bay Area. John and Duskie know pork, so much so that in 2011 they were part of a regional chefs' competition that focused on heritage pork, leading to their win at the Grand Cochon (pig) national finals in Aspen.

Olive Growers

DaVero, 766 Westside Rd., Healdsburg, CA 95448; (707) 431-8000; www.davero.com. Using certified organic and biodynamic techniques, Colleen McGlynn and Ridgely Evers grow and make oil from olive trees that began as cuttings from 800-year-old trees in Tuscany. That explains the remarkable flavor, and how in 1997 DaVero's extra-virgin olive oil was the first American-made oil to win a blind tasting in Italy. The awards have piled up ever since, and Chef Mario Batali once came to the DaVero farm to film a cooking show. Even though Colleen and Ridgely have 4,500 olive trees on 22 acres, the business remains small and intimate. It's not all about olives—the couple also grows citrus, apples, figs, persimmons, lavender, and other crops. (And when you can get your hands on the Meyer lemon olive oil, by all means, buy a couple of bottles then and there.) The tasting room is for trying their many oils, vinegars, preserves, and also their wines—a rare varietal called Sagrantino and small quantities of red and rosé Sangiovese. The olive oil and wine tasting room is open daily from 10 a.m. to 5 p.m. See DaVero's recipe for **Disappearing Chicken** on p. 273.

Dry Creek Olive Company, 4791 Dry Creek Rd., Healdsburg, CA 95448; (707) 431-7200; www.drycreekolivecompany.com. Cleanse your palate after wine tasting by savoring the complex flavors in olive oil. Dry Creek Olive Company gathers its harvest from a combination of old trees, some dating back a century, and newer plantings. Our dry Mediterranean-style climate is ideal for growing olives for oil, and now that Sonoma County has conquered the world of wine, we're giving Italy some stiff competition in the olive oil market. In 2011, this company won a double-gold award from the Sonoma County Harvest Fair for its Three Orchards Blend olive oil. The facility combines two pressing techniques: a traditional granite mill and a hammer mill. The olive oil tasting room is open daily from 11 a.m. to 4:30 p.m. Tours are offered, too—just ask.

Community Supported Agriculture Programs (CSAs)

Foggy River Farm, 8194 Eastside Rd., Healdsburg, CA 95448; (707) 838-4948; www.foggyriverfarm.org. The diversity of vegetables grown on this small family farm should keep your CSA box brimming with interesting possibilities. Boxes cost $22 per week, and u-pick items can also be added.

Food & Wine Pairings/
Landmark Wineries

Chalk Hill Estate, 10300 Chalk Hill Rd., Healdsburg, CA 95448; (707) 657-4837; www.chalkhill.com. This hilltop chateau-style winery overlooks more than 1,400 acres with exceptional views. In the early 1970s, founder Fred Furth envisioned a spectacular winery and vineyard in this spot, and a few years later his wish became reality. The winery bottles Merlot, Syrah, Semillon, Pinot Gris, Viognier, Chardonnay, and Sauvignon Blanc. In addition to coaxing premium wine grapes from the vines, Chalk Hill has on-site organic gardens planted with vegetables, herbs, and fruit—many of them heritage and heirloom varieties. Take a culinary tour lasting more than 2 hours ($75 per person) that includes a sit-down tasting of wines with small plates of food prepared by the winery chef using ingredients from the gardens. A less expensive, 1-hour cheese-and-wine tasting ($40) is available, too. Gather together at least four friends for the estate luncheon option ($175), when a full meal is matched with Chalk Hill wines. This option includes a driving tour around the estate. All food-and-wine pairings require advance reservations. Chalk Hill is open every day from 10 a.m. to 4 p.m.

Ferrari-Carano Vineyards & Winery, 8761 Dry Creek Rd., Healdsburg, CA 95448; (707) 433-6700; www.ferrari-carano.com. This beautiful hospitality center is an Italian-style villa with a first-floor tasting room and wine shop, and a cellar beneath where limited-release and reserve wines are sampled. The winery is known for its Chardonnay, Pinot Noir, Zinfandel, Merlot, Cabernet Sauvignon, a red blend called Siena, and a white blend known as Bella Luce. Several private tastings by appointment are offered: the winery's white wines paired with artisan cheese, a red-wine tasting accompanied by chocolates and dried fruit, a pairing of four wines with small plates of food using seasonal ingredients, and a couple of others that match wines with charcuterie plates. These tastings range from $25 to $35 per person and take place Tues through Sat from 11 a.m. to 2:30 p.m., based on availability. The winery won a double-gold award in 2011 from the Sonoma County Harvest Fair for its mountain estate olive oil, so try to score a taste, if samples are available. Ferrari-Carano has the type of gift shop that overcommercializes the wine-tasting experience, in my opinion, but they make up for it with the exceptional gardens and landscaping throughout the property. So if you're weary of shuffling past shelves of logo T-shirts, coasters, and corkscrews, don't miss a stroll through the "enclosed" garden outside. It's sort of an enchanted forest of more than 2,000 species of trees and shrubs, including finicky Portuguese cork trees. Open daily from 10 a.m. to 5 p.m.

Foppiano Vineyards, 12707 Old Redwood Hwy., Healdsburg, CA 95448; (707) 433-7272; www.foppiano.com. Another of Sonoma County's venerable and historic wineries is Foppiano Vineyards, still being run by descendants of the original founder, Giovanni Foppiano. Dating to 1896, many of the vines here are still producing excellent grapes. The winery made it through the Prohibition years by growing other crops, such as pears and apples, within the vineyards. Treasury agents still made a raid on the property in 1926 and destroyed more than 100,000 gallons of red wine. Yet the family continued to produce wine illegally while the law was still in effect. When Prohibition was over, the Foppianos had 83,000 gallons of wine ready to go for the new markets that emerged. By the 1970s, the winery had transitioned to producing fine wine instead of jug wine, and today Foppiano is known for Petite Sirah, Pinot Noir, Chardonnay, Sauvignon Blanc, and a rosé. The tasting room is open daily from 11 a.m. to 5 p.m.

Francis Ford Coppola Winery, 300 Via Archimedes (at the Independence Lane exit off US Hwy. 101), Geyserville, CA 95441; (707) 857-1400; www.francisfordcoppolawinery.com. You know the films: *The Godfather, Apocalypse Now, Bram Stoker's Dracula, Marie*

Antoinette. You know the filmmaking Coppolas: Francis Ford and his daughter, Sofia. Francis also makes wine, and has for several decades. When he bought this property in Geyserville a few years ago, formerly known as Chateau Souverain, he wanted to turn it into a fun experience for families and visitors of all ages. It took some time to make it happen, but it's now the coolest must-see attraction between Healdsburg and Cloverdale. The wines are good (sip at one of two tasting bars), and the restaurant is excellent (see the listing for **Rustic—Francis's Favorites** under the Foodie Faves category, p. 172). Coppola bottles several wines, including the inexpensive "everyday" Rosso and Bianco labels. Many varietals are produced: Cabernet Sauvignon, Chardonnay, Pinot Noir, Syrah, Viognier, Petite Sirah, and a late-harvest Semillon. But the attraction for many visitors is the movie memorabilia. Much of what's on display was once housed in Coppola's Napa Valley winery. When he took that property more upscale to focus on his pricier wines, he put treasures such as Vito Corleone's desk and chair into mothballs. Now the movie stuff is all here: the five Academy Award statues, the Golden Globe trophies, and numerous other honors from his filmmaking heyday. There are other props from the *Godfather* movies; iconic wardrobe pieces such as the hat and boots worn by Robert Duvall in *Apocalypse Now* ("I love the smell of napalm in the morning"); the red, sinewy armor inhabited by Gary Oldman in *Dracula*; and the 1948 Tucker automobile from the movie *Tucker*. Sofia's work is also represented by furniture, paintings, and the miniature ships seen in her movie *Marie Antoinette*. It's part museum, part retail store, with books, tableware, kitchen linens, and much more for sale. Outside, it seems like a little slice of Italy, with a line of colorful and elegant cabanas (open seasonally) facing a huge swimming pool and bocce courts. Pack your bikini to take a swim for a modest fee, and bring the whole family. There's also a covered outdoor stage patterned after the Lake Tahoe pavilion from *The Godfather, Part II*. A round outdoor cafe supplies the snacks, in season. Open daily from 11 a.m. to 9 p.m. (wine tasting until 6 p.m.).

Hop Kiln Winery, 6050 Westside Rd., Healdsburg, CA 95448; (707) 433-6491; www.hopkilnwinery.com. Housed in a California Historic Landmark dating to 1905, this winery was once a hop kiln, processing the grain for beer. By the mid-1970s the hops had been replaced by vineyards, and the structure was reworked to become a spacious tasting room. Hop Kiln bottles under two labels: Hop Kiln and HKG. The former includes the popular Thousand Flowers, Rushin' River, and Big Red products—all proprietary red and white blends. HKG wines are ultra-premium, made from the vineyards on 250 acres in the Russian River Valley nearby. The HKG collection includes Chardonnay, Pinot Noir, Pinot Grigio, and rosé of Pinot Noir. Both labels can be tasted at the Westside Road tasting room, which also is packed with Hop Kiln–label mustards, oils, vinegars, pestos, vinaigrettes, and dessert sauces. There's also a deli case with selections of cheese, meat, and bread for making a picnic outside by the pond. Open daily from 10 a.m. to 5 p.m. The HKG tasting room

is in the Sonoma Valley at 13647 Arnold Dr. in Glen Ellen, (707) 938-7622. It's where you can taste the ultra-premium line of wines produced by Hop Kiln and also reserve a food-and-wine flight, such as crab and curry mustard crème fraîche cannoli with Chardonnay, duck confit with raspberry preserve and polenta matched to Pinot Noir, and bacon gelato with a balsamic reduction paired with the rosé. Another option is a chocolate pairing, or purchase some small desserts and pies to go. The Glen Ellen tasting room is open Thurs through Sun from noon to 6 p.m. See the recipe for Hop Kiln Winery's **Zuppa de Pesce (Seafood Stew)** on p. 270.

J Vineyards' Bubble Room, 11447 Old Redwood Hwy., Healdsburg, CA 95448; (707) 431-5430; www.jwine.com. J sparkling wine goes down soooo easy, you won't know what hit you. That's why it's best experienced with food. The Bubble Room is open Friday, Saturday, and Sunday for 3-course food-and-bubbly pairings, when J's sparklers, Pinot Gris, Pinot Noir, and other varietals are matched to house-made ricotta gnocchi, squash soup, pan-seared duck breast, braised pork belly, and roasted pumpkin trifle, among other tasty bites (reservations recommended). J Vineyards is a relative youngster among wineries in Sonoma County, founded in 1986. In addition to an excellent line of elegant brut sparkling wines, J produces still wines such as Pinot Noir, Chardonnay, and Pinot Gris. Open daily from 11 a.m. to 5 p.m.

Kachina Vineyards, 4551 Dry Creek Rd., Healdsburg, CA 95448; (707) 332-0854; www.kachinavineyards.com. Open to the public on weekends only, Kachina bottles Cabernet Sauvignon, Zinfandel, Chardonnay, Charbono, and a port. The winery is named for the Hopi Indian spirits that were believed to be supernatural beings (Kachina dolls are popular throughout the American Southwest). Kachina operates exclusively on solar power, and is green in many other ways, too. The wine grapes are from the estate vineyards and other vineyards within Dry Creek Valley. On weekends Kachina puts together small bites of food to pair with the wines ($10 per person). A more extravagant experience, called the Tuscan Lunch, includes cheese, bread, meat, olives, fruits, nuts, and a port-infused truffle, all paired with the winery's varietals ($45 per person.) Reservations are required for these pairings, which take place between 11 a.m. and 4 p.m. Sat and Sun.

Lambert Bridge Winery, 4085 W. Dry Creek Rd., Healdsburg, CA 95448; (707) 431-9600; www.lambertbridge.com. Many of the wines produced here are available only in the tasting room (check out the wine-stained bar made from oak casks). Lambert Bridge produces both red and white wines—Viognier, Merlot, Chardonnay, Cabernet Franc, Cabernet Sauvignon, and Zinfandel. Fortunately, Lambert Bridge offers opportunities to pair the wines with food in the barrel room on the property. On Saturday and Sunday, the staff conducts a 45-minute pairing of wine flights with artisan cheese and small nibbles ($40 per person, for small groups). Larger groups (inquire for more details) have more options: a premium wine-and-cheese tasting ($50), a custom group tasting ($30) that includes cheese and locally baked breads, and a pizza class ($70), in which seasonal vegetables are combined with other ingredients in a demonstration of pizza making in one of the three wood-fired ovens on the property. Call the winery for more details and to make reservations. Depending on the weather, you might enjoy the toasty fireplace inside—on other days, perhaps the outdoor tables. The tasting room is open daily from 10:30 a.m. to 4:30 p.m.

Locals Tasting Room, 21023 Geyserville Ave. (at the intersection of Hwy. 128), Geyserville, CA 95441; (707) 857-4900; http://taste localwines.com. Wine "collectives" have sprung up like mushrooms in the region in the past few years, but this independently owned tasting room in sleepy Geyserville has been welcoming visitors since 2002. Locals represents several great labels, so it can be a one-stop experience to try, say, five or six Pinot Noirs or Zinfandels made by different local wineries in a "flight" tasting. Many are small producers without tasting rooms of their own that are open to the public. It can be more interesting to taste wines in this fashion if your time is limited, or you want to try labels from small producers whose distribution may not be available outside the region. Open 11 a.m. to 6 p.m. daily.

Medlock Ames Winery, 3487 Alexander Valley Rd., Healdsburg, CA 95448; (707) 431-8845; www.medlockames.com. Producers of small lots of Cabernet Sauvignon and Merlot, Medlock Ames is a lovely setting, with a communal table for sharing a picnic with new friends as you sip the winery's nectar. A food-and-wine pairing is offered that includes a flight of current wine releases with cheese, *salumi,* or some fresh-from-their-garden produce ($10 per person, reservations required). If your timing is right, pizza samples will be passed around, pulled

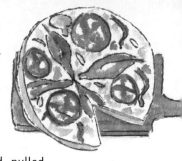

hot from the outdoor oven. Medlock Ames also bottles Sauvignon Blanc, Chardonnay, and a rosé. Open daily from 10 a.m. to 5 p.m. Behind the tasting room is something you don't usually see at a winery: a fully stocked bar that aims to feel like a neighborhood joint from yesteryear. Called the Alexander Valley Bar, you can order a seasonal cocktail, beer, or wine. Some of the signature drinks being shaken and/or stirred include a ginger thyme martini and a margarita with serrano peppers. The bar opens daily at 5 p.m.

Preston Vineyards, 9282 W. Dry Creek Rd., Healdsburg, CA 95448; (707) 433-3372; www.prestonvineyards.com. Formal food-and-wine pairings don't take place at Preston, but you'll love it here for everything else that goes on. Some wineries may crow about their green techniques, but Preston really lives it. Lou Preston has always embraced sustainability, and the grapes he grows have been certified organic for years. Nothing goes to waste on this property, from the food scraps fed to the animals (sheep, chickens, pigs, and goats), to the refuse generated by the winery, farm, and offices (chipped, shredded, or turned into compost). Even the diesel tractors are fueled by used fryer oil from local restaurants. Preston has restored 100-year-old vineyard blocks and uses only grapes that they grow. Only natural farming methods are followed, not just for the grapes, but for the vegetables, fruit and nut trees, and the olive trees on the property. Preston bottles Zinfandel, Petite Sirah, Barbera, and Mourvedre in reds; the whites include Sauvignon Blanc, Roussanne, and Viognier. Tasting at Preston usually includes a bonus: samples of Lou's fresh-baked sourdough bread, the olive oils made from the trees on the estate, and whole cured olives. The farm store has loads of other fresh goodies to use in your own cooking. Open daily from 11 a.m. to 4:30 p.m. (Read more about **Preston Vineyards** on p. 187.)

Rodney Strong Vineyards, 11455 Old Redwood Hwy., Healdsburg, CA 95448; (707) 431-1533; www.rodneystrong.com. As famous for its annual summer concert series as for its wines, Rodney Strong has been around since Sonoma County was "discovered" as a premium wine-growing region (it was one of the county's first bonded wineries, dating to 1959). The building is unlike many other wineries, with a roof that spreads like eagle wings. Rodney Strong bottles Cabernet Sauvignon, Sauvignon Blanc, Chardonnay, Pinot Noir, Zinfandel, and a couple of red blends. The summer concerts bring in visitors from far and wide to see musical acts such as Chris Isaak, Pat Benatar, Chris Botti, Michael McDonald, and the Average White Band. It's a great excuse to taste wine, feast on appetizers, and stand up in your seat and gyrate to your heart's content. Open daily from 10 a.m. to 5 p.m.; guided tours are conducted daily at 11 a.m. and 3 p.m.

Seghesio Family Vineyards, 700 Grove St., Healdsburg, CA 95448; (707) 433-3579; www.seghesio.com. On Friday, Saturday and Sunday, sit-down food-and-wine pairings are conducted at this winery northwest of downtown Healdsburg. The "Family Tables" tastings start with a tour of the winery, and then seasonal foods are matched to Seghesio varietals. A typical tasting ($45 per person) might pair pasta with brussels sprouts and bacon cream with Zinfandel; rigatoni and eggplant with Omaggio (a blend of Cabernet Sauvignon and Sangiovese); polenta with sausage matched to Venom (a Sangiovese so named because the vines grow high on Rattlesnake Hill, with the serpents); and a cheese course of Gorgonzola and *pradera* served with *Dionigia* (a red dessert wine made of equal parts Petite Sirah, Zinfandel, and Cabernet Sauvignon). Reservations are recommended for these pairings. Seghesio bottles additional varietals such as Pinot Grigio. Open daily from 10 a.m. to 5 p.m.

Simi Winery, 16275 Healdsburg Ave., Healdsburg, CA 95448; (707) 473-3232; www.simiwinery.com. Simi is one of the old-timers in Sonoma County, celebrating 135 years in 2011. It was founded by Giuseppe Simi and his brother, Pietro, Italian immigrants from Tuscany who failed to make millions from prospecting during the

Gold Rush. They took what money they had from selling vegetables in San Francisco and set about planting grapes and building a winery in the Alexander Valley. When the two brothers died of the Spanish flu in 1904, Giuseppe's daughter Isabelle, only 18 years old, took over leadership of the winery and made a success of it. The Prohibition years were tough on the winery, but Isabelle kept the business afloat. When the law was repealed, Isabelle had a large redwood tank rolled out to the side of the road and made into a tasting room. Visitors have been coming ever since. The redwood grove outside is a refreshing oasis when the weather is warm, and you might find thin-crust pizza being served that's topped with house-made sausage. Simi produces Chardonnay, Merlot, Sauvignon Blanc, and Merlot. Open daily from 10 a.m. to 5 p.m.

Twomey Cellars, 3000 Westside Rd., Healdsburg, CA 95448; (707) 942-7120; www.twomeycellars.com. The building is unusual for this valley, one of the few modern structures you'll see in the area—made of floor-to-ceiling glass to take advantage of the fabulous view. It housed another winery before it became Twomey, which also has a winery in Napa Valley. Raymond Twomey Duncan was a co-founder of Silver Oak Cellars in Napa Valley, where ultra-premium Cabernet Sauvignon is produced. Twomey Cellars was launched in 1999, with a winery and tasting room south of Calistoga. This facility in the Russian River Valley spotlights the Pinot Noirs the Duncan family has been making more recently from Sonoma County grapes. Their other varietals, Sauvignon Blanc and Merlot, may also be tasted here. With prior arrangement, enjoy a chef's board

THE MYSTERIOUS AROMAS OF WINE

Have you ever been served wine that emits unpleasant or unexpected aromas? An uncle once poured me a glass of red table wine (produced in a southern state) with an odor I feared would singe my eyebrows. It reeked of petroleum, and I looked around nervously for nearby open flames. To me, the wine was undrinkable, yet I sipped it with a smile on my face to preserve family harmony.

I learned later it's not uncommon to smell gas in wine. In fact, the Aroma Wheel created by Ann Noble, a professor at the University of California at Davis, devotes a subcategory to the scents of petroleum, such as diesel, kerosene, tar, and plastic. Ms. Noble developed the Aroma Wheel more than 20 years ago for novice and pro wine drinkers "to learn about wines and enhance one's ability to describe the complexity of wine flavor." UC-Davis is the leading school in California—and America, I dare say—for earning a degree in winemaking.

If you spend much time trying new wines, either at wineries or with friends, you may have come across a particular odd taste or odor that made the experience heavenly, or dreadful. Tasting rooms at wineries frequently have some form of the Aroma Wheel close at hand to help visitors nail down smells in the wine. Some of the wheel's categories and specific terms are to be expected (fruity, woody, herbaceous), but the wheel also offers these pungent possibilities: wet dog, wet wool, skunk, burnt toast, and even natural gas.

of bite-sized food to pair with the wines ($25 on Fri, Sat, and Sun only). The feast includes some meat, cheeses, olives, and nuts—enough for two to four people. Twomey is open Mon through Sat from 10 a.m. to 5 p.m. and Sun from 11 a.m. to 5 p.m.

Brewpubs & Microbreweries

Bear Republic Brewing Company, 345 Healdsburg Ave., Healdsburg, CA 95448; (707) 433-2337; http://bearrepublic.com. Bear Republic is a popular watering hole in downtown Healdsburg that produces a couple of standout brews: the American-style Racer 5 India Pale Ale and Red Rocket Ale. The stout is Big Bear Black Stout, and Hot Rod Rye is an IPA made with 18 percent rye malt. The beers are brewed off-site at a facility in nearby Cloverdale, but Healdsburg is where you can get all the brews and the food for pairing. Start with calamari, chicken tenders, mac and cheese (with bacon), Cobb salad, or shrimp Louis. Burgers (eight types to choose from) are featured, along with pork sliders, a crab sandwich, and a halibut sandwich. Entrees might be portobello mushrooms and polenta, shrimp scampi, baby back ribs, gumbo, and a daily pasta special. Bear Republic is open daily at 11:30 a.m., and serves until 9:30 p.m. (to 10:30 p.m. on weekends).

Ruth McGowan's Brewpub, 131 E. First St., Cloverdale, CA 95425; (707) 894-9610; www.ruthmcgowansbrewpub.com. They take darts seriously at this brewpub, with an active dart league and many devoted league members. That said, darts go better with beer, and Ruth McGowan's has that covered, too. Founded in 2002, the place was named for the owner's grandmother, and it has a strong Irish lilt. House brews include Caroline's Blonde, Cloverdale Ale, Kong Brown Ale, and Floyd India Pale Ale (get a growler of your favorite to go). If you plan to be a regular, save loads of cash by joining the Mug Club (ask for the details). Traditional pub food here might be burgers done several ways, fish and chips, wings, brats, soups, and salads. Musicians are invited to bring their instruments and join in on session nights—the music could be blues or folk, or old Irish and Scottish standards. (Stink at darts? Ask to play shuffleboard instead.) The brewpub is open Mon through Thurs from 3 to 9 p.m., Fri from 11 a.m. to 10 p.m., Sat from 10 a.m. to 10 p.m., and Sun 10 a.m. to 9 p.m.

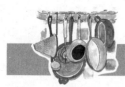

Learn to Cook

Relish Culinary Center, 14 Matheson St., Healdsburg, CA 95448; (877) 759-1004 or (707) 431-9999; http://relishculinary .com. Master the art of making paella or craft your own mozzarella and *burrata*. At Relish, many demonstration and hands-on classes are available, such as learning to bake bread, make perfect pies, and create appetizers. Classes are led by local chef instructors, and locally grown produce and organic ingredients are used whenever possible. Prices for the 3-hour classes can range from $50 to $96 per person. The culinary center has space for 20 students for hands-on instruction and up to 36 participants in demonstration classes. Each student receives copies of all the recipes being prepared and a full meal. Affordable culinary adventures are also available, which include visits to local farms and wrap up with a 3-course lunch. Private cooking parties can also be arranged, so call the center for the details.

West Sonoma County & the Coast

I remember the first time I took a leisurely drive through west Sonoma County on my way to the Pacific Ocean. The views from the narrow and twisty rural roads were beautiful, alternating between sunny and expansive vineyards, dark tunnels created by towering redwood trees, and the gentle green and rolling hills nearer to the water. Slowing down in the small communities to take in the sights, I spied many colorful characters lounging around and hitchhiking who looked as if they had just stepped out of the cast of *Hair*.

The clothes and the coifs might be more stylish now, and the ponytails are mostly gray, but in certain parts of Sonoma County—particularly where those groves of tall trees grow—it still feels like 1970.

The West County, as everyone here calls it, has always been identified as a counterculture retreat, where alternative lifestyles are openly encouraged and celebrated, a place for "letting your freak flag fly," as a man once set to music.

Nowhere is this more visible than around the community of Guerneville (population 4,500), in the heart of the Russian River resort region. Named for George Guerne, a Swiss immigrant who owned a sawmill, the town was a popular destination for well-to-do San Francisco families in the late 19th century. They came by ferry and train to stroll through the redwoods, sleep in quaint riverside cabins and cottages, and splash in the water. As the decades passed, occasional major floods along the river brought a steady decline to many of the structures and businesses, and by the 1960s the town was attracting unsavory characters and widespread illegal drug activity.

In the 1970s, San Francisco's gays and lesbians began vacationing in Guerneville by the thousands, drawn by the town's liberal environment and recreational opportunities. Many stayed permanently to open businesses and remodel some of the run-down resorts to attract an all-gay clientele. In the 1980s, the AIDS epidemic changed the face of Guerneville forever, and a decade later many more families, straight couples, and retirees had moved in to live in the cottages year-round. Resorts that were once gay-only now attract people of all ages and from all walks of life, and the town's Main Street has been refreshed to include trendy restaurants and funky boutiques.

Sebastopol is the Sonoma County city most associated with apples, particularly the Gravenstein variety (read more about apples on p. 244). Many people come to visit Sebastopol and never leave. It has the feel of a small community (population 7,400), but with enough sophistication, fine dining, and culture to keep the towns-folk engaged and inspired. Most of the thousands of acres of apple orchards that once encircled Sebastopol have now been replaced by vineyards.

The smaller communities of Graton, Forestville, Occidental, Freestone, Valley Ford, Bodega, Cazadero, and Duncans Mills all have their individual charms and interesting diversions: restaurants, art galleries, nightclubs, quirky lodgings, and luxury inns. "Hippie chic" might be the best way to describe the overall vibe.

At the Pacific Ocean, the seaside towns of Bodega Bay (population 1,100) and Jenner (fewer than 100 residents) attest to the non-commercialization of this part of the northern California coast—the opposite of the southern half of the state. This unspoiled coastline offers visitors outstanding views and several opportunities to enjoy good food.

Landmark Eateries

Applewood Inn & Restaurant, 13555 Hwy. 116, Guerneville, CA 95446; (707) 869-9093; www.dineatapplewood.com; $$$$. It was an exclusive inn before it became known as a destination restaurant, too. Applewood Inn's restaurant earned a Michelin star in 2012, and it's no surprise. The cuisine has always been top-drawer, with a choice of a la carte entrees (seared albacore tuna, duck breast, rack of lamb, and pan-seared scallops), or a 5-course chef's tasting menu ($75 per person excluding wine pairings). With prior arrangement, Applewood will also gather together a delicious picnic lunch with all the food, napkins, flatware, and other accessories you will need. Choose from three menus—all come with a fresh baguette, too. Take your picnic to the coast, into a nearby redwood forest, or to your private room for a balcony lunch or dinner. Applewood is open for dinner Wed through Sun from 5:30 to 8:30 p.m. (breakfast is served daily for guests of the inn only).

Bay View Restaurant at Inn at the Tides, 800 Hwy. 1, Bodega Bay, CA 94923; (707) 875-2751; www.innatthetides.com; $$$. More elegant than its sister restaurant on the bay side of the highway, the views from the dining room higher on the hill are magnificent, and a room at the inn can be nifty, too. On the menu, the priciest dish is the cioppino, a heavenly broth loaded with lobster, mussels, and whatever local seafood is available fresh that day. Other options are orecchiette pasta with spicy Italian sausage, lasagne, eggplant or chicken parmigiana, and veal available four ways: Milanese, scaloppine, piccata, or Sorrentino. If you love the film *The Birds*, which was shot in 1962 at the Tides Wharf, order the filet mignon Hitchcock. A salute to the movie's director, it's a steak stuffed with Dungeness crab and served with mashed potatoes and béarnaise sauce. You might prefer instead a pizza, a caprese salad, an arugula salad with gorgonzola and candied walnuts, and desserts such as tiramisu and *panna cotta*. The restaurant also hosts monthly "winemaker" dinners, when a local winery presents a special pairing of wines with a fixed-price dinner, which can cost from $89 and up per person. These are popular events, so reserve early. The inn, too, is pretty great—I've stayed here and once had the pool all to myself on a starry night. Bay View is open for dinner Wed through Sun.

Farmhouse Inn & Restaurant, 7871 River Rd., Forestville, CA 95436; (800) 464-6642 or (707) 887-3300; www.farmhouseinn .com; $$$$. The fixed-price tasting menu is worth the drive to the charming roadside inn with its pale yellow buildings and beautifully landscaped grounds. One of the dishes in the 3-course tasting menu ($69 per person) or the 4-course menu ($84) might be grilled Mediterranean octopus accompanied by bacon, fresh chickpeas, grilled cherry tomatoes, and arugula, doused with a bit of vinaigrette. The pork tenderloin could be crusted with black trumpet mushrooms and served on a bed of chanterelle mushrooms and corn kernels. Other courses may be wild king salmon baked in a macadamia nut crust and served with bok choy and leeks, or an elk tenderloin. The dining room is intimate and the seats are coveted— the restaurant earned a Michelin star in 2012, so reservations are a must. Open for dinner Thurs through Mon.

K&L Bistro, 119 S. Main St., Sebastopol, CA 94972; (707) 823-6614; http://klbistro.com; $$$. This restaurant earned a Michelin star recently, and for several years it's been a destination for San Francisco foodies and others coming from faraway places who follow those elusive Michelin stars. The cuisine is mostly French-inspired, with a few Italian influences. One dish to try is the smoked salmon terrine, with the fish fillet wrapped in black seaweed and formed into the shape of a salmon steak. It's accompanied by fresh crab-meat and a celery root remoulade. The roasted baby beet salad and cream of cauliflower soup are beautifully presented—the salad accessorized with candied kumquats and the soup topped with a bit of tapenade and a swirl of olive oil. The potato gnocchi is always a hit, and the lamb chops are cooked medium rare with salsa verde and sautéed greens on the side. Comfort food includes a large ramekin of creamy macaroni and cheese made with gruyère and sprinkled with toasted bread crumbs. If it happens to be on the menu, try the *hiramasa,* a yellowtail kingfish that's thinly sliced and served with cold radishes and a green avocado cream. K&L is open for lunch and dinner Mon through Sat.

The Tides Wharf Restaurant, 835 Hwy. 1, Bodega Bay, CA 94923; (707) 875-3652; www.innatthetides.com; $$$. I've happily consumed more than my share of clam chowder and calamari here over the years. (The chowder comes two ways: traditional New England style and Bodega Bay style, loaded with locally sourced seafood.) It's hard to beat the appeal of the Tides. In Bodega Bay, it's where most people stop for a quick bite at the snack bar, grab a table in the lounge inside or outside for a beer or glass of wine, or order from the menu in the main restaurant. In every case, the views are delightful, no matter where you sit. Diners in the main restaurant have lots of menu choices, even a surf-and-turf option or two. The crab cioppino is always a safe bet, as well as the poached salmon with béarnaise sauce. The hot crab sandwich has been a favorite of mine in the past, and the Louie salad, too, which comes with shrimp on top, or a combination of crab and shrimp, or all crab. The Tides Wharf is part of the Inn at the Tides complex, including the restaurant called **Bay View** across the highway (see the listing in this category). The Tides Wharf's main restaurant is open daily—even holidays—for breakfast, lunch, and dinner. The snack bar is open limited hours every day except Wednesday. Read more about the Tides Wharf Market in the Specialty Stores & Markets category.

Foodie Faves

Agriculture Bar & Kitchen at Dawn Ranch Lodge, 16467 River Rd. (Hwy. 116), Guerneville, CA 95446; (707) 869-0656; http://dawnranch.com; $$. It's hard to go wrong with the hamburger, the house-made fettuccine, the gnocchi with pan-seared duck, or the pulled pork ravioli with sautéed Granny Smith apples and toasted almonds. Start with a roasted beet salad or salmon flatbread, or try the artisan cheese board with all locally produced *fromage* to choose from. Inventive cocktails, too: ask for a jalapeño orange drop or a chipotle Bloody Mary. Agriculture is part of the Dawn Ranch Lodge resort, within walking distance to the other attractions along Guerneville's main street. Open for lunch Fri through Sun; for dinner Thurs through Mon; and the bar menu is available after 4 p.m. on Tues and Wed.

Alexander's at Timber Cove Inn, 21780 Hwy. 1, Jenner, CA 95450; (707) 847-3231 or (800) 987-8319; www.timbercoveinn .com; $$$$. Sonoma County's coastline north of Jenner has been compared to Big Sur in central California. It's certainly dramatic, with high cliffs and a winding highway. So by the time you reach Timber Cove Inn, you're ready to pull over and check in. Before calling it a night, have a glass of wine at the long bar in the main lobby, then tuck into dinner at Alexander's. I've been an overnight guest at this inn a couple of times, and dined in the restaurant when it was overseen by a previous chef. The newest executive chef is keeping the menu simple, not trying to cover too much ground. Start with an heirloom tomato salad with fresh mozzarella, then segue into the seafood-filled cioppino or the marinated ono. Other choices could be braised beef ribs, Tuscan brined pork chop, and braised lamb shank. In season, the Dungeness crab salad is heavenly. The scenery at Timber Cove is awe-inspiring, particularly if you make the short hike to the open firepit or the totem pole, breathe in the ocean air, and relax to the sound of the waves breaking on the rocks below. Open for breakfast, lunch, and dinner daily.

Aubergine Vintage Emporium & Cafe, 755 Petaluma Ave., Sebastopol, CA 95472; (707) 827-3460 or (707) 861-9190; http://aubergineafterdark.com; $. Aubergine began as a small vintage clothing shop in Occidental, a cubbyhole filled with classic couture, old rock tour T-shirts, fake fur coats, and black velveteen newsboy caps (I own one of these myself). Instead of paper or plastic shopping bags, they wrapped my purchases in colorful scarves (I still have those, too). Then a few years ago the owner seized on the opportunity to move into this much larger space in Sebastopol that would receive greater exposure, and could house a cafe and a stage for live music, too. The building was once a huge antiques collective, with a cute tea shop at one end. Now the whole place is Aubergine. Let your fingers do the walking through hanger after hanger of gently worn clothing for women and men (along with shoes, purses, hats, bustiers, crinolines, and other accessories), then hang around for a light meal and watch a kickin' band. The food ranges from six different pizzas (with lots of add-ons possible), to wraps, satays, and Greek and Caesar salads. Shows are staged nearly every night starting about 7:30 p.m. Food is served from 4 p.m. to midnight on weekdays (and to 1 a.m. on Fri and Sat).

Bar-B-Que Smokehouse Bistro, 6811 Laguna Park Way, Sebastopol, CA 95472; (707) 575-3277; www.bbqsmokehouse catering.com; $$. Something you don't see frequently in Sonoma County is Southern-style barbecued meats slowly smoked over a genuine Texas-style barbecue pit. Owner Larry Vito is a professional caterer and classically trained chef who's shared time in commercial kitchens with Paul Prudhomme, Wolfgang Puck, Emeril Lagasse, and Alice Waters. The most expensive meals on Larry's menu ring up at $15.95—the burnt beef brisket ends, or the 20-hour Texas beef brisket, both served with all the fixins. Lighter appetites might prefer the smoked salmon salad or the "drunk and stoned shrimp," which are soaked in whiskey before being smoked on the pit. Add a basket of cornbread and the cheese-filled baked new potatoes—both award-winners at the Sonoma County Harvest Fair. Larry's Memphis-style pork ribs took a double-gold award at the fair in 2011, too. Huge to-go packages of the ribs and sides are perfect for feeding the family or a whole family reunion—ask Larry for details. Open daily from 11:30 a.m. to 8:30 p.m. (to 9:30 p.m. on Fri and Sat).

Black Point Grill at the Sea Ranch Lodge, 60 Sea Walk Dr., Sea Ranch, CA 95497; (800) 732-7262 or (707) 785-2371; www .searanchlodge.com; $$$. The views are magnificent, particularly if your meal coincides with sunset. Start with the crab cakes, dolled up with a bit of celery root salad and paprika-dusted aioli. These are light and fluffy cakes, not over-fried and dry. Follow with an artisan cheese plate, with all of the *fromage* made by nearby producers and complemented with apple slices, grapes, crackers, honey, and almonds. Then order the oysters Rockefeller, broiled and accompanied by spinach and butter and bread crumbs. Mains might be grilled pork medallions or filet mignon, a bricked half chicken, stuffed lamb chops, vegetable risotto, or roasted halibut. If you've come this far from "civilization" to dine, plan to spend the night. The stretch of Sonoma County coastline north of Jenner, while beautiful, is not as commercially developed as areas farther south. The options for dining (and even a potty break) are few and far between. So after a bottle of wine with dinner here, you don't want to drive if it involves a long journey south on Highway 1 in the dark, which at times can be like an obstacle course. Stay close by—in a room at this lodge, or a few miles north in the town of Gualala, accessed on a straighter, flatter ribbon of asphalt. Open for breakfast, lunch, and dinner.

Bluewater Bistro, 21301 Heron Dr. (located at The Links at Bodega Harbour), Bodega Bay, CA 94923; (707) 875-3513; www .bodegaharbourgolf.com; $$. Perched high over the coast south of Bodega Bay proper, Bluewater is located in the Links at Bodega Harbour golf course complex, with the mesmerizing view of the Pacific Ocean all around. The menu offers some of the usual seaside appetizers: fried calamari, steamed clams, and Dungeness crab cakes. Pizza is also an option, such as one topped with andouille sausage and pepperoni. Entrees include braised lamb shank, baby back ribs, seared scallops, and pan-roasted salmon on a bed of fresh lentils and spinach. Open daily for lunch, breakfast on weekends, and dinner Thurs through Sat.

Boon Eat + Drink, 16248 Main St., Guerneville, CA 95446; (707) 869-0780; www.eatatboon.com; $$. Chef-owner Crista Luedtke livened up the culinary scene in Guerneville by opening this hip eatery that grows many of the vegetables and herbs used in the meals. Two sizes of artisan cheese and *salumi* plates are offered, several small plates (such as flash-fried polenta sticks with marinara), and main dishes like grilled halibut with fennel-braised gigante beans. Panini sandwiches are served on locally baked bread and are filled with grilled eggplant, prosciutto, or house-cured coppa and salami with provolone. Desserts are delicious: *panna cotta* topped with a wild organic blueberry compote, fudge brownies with olive oil ice cream on the side, and seasonal fruit cobbler and ice cream. Open daily for lunch and dinner, and weekend brunch starting at 10 a.m.

Brisas del Mar, 2001 Hwy. 1 (in the Ocean View Center), Bodega Bay, CA 94923; (707) 875-9190; www.brisasdelmar-bodegabay.com; $$. Order your seafood with a Mexican twist, along with traditional south-of-the-border dishes. The dinner menu is divided between familiar seafood dishes on one side (Dungeness crab cakes, clam chowder, fried calamari, barbecued oysters, and entrees such as fish-and-chips and fried shrimp), and Mexican specialties on the other, prepared primarily with seafood. The restaurant's signature paella features prawns, clams, mussels, and chicken with spicy chorizo sausage added. Brisas del Mar is on the north edge of Bodega Bay next door to the community center. Open Wed through Mon for lunch and dinner.

Cape Fear Cafe, 25191 Main St., Duncans Mills, CA 95430; (707) 865-9246; www.duncansmills.net; $$. I have a soft spot for Cape Fear Cafe. It's one of those places I've made a beeline for to deal with a life crisis, or celebrate a small victory, or acknowledge a birthday or anniversary. There might be trendier places to run to, but I'm comfortable here, ordering grilled grits served under poached eggs or shrimp. The french toast is awesome, too. You might prefer an oyster po' boy or the BLT plus egg. But it's the variety of eggs Benedict on the weekends that deserve your attention—none disappoint. Open daily Mon through Thurs from 10 a.m. to 3 p.m., Fri from 10 a.m. to 8:30 p.m., Sat from 9 a.m. to 8:30 p.m., and Sun from 9 a.m. to 7 p.m.

Casino Bar & Grill, 17000 Bodega Hwy. (Hwy. 12), Bodega Bay, CA 94922; (707) 876-3185; $$. The CASINO neon sign might give the wrong impression. Not a casino, it's the town hangout in the little burg of Bodega, a place so small it has to share its name with the larger town on the water 5 miles away. Lately, the food being created by Chef Mark Malicki is the main attraction at the old building Alfred Hitchcock reportedly checked out one day while he was filming *The Birds* up on the hillside. Chef Malicki was born and raised on the East Coast, trained in Manhattan restaurant kitchens, and even served as personal chef to Richard Avedon for a time. He's been cheffing in Sonoma County for many years, running his own restaurants with some success. Lately he's been coming up with new dinner menus for the Casino, making them up the night before, depending on what ingredients he can source on any given day. One night the choices could be corn soup with chanterelle mushrooms, wild boar prosciutto with peaches and arugula, rock cod with wild fennel, and roasted pork shank. The next night, it's an entirely different list. Dinner is served nightly from 5 to 9 p.m.; follow the chef's updates on Facebook. Casino Bar opens at 8 a.m. and closes late, typically at 2 a.m.

Dinicci's Italian Restaurant, 14485 Valley Ford Rd., Valley Ford, CA 94972; (707) 876-3260; $$. In a big white building constructed as a hotel in 1908 with ITALIAN DINNERS painted on two sides, you can't miss this restaurant. Dinicci's has been serving food almost continuously since 1939, and it still bears the Dinicci name, though another family now operates it. Expect the usual selection of pasta dishes, deep-fried or grilled seafood, fried chicken (a comfort food that has all but disappeared on local restaurant menus), and some vegetarian options. The entrees come family-style with antipasto, bread, minestrone, and salad. Tiramisu, spumoni, or chocolate mousse round out the traditional meal. Dinicci's is open for dinner Thurs through Mon, and Sun for lunch.

East West Cafe, 128 N. Main St., Sebastopol, CA 95472; (707) 829-2822; www.eastwestcafesebastopol.com; $$. As the name implies, the cuisine is both American and Mediterranean inspired, so you can order a hamburger, or baba ghanoush and dolmas. Many breakfast options are offered (Benedicts and omelets), some with tofu in place of meat. The pancakes are made from organic flours, and the french toast from organic sprouted wheat or white sourdough bread. One of my favorite meals is a simple bowl of the delicious soup of the day, always good, and with a yummy fresh roll on the side. Dinners include chicken samosa, salmon, falafel pockets, grilled eggplant sandwich, and a couple of quesadilla options. Open Mon through Sat from 8 a.m. to 9 p.m., and Sun from 8 a.m. to 8 p.m. Another East West Cafe is in Santa Rosa at 557 Summerfield Rd., (707) 546-6142.

French Garden Restaurant & Bistro, 8050 Bodega Ave., Sebastopol, CA 95472; (707) 824-2030; www.frenchgardenrestaurant .com; $$$. Looking at it now, it's difficult to imagine that this building was once Marty's Top o' the Hill, a legendary casual bar and restaurant that featured live rock or country music on weekends. My husband's band even played here a few times. When Marty closed the place so he could finally retire, it sat empty for a spell, then was lavishly remodeled in anticipation of a new beginning as an upscale eatery. The restaurant that moved in was out of business so fast I can't even remember its name, and the building sat unoccupied and unloved for a while longer. Then along came Dan Smith, who might be known as much for his produce as for his restaurant. A couple of chefs have come and gone since the French Garden opened its doors, but the menu remains one of the best in the region, full of fresh produce from Dan's farm, 5 miles west of Sebastopol. The old red farm tractors out front are a bit hokey but they drive home the farm-to-table mantra here. Starters might be squash ravioli, grilled artichokes, or a salad made from greens from the nearby farm. Mains are grilled beef tenderloin, pan-seared scallops, roasted acorn squash, and roasted squab. Don't miss the side dishes of kale, chard, or carrots. The live music on weekends has survived all the changes since Marty's era—check the website for the latest entertainment calendar. French Garden is open for lunch and dinner Wed through Sun, and brunch on Sun from 10 a.m. to 2 p.m. The weekly farm market, when the produce from Dan's farm is sold to customers, coincides with Sunday brunch.

GTO's Seafood House, 234 S. Main St., Sebastopol, CA 95472; (707) 824-9922; www.gtoseafoodhouse.com; $$. The G-T-O moniker stands for Gene and Tess Ostopowicz, who opened this restaurant in 2001. As a New Orleans native, Tess had access to great seafood growing up. After she met Gene at Mardi Gras one year, the couple married and worked around the country before settling into Sebastopol and creating the type of restaurant they hoped customers would love as much as they do. Oysters, New Orleans–style okra gumbo, or Dungeness crab fondue can start off your meal, followed by chicken and sausage jambalaya, fish-and-chips, pan-seared sea bass, or lobster spaghettini. Steak, risotto, and chicken are also options. For dessert, try the New Orleans–style bread pudding drizzled with bourbon sauce, or the salted caramel cheesecake. Gene is the bartender, mixing up expert cocktails every night (on Wednesday, happy "hour" goes on all evening). Oysters prepared as sliders, charbroiled, or chilled on the half shell are all available on the bar menu, along with calamari, blue cheese fries, and citrus-cured cod. Much of the seafood is sourced locally, including the oysters from nearby Tomales Bay. Open for dinner Tues through Sat.

Howard's Station Cafe, 3811 Bohemian Hwy., Occidental, CA 95465; (707) 874-2838; www.howardstationcafe.com; $$. Occidental is the coolest little town, off the beaten track but full of interesting places to eat and shop. Howard's is one of them. It's legendary for breakfasts, so come hungry. Omelets are served all day, with many varieties to choose from and the build-your-own option, too. The salmon Benedict is delicious, and the *huevos rancheros*. Smaller breakfast combos, and old standbys like hot oatmeal and homemade granola, are favorites. Lunch includes several main-dish salads (the classic Cobb is great), sandwiches, and hamburgers. No credit cards are accepted, so be prepared to pay with cash. Open daily from 7 a.m. to 2:30 p.m. (to 3 p.m. on weekends).

Island Style Deli, 599 Hwy. 1, Bodega Bay, CA 94923; (707) 875-8881; $. Park your surfboard outside and come on in for a little bit of Hawaii on the California coast, specifically Hawaiian plate lunch. The salmon burgers can also be excellent, and the fish-and-chips, prawns-and-chips, and chowder, too. The aloha atmosphere is accentuated by continuous entertainment on the TV monitor that ranges from surfing films to ukulele performances. Island Style Deli shares a driveway with **Lucas Wharf** restaurant (see next listing). Open from 11 a.m. to 6 p.m. every day.

Lucas Wharf, 595 Hwy. 1, Bodega Bay, CA 94923; (707) 875-3522; http://lucaswharfrestaurant.com; $$$. In Bodega Bay, you can count the best restaurants in town on one hand. Lucas Wharf is one of them. The menu has evolved over the years, and no longer includes a rich, decadent appetizer that I dearly, dearly loved, so I won't even bother describing it. But you can still wait for a window seat that overlooks the bay (time your meal for one of the cool sunsets), and order fresh oysters or garlic butter oysters to start your experience. (During the day, try one of the outdoor tables—these are well protected from any chilly breezes that might blow in.) Blackened mahi mahi, angel-hair pasta and prawns, or fresh local halibut might all be on the menu. On another day it could be stuffed sole Florentine, or risotto and prawns. If munching on the tentacles of calamari bothers you, get your squid fix another way: the calamari steak sandwich, breaded, grilled, and served on an onion roll. Expect surf-and-turf combos and seafood pastas, too. Look for the most recent specials described on Lucas Wharf's Facebook page. Open daily for lunch and dinner.

Mom's Apple Pie, 4550 Hwy. 116 North, Sebastopol, CA 95472; (707) 823-8330; www.momsapplepieusa.com; $. There's no doubting what Mom's sells: pies. Double-crust fruit pies are the main attraction, and people come from far and wide to get a whole pie to go for special occasions or just for a good pig-out. But as long as you're in the store, sit down for lunch and select from several salads, a daily soup, and sandwiches, too. Betty Carr is the genius behind the handmade pies. Betty and her late husband started the business as a fruit stand in 1979, then added a deli. The property was blessed with 8 acres of Gravenstein apple trees, too, so Betty (Mom) started baking pies and selling them at the deli. That was in 1984, and she's still baking. The store evolved into this cute place along the highway that can supply all your pie needs during the holiday season. Open daily from 10 a.m. to 6 p.m.

Negri's Restaurant, 3700 Bohemian Hwy., Occidental, CA 95465; (707) 823-5301; www.negrisrestaurant.com; $$. Dating to 1938, this restaurant was founded by Joe and Theresa Negri, and their children still run the place, along with the grands and the great-grands. You get a lot of food with your family-style plate of pasta (minestrone, salad, antipasto, and bread), so you never leave hungry. There are all the popular favorites of a good Italian restaurant, along with chicken and duck, steak and hamburger, seafood, and pizza, too. Negri's is open every day for lunch and dinner.

Peter Lowell's West County Organic, 7385 Healdsburg Ave., Ste. 101, Sebastopol, CA 95472; (707) 829-1077; http://peter lowells.com; $$$. Lowell Sheldon, the proprietor, opened this restaurant in 2007 with what he refers to as a "slightly off-kilter" attitude toward business. Meaning the restaurant puts people, animals, and the environment before profit while also sourcing organic ingredients and making high-quality cuisine the top priority. The menus at Peter Lowell's give credit to the local farmers and grape growers who supply some of the building blocks in each dish and the wine list. Many of the photographs on the walls bring those nearby plots of land to life, so they aren't just footnotes on a piece of paper. And as you dip into your Italian-inspired duck egg raviolo or broccoli Romanesco, one of those farmers might stroll in with a box of freshly picked produce, heading to the kitchen. Peter Lowell's began as a mostly vegetarian restaurant, but has evolved to offer several meat dishes using locally raised lamb, beef, pigs, and chickens. The restaurant is well loved for macro bowls: a choice of vegetarian protein and a house-made sauce, served in a soapstone pot warmed on the hearth oven. Pizzas include the *salsiccia,* with house-made pork sausage and fontina cheese. The California black cod might have been pulled from the waters of Bodega Bay only hours earlier. It's marinated in balsamic vinegar and garlic and roasted with carrots and king trumpet mushrooms. Ask about the Zero Kilometro dinner, a fixed-price 3-course meal using ingredients sourced very close by, with some of the proceeds donated to local farms. Open for breakfast, lunch, and dinner on weekdays, and brunch and dinner on Sat and Sun.

River's End, 11048 Hwy. 1, Jenner, CA 95450; (707) 865-2484; www.ilovesunsets.com; $$$. Reserve a window table for sunset—the view is sensational. If you can tear your gaze away from the ocean, try the duck confit rolls as a starter, followed by clam chowder or cream of mushroom soup. For your main course, order the pork tenderloin with local apples, or the lamb in *chimichurri* sauce, white prawns and pasta, or pan-seared black cod with butternut squash puree and roasted beets. River's End is also an inn, with several cottages boasting ocean views. In both the restaurant and the rooms, the management discourages bringing children younger than 12 so that couples can enjoy a romantic meal and a quiet getaway. The restaurant is open for lunch and dinner year-round, Thurs through Mon.

Rocker Oysterfeller's, 14415 Hwy. 1, Valley Ford, CA 94972; (707) 876-1983; www.rockeroysterfellers.com; $$$. A restaurant has to be good to justify an out-of-the-way drive for most of us city dwellers. This one is along a lonely stretch of road, dipping and swerving through rolling pastures. The tiny wide spot in the highway known as Valley Ford got a hip restaurant a few years ago, and it's become a destination eatery that makes the drive worth it. Dishes such the chicken-fried duck with gravy, potato hash, and two eggs (followed by fresh beignets for dessert) are only the beginning. The rabbit smothered in mushrooms and served with cornmeal dumplings is also tasty. Open Wed through Sun for dinner, and weekends for brunch.

Sandpiper, 1400 Hwy. 1 (in the Pelican Plaza), Bodega Bay, CA 94923; (707) 875-2278; www.sandpiperrestaurant.com; $$. The Sandpiper always remembers me on my birthday, when they send a postcard offering a special discount during September. They're persistent, too: one year I couldn't redeem the coupon that month, so they extended the discount for two months beyond. You gotta love these guys. Sandpiper is off the water, in the small Pelican Plaza complex overlooking the bay. Like many seafood restaurants, the Sandpiper crows about its clam chowder being the best, and well, it is really good. All the traditional good seafood plates are here, too: fried calamari, salmon fish-and-chips, tempura prawns, crab ravioli, red snapper, and crab stew. Open every day from 8 a.m. to 8 p.m. (to 8:30 p.m. on Fri and Sat).

Spud Point Crab Co., 1860 Westshore Rd., Bodega Bay, CA 94923; (707) 875-9472; http://spudpointcrab.com; $. You might rub elbows with a couple of salty dogs in this small eatery, as the marina is just across the road. But instead of rum and women, they have a powerful thirst for espresso, and maybe a tri-tip sandwich. With its inviting picnic tables, Spud Point is a morning meeting place for commercial and recreational fishermen, where they can grab coffee and doughnuts before heading out to sea. The fresh crab and wild king salmon on ice in the display case were likely caught by the owner's own fishing boats. The salmon is smoked on-site, and you can watch the crabs being cooked outside. Spud Point's clam chowder is some of the best in whole region, too, and they whip up chili and seafood cocktails, as well as crab cakes on weekends. Open daily from 9 a.m. to 5 p.m. (except Wed).

Terrapin Creek Cafe, 1580 Eastshore Rd., Bodega Bay, CA 94923; (707) 575-2700; www.terrapincreekcafe.com; $$$. Celebration was in the air recently when Terrapin Creek Cafe earned a Michelin star for 2012. They did it by offering exceptional cuisine creatively presented on the plate and using as much local produce and ingredients as possible. Lunch options might include sausage and white bean cassoulet, a Mediterranean fish stew in fennel-saffron broth, and rotelle pasta with smoked bacon and cremini mushrooms. Dinner entrees are just as inventive: squash soup with coconut milk and mint oil, homemade fettuccine with Maine lobster, and blackened swordfish. Open Thurs through Sun for lunch and dinner.

Underwood Bistro, 9113 Graton Rd., Graton, CA 95444; (707) 823-7023; www.underwoodgraton .com; $$$. For more than 15 years, this popular bistro has been drawing people from far and wide to the tiny community of Graton, the sister restaurant to **Willow Wood** across the street. Choose from four types of oysters on the half shell, or a cheese plate with several selections, including goat cheese crottin made by Redwood Hill Farm nearby. Dip into the Catalan fish stew that's infused with extra flavor from chorizo and saffron rice. An order of Chinese broccoli (with pork and oyster sauce) is delicious alongside the grilled rib-eye steak or Moroccan chicken. A small plates menu is also available, with goodies such as Thai lettuce cups filled with ground pork, and the white anchovy crostini. The lunch menu includes the Underwood sandwich, stuffed with Serrano ham, white anchovy, and Manchego cheese from Spain and presented on warm *pugliese* bread. Open for lunch and dinner Tues through Sat.

Union Hotel Restaurant, 3731 Main St., Occidental, CA 95465; (707) 874-3555; www.unionhoteloccidental.com; $$. Red-checked tablecloths and candles in Chianti bottles—there's no mistaking that this is a family-style Italian restaurant, serving big meals and pizza since the 1940s. Each entree includes antipasto, salad, minestrone, and sourdough bread. If you can't decide from one of the many special pasta dishes, build your own bowl from six pasta choices (angel-hair to shells), top with one of six sauces, then add the extras such as prawns or the "grand" meatballs. Roast chicken with herbs and a side of ravioli is also a favorite, and a bowl of clam chowder with an order of bruschetta makes a great combination, too. The pizza menu covers a lot of ground—choose your own toppings or select from specific combos, such as the Four Seasons, with each quarter of the pie topped a different way. Open daily at 6 a.m., serving baked goods and coffee in the cafe and bakery; the restaurant is open daily from 11 a.m. to 9 p.m.; and the saloon stays open much later. Union Hotel is great for big family gatherings, and it also has two locations in Santa Rosa with similar menus: at 280 Mission Blvd., (707) 538-6000, and at 1007 W. College Ave. in the G&G Supermarket shopping center, (707) 544-3444.

Willow Wood Market Cafe, 9020 Graton Rd., Graton, CA 95444; (707) 823-0233; http://willowwoodgraton.com; $$. For such a small community, Graton is blessed with at least two good places to eat (this one and **Underwood Bistro,** p. 229), both run by the same proprietors and across the street from each other. Willow Wood is popular for its wonderful breakfasts, such as the french toast made with challah bread, baked eggs atop a huge stack of Black Forest ham dotted with goat cheese, the creamy polenta with butter and warm syrup (I'm swooning), and the house-made granola served on a bed of yogurt. Steamy hot cocoa is served in a bowl, too. In the past the restaurant has received both Best Breakfast and Best Brunch awards from a local newspaper. Lunch and dinner menus include black bean soup, smoked trout salad, pork tenderloin ragout, roasted half chicken, and plenty of hot sandwiches, too. Willow Wood is open Mon through Sat from 8 a.m. to 9 p.m., and Sun from 9 a.m. to 3 p.m.

A CRABBY DELIGHT

One of the joys of living in Sonoma County or visiting in the off-season (typically November through April) is the availability of fresh Dungeness crab, pulled by the ton from the waters of the Pacific Ocean (19 million pounds during the 2010–2011 crab season along the California coast). The crabs are sold in Bodega Bay at the Tides Wharf market, and also distributed all over the region at supermarkets and specialty grocers. G&G Supermarkets frequently advertise the lowest price per pound, but check around for other deals.

Most of the crabs are already cooked when you buy them, although live crabs may be offered, too—just ask. In that case you will need to do the cooking yourself. I prefer to buy a freshly cooked crab at my grocery store's fish market, and have them clean and lightly pre-crack the shells for ease in pulling out the meat.

The Dungeness crab season breaks wide open before Thanksgiving, and many locals pre-order the delicacies for their Thanksgiving Day feasts. Winter months are also when many of the numerous all-you-can-eat crab fund-raisers take place for children's charities, school foundations, and the like. Ticket prices typically run from $40 to $50 per person, and the festivities might also include music and dancing, live and silent auctions, wine and cocktails, and raffles for prizes.

During a prosperous crab season, nobody walks away from the fish counter empty-handed—there's plenty for all. Yet the supply can ebb and flow with the weather. On stormy days, the fishing boats stay at the docks to avoid the dangerous conditions.

Big Bottom Market, 16228 Main St., Guerneville, CA 95446; (707) 604-7246; www.bigbottommarket.com. It's not named for the Spinal Tap song, in case you were wondering. Because Guerneville is in an alluvial floodplain, the town was called the Big Bottom about 150 years ago. The owners of this market also want you to know that biscuits are the new cupcakes, so be prepared to experience a heavenly pillow of buttery bread used in several menu items, including the chicken potpie made with lemon thyme biscuits, and other savory dishes. The market also has intriguing products for sale on its shelves, including its own line of olive oil, plus Rancho Gordo dried beans and herbs, case after case of wine, and jams and crackers.

Guayaki Yerba Maté Bar, 6782 Sebastopol Ave., Sebastopol, CA 95472; (707) 824-6644 or (888) 482-9254; http://guayaki .com. You'll see the bottles of yerba maté in many stores in the area, and you can try it here, too, during limited hours, at the company's headquarters and tasting bar. Yerba maté is a naturally caffeinated drink made from the leaves of a holly tree found in the South American rain forest. A long, long time ago, people living in the rain forest discovered that the leaves could be steeped as a tea that would help boost their energy, in much the same way as coffee. It's been said that yerba maté has the health benefits of tea, the euphoria from chocolate, and the strength of coffee. In addition to supplying a stimulant that seems to have some health benefits, this company also aims to help save and restore the South American rain forest—200,000 acres of it—while creating jobs for indigenous peoples. Guayaki is reportedly the leading producer of yerba maté drinks in the United States, with its bottled beverages found in major grocery store chains such as Safeway and Raley's. Open weekdays from 11 a.m. to 3 p.m.

Infusions Teahouse, 6988 McKinley St., Sebastopol, CA 95472; (707) 829-1181; www.infusionsteashop.com. Black, green, white, herbal—more than 100 teas of the world can be found at Infusions, available for taking away loose or for sipping on the spot. The store hosts a high tea a couple of times a month, and offers a light daily menu that might include a pita sandwich for lunch, and granola or muffins for breakfast. Add a sweet finish with a few chocolates from their **Sonoma Chocolatiers** line (see listing in this category). Open daily from 9 a.m. to 7 p.m. (to 8:30 p.m. on Fri and Sat), and Sun from 10 a.m. to 6 p.m.

Mr. Trombly's Tea, 25185 Main St., Duncans Mills, CA 95430; (707) 865-9979; http://mrtromblystea.com. You don't have to like tea to be blown away by the huge assortment of teapots on display, including the fanciful Franz line of collectible pots that are more like works of art than something to pour boiling water into. Browse through row after row of loose teas in canisters, and try the special tea that's always brewing—the flavor changes every day. Ask Mr. Trombly (you can call him Brian) for assistance in picking a flavor of tea that might be your new favorite.

Raymond's Bakery, 5400 Cazadero Hwy., Cazadero, CA 95421; (707) 732-5336; http://raymonds-bakery.com. It's a long way to go for superb baked goods, so grab your lemon bar and blueberry scone and take a seat outside, if the weather cooperates. Surrounded by an old-growth redwood forest and far from any city, Raymond's is a cool destination, an oasis of shady tranquility. Owners Mark and Elizabeth bake loads of bread loaves, including ciabatta, semolina raisin, pumpernickel rye, cinnamon-raisin swirl, and onion rolls, too. The breakfast goods are plentiful, as well, with cinnamon rolls, croissants, coffee cakes, turnovers, and brownies all lined up in the case. More than just a bakery, Raymond's also makes sandwiches and pizza, pours beer and wine on Friday night, and occasionally offers mellow live music from local bands such as Without Mirrors. You may not want to leave, and you don't have to: ask about renting one of the charming cottages on the property for the night. Open Fri from 8 a.m. to 9 p.m., Sat and Sun from 8 a.m. to 3 p.m. Depending on the season, the bakery may be open other days, too—call for the latest.

Screamin' Mimi's Ice Cream, 6902 Sebastopol Ave., Sebastopol, CA 95472; (707) 823-5902; www.screaminmimisicecream.com. On a busy street corner downtown, Screamin' Mimi's is painted pink and sports a big ice cream cone hanging outside. The shop has been in business since 1995, making fresh ice cream and sorbet every day. At any one time there are 16 flavors of super-premium ice cream behind the counter (super-premium means it has at least 14 percent milk-fat content) and eight sorbets. "Mimi's Mud" is owner Maraline (Mimi) Olson's most popular ice cream, an espresso-based concoction with Belgian chocolate chips. Also available most days is "Mimi's Mistake," first created when she added the wrong ingredients together ("I was unsuccessfully multi-tasking," she explains) and came up with a new mixture infused with peanut butter. At Mimi's, you pay by weight, not by the scoop. Open daily from 11 a.m. to 11 p.m.

Sonoma Chocolatiers, 6988 McKinley St., Sebastopol, CA 95472; (707) 829-1181; www.sonomachocolatiers.com. You'll see packages of these delicious chocolates in retail stores around Sonoma County, and this is where they are made. Inside the **Infusions Teahouse** (see listing in this category), a husband-and-wife team operates the two businesses under one roof. (Peek into the kitchen to see the chocolates being made.) A huge assortment of truffles, caramels, clusters, bars, and other goodies are on display, all made with Scharffen Berger dark chocolates of at least 62 percent cacao, and some as high as 85 percent cacao. The Citrus Earl truffle won a double-gold award in the 2011 Sonoma County Harvest Fair competition. The store is open daily from 9 a.m. to 7 p.m. (to 8:30 p.m. on Fri and Sat), and Sun from 10 a.m. to 6 p.m.

Sonoma County Fish Bank, 11435 Hwy. 1, Valley Ford, CA 94972; (707) 876-3474; www.sonomacountyfishbank.com. A fish bank? It's in a 100-year-old building that had been empty for some time, once called the Dairyman's Bank and complete with a vault and lots of architectural character. After a renovation, the owners of **Rocker Oysterfeller's** next door went into the fresh seafood business, outfitting the old bank with local fish and shellfish by the pound, local cheeses, gumbo, clam chowder, panini sand-wiches, oysters, and picnic supplies, too. Open Wed through Sun from 11:30 a.m. to 6 p.m.

The Tides Wharf Market, 835 Hwy. 1, Bodega Bay, CA 94922; (707) 875-3554; www.innatthetides.com. Eventually, every new visitor to the Sonoma Coast (and most of us locals, too) pulls into the Tides Wharf to have a look around, buy a few seashells, grab a bite to eat, and take away cheese and wine for consuming later. Goodness knows there's enough here to choose from. The fresh fish selection is always changing, depending on the season and the availability of certain types, but on a recent visit I found smoked salmon and herring, shrimp, mussels, and fresh oysters. During Dungeness crab season (November to June, officially), those beautiful orangey-pink crustaceans will be on ice, too. The market has a bit of everything you need to improvise a picnic or a meal back in your hotel room: local cheeses (Spring Hill, Bellwether, Laura Chenel brands), jar after jar of stuffed olives, and fresh bread from the **Franco American Bakery** (p. 132) in Santa Rosa. Get a couple of pints of clam chowder to go, and a shrimp cocktail, too. The shelves are lined with imported Italian dry pastas, olive oils, cioppino sauces, and even some health and beauty products (such as ibuprofen, if all this sensory overload is giving you a headache). The  Tides was one of the locations for Alfred Hitchcock's film *The Birds,* so there are plenty of kitschy movie souvenirs for sale, including bottles of wine with actress Tippi Hedren on the labels (the proceeds benefit a wildlife sanctuary).

Valley Ford Market, 14400 Hwy. 1, Valley Ford, CA 94972; (707) 876-3245. As you enter through the ancient wooden door, you half expect to see Clint Eastwood in a wool poncho squinting back at you. This place has a wild west feel to it at first glance, aged and weathered, much like Clint himself. The store is handy for the scattered residents who live around Valley Ford, and for visitors, too. It's a convenient stop if you need beer and soft drinks and a freshly baked pie to take home, or the fixings for a picnic at the coast.

The owner makes his own sausages (German-style brats, Italian, and beer and garlic flavors, for instance), and there are numerous fresh salads in the deli case and fresh beef and other meats ready to take away for grilling. Open daily from 6 a.m. to 7 p.m.

Wild Flour Bread, 140 Bohemian Hwy., Freestone, CA 95472; (707) 874-2938; www.wildflourbread.com. If you love warm, hand-crafted bread pulled fresh from wood-fired ovens, plan to spend a morning at Wild Flour. Just off Highway 12 at the turnoff to Freestone, the bakery offers several breakfast goodies, like sticky buns and a few different flavors of its trademark whipping cream scones. By midmorning, there are stacks of bread loaves, at least 10 to 12 kinds that were all started with organic sourdough starter (even the sweet breads). The setting at Wild Flour is lovely, with gardens surrounding the building and goats and chickens frolicking nearby, too. Bring cash for your purchases—they don't take plastic. Open Fri through Mon from 8:30 a.m. to 6 p.m.

Made or Grown Here

Farmers' Markets

Bodega Bay Farmer's Market, Community Center, 2255 Hwy. 1, Bodega Bay, CA 94923. A small market, it lasts only a few weeks at harvest time. But it may be worth checking out if you are seeking a Sunday morning shopping opportunity, from 10 a.m. to 1 p.m. Local growers such as Bloomfield Farms Organics might display their salad greens, tomatoes, beets, kale, beans, and other colorful vegetables and herbs. Raymond's Bakery from nearby Cazadero supplies the fresh-baked goods for munching at the market and taking home to devour later.

Occidental Bohemian Farmers' Market, downtown Occidental, CA 95465; (707) 793-2159; www.occidentalfarmersmarket.com. Running from 4 p.m. to dusk on Friday, between June and October, this market stretches for more than two blocks along the tiny town's main drag, the Bohemian Highway. Several farmers you won't find at other area markets come together here to showcase their wild and cultivated mushrooms, kale and kohlrabi, flower bouquets, meats, fruits and jams, and plants and seedlings.

Sebastopol Farm Market, corner of Petaluma and McKinley Avenues, Sebastopol, CA 95472; (707) 522-9305; www.sebastopol farmmarket.org. Clear your schedule on Sunday morning for this market, from 10 a.m. to 1:30 p.m., year-round. Some of the gems that may be found here are chicken eggs, goose eggs, and even duck eggs. Greens (actually, these days they are all colors), beets, broccoli, garlic, leeks, and French sorrel may be offered, along with honey, locally grown citrus, goat cheese, sheepskins, spring plant starts, flowers, and pastries to eat on the spot.

Hybrid vs. Heirloom

The displays of heirloom tomatoes at farmers' markets burst with color, from brilliant reds to greens and yellows, and even striped types. Some of their names are just as vibrant: Brandywine, Green Zebra, Black Elephant, Purple Calabash, Violet Jasper. They sound more like crayon colors than tomato varieties.

But what sets an "heirloom" apart from an ordinary tomato? It depends whom you ask. We've all eaten hybridized tomatoes, those oftentimes tasteless orbs of uniform size and questionable color, picked too soon in faraway places. They will do in a pinch, but the taste is almost always disappointing.

Some tomato experts divide heirloom tomatoes into categories and subcategories based on pollination and cross-breeding. This gets really complicated unless you wish to seriously plant many varieties of heirlooms, and you live in the ideal climate to do so. A simpler definition for an heirloom tomato is it's any variety that is a self-pollinator, not a hybrid, and has been grown steadily for 50 years or longer.

Farms & Farm Stands

Andy's Produce Market, 1691 N. Gravenstein Hwy. (Hwy. 116), Sebastopol, CA 95472; (707) 823-8661; www.andysproduce.com. Andy's is legendary in the west county, one of the last remaining open-air markets in northern California and chock-full of great

Sonoma County has countless microclimates, some of which are sunny and hot enough to successfully grow tomatoes in the ground without protection from the elements. But many parts of the county cool down at night during the growing season because of ocean influences and banks of coastal fog. These are not great conditions for most tomatoes, which crave abundant sun and consistent warmth.

Heirlooms usually cost more at farm stands and in supermarkets because the plants produce lower volumes of fruits (yes, the tomato is technically a fruit, not a vegetable, but we all think of it as a veggie). Most people swear that heirloom tomatoes are more flavorful and juicy than hybridized varieties. The bottom line on tomatoes is, if you grow them in your own yard, they will always taste better than what you buy at the supermarket.

produce, groceries, bulk foods, cheeses (the Redwood Hill Farm line, for instance), wine, and even natural health and beauty products. What began as a small fruit stand almost 45 years ago has grown to be a must-stop along the highway for locals and visitors. Andy Skikos started the business with his wife Katie, and his children and grandchildren (and in-laws) are still involved, managing and looking after the inventory. Andy's private-label items include corn chips, red-apple balsamic vinegar, and a Greek balsamic vinaigrette. The store is open daily from 8:30 a.m. to 8 p.m.

Bloomfield Farms Organics, Highway 116 at Bloomfield Road, Sebastopol, CA 95472; (707) 876-3261; www.bloomfieldfarmsorganics.com. Farmers Michael and Karen Collins grow vegetables, flowers, herbs, and eggs on this 22-acre ranch south of Sebastopol in the unincorporated area of Bloomfield, and they operate a CSA, too (see that category). During the harvest season you will find their produce at area farmers' markets, and they also run a seasonal farm stand at the corner of Highway 116 and Bloomfield Road, Thurs through Sun from 10:30 a.m. to 5:30 p.m. Individuals who wish to buy vegetables at the farm itself may call for directions.

New Family Farm, 669 Ferguson Rd., Sebastopol, CA 95472; (707) 478-5802. In a throwback to an earlier time, the young farmers who work the land here prefer draft horses to tractors. Three of the 12 acres are devoted to growing vegetables, and the farmers also raise their own meat, dairy products, and eggs, and make preserves. Their produce can be found at the **Farmers' Market at Veterans Hall** (p. 139), where Adam, one of the farmers, will explain their methods of growing food and why the horses have less impact on the land than heavy machinery. To visit the farm, please call ahead.

Apples & Berries

Apple-a-Day Ranch, 13128 Occidental Rd., Sebastopol, CA 95472; (707) 823-0538. Getting your apple a day is easy at this farm, a "u-pick" enterprise growing Gravenstein, Golden Delicious, and Rome varieties. Count on Bartlett pears, too, along with fresh-frozen apple juice. Call ahead to make certain someone will be there to greet you, usually year-round.

Dutton Ranch, 10717 Graton Rd., Sebastopol, CA 95472; (707) 823-0448; www.duttonranch.com. The Dutton name is widely known in these parts, dating back to the 1880s. Revered for growing wine grapes, the Duttons also farm 250 acres of apples, including the Gravenstein variety. The orchards are certified organic, too. The farm is open from Aug through Oct, weekdays from 8 a.m. to 5 p.m. The family also operates **Dutton Estate Winery** (p. 255). See the recipe for Gail Dutton's **Apple Prune Cake** on p. 277.

Gabriel Farm, 3175 Sullivan Rd., Sebastopol, CA 95472; (707) 829-0617; www.gabrielfarm.com. Who knew 14 acres could produce so many different fruits: eight varieties of Asian pears, apples (McIntosh, Fuji, and Rome), Fuyu persimmons, plums, several varieties of berries, and lavender, too. This is a pick-your-own-apples farm, at $2 per pound. Bring along extra cash for the other products sold by the family, such as jams, juice, and the dried lavender.

THE GRAVENSTEIN:
A HERITAGE APPLE WITH ITS OWN FESTIVAL

They don't travel well or keep for long, their stems are short, and their color is sometimes more ho-hum green than a snappy red. Characteristics like these have kept the Gravenstein apple from being widely grown throughout the world. In fact, this apple variety is found mostly on the West Coast, and specifically in Sonoma County.

Apple orchards ruled here at one time, accounting for approximately 13,000 acres. In the early 1900s, growing apples was prevalent throughout the western part of Sonoma County, with as many as 25 warehouses processing and packing the fruit. The apples were shipped by rail by the millions to the East Coast, and Sonoma County supplied the primary source of dried apples and applesauce that fed American troops during World War II.

With the increased planting of more profitable vineyards and the encroachment of housing developments, fewer than 3,000 acres of apple orchards exist here today. The processing plants are gone,

Kozlowski's Farms, 5566 Gravenstein Hwy. (Hwy. 116), Forestville, CA 95436; (800) 473-2767; www.kozlowskifarms.com. The Kozlowski family opened a small farm store several decades ago that has evolved into a major local producer of more than 100 gourmet food products. Many visitors come for the pies, made with fruit grown on the farm, such as Gravenstein apples and cherries. Much of the Kozlowski line is fruit-based (chutneys, jams, preserves, but the apples are still a huge part of Sonoma County's heritage and identity. The apples are available from numerous farmers and some area grocery stores, and the trees can also be found in hundreds of urban backyards. There are two Gravenstein apple trees living next door to me that supply an abundance of the fruit for making apple crisp, applesauce, and tasty pies.

The Gravenstein apple was selected by the Slow Food Foundation for Biodiversity as a heritage variety for its outstanding taste and quality. Sonoma County also celebrates the apple annually with the Gravenstein Apple Fair in Sebastopol. The first apple fair was held in 1910 and every year since then it has grown larger and more fun, with pie-eating contests, apple juggling, a no-hands caramel apple–eating contest, and similar hijinks. More details about the fair can be found in the Food Events & Happenings list.

spreads, syrups, and sauces), but they produce savory items, too (salad dressings, tapenades, cioppino seafood sauce, barbecue sauce, and so on). What about wine? Yes, the family bottles Pinot Noir made from grapes grown in the Russian River Valley, not far from the store. Kozlowski's is also popular for its big selection of gift baskets, and online ordering. The store is open daily year-round from 9 a.m. to 5 p.m.

Munch Apples, 2061 Pleasant Hill Rd., Sebastopol, CA 95472; (707) 824-6939. When you see "open" on the red and yellow sign by the road, pull in for freshly picked apples, peaches, plums, pears, persimmons, walnuts, and almonds at the self-serve stand. Munch adheres to organic methods to farm these orchards.

Sebastopol Berry Farm, 9201 Ross Station Rd., Sebastopol, CA 95472; (707) 694-2301; www.sebastopolberryfarm.blogspot .com. Blueberries, blackberries, and raspberries—boysenberries and strawberries, too. If it has the word "berry" in its name, chances are you will find it at this farm. Growing berries for more than 25 years, the farm is certified organic. Expect to see these berries at local farmers' markets, and visit the farm, too. It's always a good idea to call ahead to avoid disappointment.

Sonoma Swamp Blueberries, 7000 Occidental Rd., Sebastopol, CA 95472. The eight varieties of certified organic berries are grown on 21 acres adjacent to the Laguna de Santa Rosa, a huge fresh-water wetlands near Sebastopol. The stand is open daily from 9:30 a.m. to 6 p.m. during blueberry season, generally until the end of August. If you time it right, you might catch a bald eagle in the air or nesting nearby. Owners Andy and Mamta Landerman can usually be found selling their berries at the area farmers' markets, too, and local stores such as Oliver's Markets, G&G Supermarkets, and Andy's Produce also carry the berries.

Walker Apples, 10955 Upp Rd., Sebastopol, CA 95472; (707) 823-4310. Gravenstein, Golden Delicious, Fuji, Rome, Pippin, Baldwin, Winesap, Granny Smith, and Northern Spy—apples are the mainstay on this farm. Expect to see the Walker Apples stand at the **Farmers' Market at Veterans Hall** (p. 139) and others, or call ahead if you wish to visit the farm and pick up the fruit there.

Cheesemakers

Bleating Heart Cheese, Sebastopol, CA 95472; (858) 245-1682; http://bleatingheart.com. One of the newest producers on the cheese scene in Sonoma County is Seana Doughty, who went out on a limb to take up cheesemaking, and so far is getting rave reviews for her efforts. She won double-gold awards at the 2011 Sonoma County Harvest Fair for two of her sheep milk cheeses, Fat Bottom Girl and Shepherdista. Two of her Jersey cow cheeses also won recognition. Seana began her enterprise using milk from another farmer's sheep, but she now has her own flock.

Redwood Hill Farm & Creamery, Sebastopol, CA 95472; (707) 823-8250; www.redwoodhill.com. The Bice family began the business in 1968, and they continue to oversee this exceptional goat dairy, the first to be certified humane in the United States, which earns them the right to add the "Certified Humane Raised and Handled" label to their products. The company's 300 goats supply the milk that makes it possible to create the award-winning cheese, yogurt, and kefir. The creamery is certified organic, and the free-range goats eat a diet of organic hay and vegetarian grain mix. Redwood Hill's line of cheese is varied and includes a raw-milk feta, cheddar and smoked cheddar, three-peppercorn chèvre, garlic chive chèvre, bucheret, camellia, and crottin. Goat cheese pairs well with wine, and it's usually easier on the digestive system than cheese made from cow's milk. Redwood Hill walked away with numerous awards at the Sonoma County Harvest Fair in 2011, including a gold for its cheddar. In spring, special tour weekends at the farm are held for visitors—check the website for more information. See Redwood Hill Farm's recipe for **Portobello Dumplings with Goat Cheese Sauce** on p. 271.

Valley Ford Cheese Co., Valley Ford, CA 94972; (707) 293-5636; www.valleyfordcheeseco.com. Cheesemaker Karen Bianchi-Moreda was born into a dairy family, so being around cows comes naturally. Her products include a raw cow's milk cheese called Estero Gold, and a fontina called Highway One. Karen won the Best of Show Dairy award at the Sonoma County Harvest Fair in 2011, and two of her cheeses won double-gold awards. The cheese can be found in numerous local grocery stores, at farmers' markets, and it's featured in some area restaurants, too. Call for an appointment if you wish to visit the farm.

Poultry & Eggs

Salmon Creek Ranch, 1400 Bay Hill Rd., Bodega, CA 94922; (707) 876-1808; www.salmoncreekranch.com. Did you know that duck eggs are richer and creamier than chicken eggs, and as such can make fluffier omelets and bouncier baked goods? On a 400-acre certified organic ranch between the small towns of Bodega and Bodega Bay, John and Lesley Brabyn raise Muscovy ducklings, a heritage breed known for having twice the breast meat and much less fat than the common Pekin variety. The ducks are raised humanely, fed only organic feed and allowed to forage freely in grassy pastures. The ranch supplies the duck meat and eggs to many restaurants, and also sells the products at local farmers' markets. The Brabyns also raise grass-fed beef and goats. To visit the farm, please call ahead.

Meats & Butchers

Victorian Farmstead, 1220 N. Gravenstein Hwy. (Hwy. 116), Sebastopol, CA 95472; (707) 332-4605; www.vicfarmmeats.com. Just north of the intersection of Gravenstein Highway and Mill Station Road you'll see the large white sign for this establishment. The beef they raise is grass-fed on area ranches, and they also market lamb and pork raised in Sonoma County and processed for meat out of the area, per USDA requirements. If you're seeking fresh chicken, try the Cornish Cross breed raised on the premises humanely, then processed on-site and sold at the farm. Stop by to see the grazing sheep, chickens, and turkeys—and buy a Christmas tree, too, if it's the season. Victorian Farmstead is also a holiday tree farm that's been in the same family for decades. The farm is open Mon, Thurs, and Fri from 3 to 6 p.m. and Sat and Sun from 1 to 6 p.m.

Williams Ranch Lamb, (707) 829-9316; www.williamsranches .com. Rex and Kerry Williams raise approximately 300 head of sheep, many of which end up as delicious lamb served in restaurants. Some wool products are produced, too. The Williamses sell their products at the **Farmers' Market at Veterans Hall** (p. 139), or call them directly to order fresh lamb.

Oysters & Fresh Fish

Hog Island Oyster Company, 20215 Hwy. 1, Marshall, CA 94940; (415) 663-9218; www.hogislandoysters.com. Indulge me while I include this fresh oyster farm in a listing of Sonoma County businesses, when in actuality it's located in the Tomales Bay region of Marin County. (We locals like to the blur the county lines as we go westward toward the Pacific Ocean.) Hog Island has been in business almost 30 years, and raises more than 3 million oysters annually (the Pacific, Atlantic, and Kumamoto species), along with Manila clams and mussels. Once "seeded," the oysters take quite a long time to grow to maturity, from 18 months to 3 years on average. You can buy fresh oysters from the source to take home in a cooler, as well as order a dozen on the half-shell at the oyster bar—made from an old boat—with its ever-changing menu. Hog Island has restaurants in Napa and in the Ferry Building in San Francisco, and many Sonoma County restaurants feature Hog Island seafood on their menus. The farm is open daily from 9 a.m. to 5 p.m.; the oyster bar is open Fri through Sun from 11 a.m. to 4:30 p.m.

The Tides Wharf Market, 835 Hwy. 1, Bodega Bay, CA 94923; (707) 875-3554; www.innatthetides.com. Bodega Bay is one of the busiest commercial fishing port on the coast of California north of San Francisco, and both commercial and recreational boats haul in millions of pounds of Dungeness crab every year. On a recent after-noon, hundreds of colorful crab pots were stacked in readiness on the piers and in the parking lot of the Tides Wharf for the opening day of the crab season. The market inside the complex is your best source for the crustaceans in Bodega Bay, along with shrimp, mussels, oysters, smoked salmon and herring, and clam chowder, too. Read more about **The Tides Wharf Market** in the Specialty Stores & Markets category (p. 236).

Honey Producers

Beekind Honey & Supply, 921 S. Gravenstein Hwy. (Hwy. 116), Sebastopol, CA 95472; (707) 824-2905; www.beekind.com. Beekind isn't only about the honey—the business also sells beekeeping supplies for anyone who wants to try their hand at the craft (more like a lifestyle), along with classes for beginners. About 20 varieties of their own honey can be tasted at the store, which is open year-round Mon through Sat from 10 a.m. to 6 p.m. and Sun 10 a.m. to 4 p.m. Take a self-guided tour and pick up some pure beeswax candles, too. Beekind has a second store in San Francisco's Ferry Building, an internationally renowned foodie destination.

Bloomfield Bees Honey, 1295 Bloomfield Rd., Sebastopol, CA 95467; (707) 490-5001 or (707) 836-7278; www.bloomfieldbees honey.com. The owners of this honey farm started small with six hives and now tend to bees in 20 locations in Sonoma and Marin counties. They sell their raw honey and honey-based health and beauty products at local farmers' markets and also at the farm. Stop by daily from 10 a.m. to 5 p.m. year-round.

Community Supported Agriculture Programs (CSAs)

Bloomfield Farms Organics, Sebastopol, CA 95472; (707) 876-3261; www.bloomfieldfarmsorganics.com. From June until approximately Thanksgiving, the vegetables grown on this farm are available in a weekly box that costs $15 to $35,

depending on your needs. The selection varies, but will usually include lettuces, beets, cucumbers, tomatoes, and broccoli—all organically farmed. Flowers are extra, and might be long-lasting sunflowers, zinnias, gladiolas, or sweet peas.

First Light Farm, 1751 Bollinger Ln., Sebastopol, CA 95472; (707) 480-5346; www.firstlightfarm.com. Organic farmer Nathan Boone's CSA boxes contain, on average, 9 to 12 different vegetables and herbs each week. Nathan grows more than 100 varieties of produce each season on the farm, so there's usually plenty of variety. He also partners with nearby farmers to keep the selections interesting. Nathan's price for a box in 2011 was $24, to feed a family of four, or two vegetarians. Convenient pick-up sites are in Sebastopol, Santa Rosa, and Sonoma.

Laguna Farm, 1764 Cooper Rd., Sebastopol, CA 95472; (707) 823-0823; www.lagunafarm.com. Laguna Farm has been operating a CSA for at least 15 years, long before it became fashionable. Their produce is also widely known from their years of participating at farmers' markets and supplying fresh produce to area restaurants. Vegetables, fruits, and many add-ons are available, with prices starting at $18 weekly.

New Family Farm, 669 Ferguson Rd., Sebastopol, CA 95472; (707) 478-5802. This may be the only CSA that lets you choose exactly what you want in your box, because you load the box yourself. The farmers harvest the produce, and you visit the farm and pick out as many potatoes or carrots or beets for your box as you wish. (Read more about this farm under the Farms & Farm Stands category.)

Orchard Farms, 10951 Barnett Valley Rd., Sebastopol, CA 95472; (707) 823-6528; www.orchard-farms.com. Ken Orchard's farm outside Sebastopol is certified organic, so all of the produce in his weekly CSA boxes is farmed in that manner. The variety ranges from the old reliables such as carrots and green beans to more unusual options: bok choy, *tah tsai,* and red mustard. Ken's 2011 prices for a box for two people ranged from $72 to $80 per month, depending on the drop-off location.

Food & Wine Pairings/ Landmark Wineries

Claypool Cellars, 6761 Sebastopol Ave., Sebastopol, CA 95472; (707) 861-9358; www.claypoolcellars.com. Calling its retail shop the "Purple Pachyderm Pinot Noir tasting room" (and isn't that a mouthful?) inside a "fancy booze caboose," Claypool is all about having fun. So all you snooty wine sniffers and spitters who love the sound of your own voice can stay away from this tasting room. Les Claypool is the bass player in a world-famous rock band called Primus, whose music has been described as "thrash-funk meets Don Knotts." (It's curious, too, that some of the band's CD titles have food references: *Frizzle Fry, Sailing the Seas of Cheese, Pork Soda.*)

Les is what is known in the music biz as a slapper and a tapper on the bass guitar (those are good things). In the wine biz, he's known for making an excellent Pinot Noir, from grapes grown in the Russian River Valley. He markets these wines under the Purple Pachyderm and Pink Platypus labels. Look for Claypool Cellars in a restored caboose inside the Gravenstein Station shopping complex. It's a tight fit in the cozy rail car, with several small-scale trains from the Claypool family collection on display to add atmosphere. Visiting hours can be limited—11 a.m. to 2 p.m., roughly—or just call ahead and see if someone will be there to pour for you. On weekends it might even be Les himself.

Dutton Estate Winery, 8757 Green Valley Rd., Sebastopol, CA 95472; (707) 829-9463; www.sebastopolvineyards.com. You'll see the Dutton name on street signs and other landmarks if you spend much time driving around Sonoma County. The Dutton family has been growing wine grapes for decades, and now they bottle their own delicious Pinot Noir, Chardonnay, and Syrah varietals. Joe Dutton's parents, Warren and Gail, bought their first farmland near Graton in 1964 and built it into a grape and apple empire. In 1995 Joe and his wife Tracy founded this winery, and today Joe also oversees the Dutton family's 1,100 acres of wine grapes in the Green Valley appellation, along with 250 acres of certified organic apples (read more about Dutton Ranch on p. 243). The Green Valley appellation is one of the coolest and foggiest in the county, perfect for growing Pinot Noir and Chardonnay grapes. Open daily from 10 a.m. to 5 p.m.

Iron Horse Vineyards, 9786 Ross Station Rd., Sebastopol, CA 95472; (707) 887-1507; www.ironhorsevineyards.com. Accessed on a rural lane that gets increasingly narrower as you climb ever higher, you're suddenly rewarded with a great view—all the better for sipping the sparkling wines Iron Horse is famous for. It produces Brut, Brut Rosé, and several Cuvées (blends), such as Blanc de Noirs, some of which have been served at special dinners at the White House since 1985. The winery also bottles still wines (Chardonnay and Pinot Noir) from grapes grown in the Green Valley appellation, a small American viticultural area (AVA) bordered roughly by the towns of Forestville, Occidental, and Graton. Regardless of the White House connection, Iron Horse's tasting room is fairly rustic and oriented toward the view outside—no fancy chandeliers or tapestries, no pretense. In summer, Iron Horse hosts private "after-hours" food-and-wine tastings, with three generous food courses paired with five of the wines ($55 per person, reservations required). The menu is changeable with the available ingredients from nearby farms, but might include grilled asparagus, wild mushroom ragout, beef Wellington bites, and dark chocolate. Open daily from 10 a.m. to 4:30 p.m.

Korbel Champagne Cellars, 13250 River Rd., Guerneville, CA 95446; (707) 824-7316; www.korbel.com. It's one of the most touristy attractions in Sonoma County, yet stopping at Korbel is still a must for first-time visitors. The sparkling wine is widely distributed—everyone has had a glass at some point, I'm sure, even if they didn't know it (wedding toasts, etc.). There is much to do at Korbel before you even enter the tasting room, from admiring the lovely flower gardens to taking a free guided tour that describes the colorful history of the place, founded in 1886 by three Czech brothers named Korbel. Once inside where the tasting takes place, you'll be delighted to learn that it's complimentary. After sipping the various bubblies and Chardonnay, pop into the deli and market for a bite to eat, or to gather up some picnic supplies. The deli won two double-gold awards in 2011 from the Sonoma County Harvest Fair for these two sandwiches: Fork in the Road pastrami, and the barbecued pulled pork on focaccia. Try to visit Korbel on a weekday when it tends to be less crowded. Open daily from 10 a.m. to 5 p.m.

Lynmar Estate Winery, 3909 Frei Rd., Sebastopol, CA 95472; (707) 829-3374; www.lynmarwinery.com. Lynmar was founded by businessman Lynn Fritz in 1980, where he produced small amounts of Pinot Noir and Chardonnay. Many years later the beautiful hospitality center and 11,000 square feet of caves were added. The gravity flow winemaking process ensures the juice from the grapes is treated gently on its way to the aging barrels and the caves. Food is an important component of Lynmar Estate's business. A cheese plate with crackers and crostini is offered daily for $20 (reservations recommended), and during summer months a more elaborate picnic-and-wine experience can be purchased. The cuisine might be truffled popcorn, a fresh salad made from greens picked that morning in the winery's vegetable garden, and a choice of sandwiches. The meal is paired with Lymnar's Russian River Valley Chardonnay and Pinot Noir. Another popular attraction at Lynmar (available in summer) is the Pizza & Pinot tasting on Saturday afternoon. For $55 per person, enjoy pizza baked over French oak barrel staves and topped with veggies from the gardens, matched with the winery's finest Pinots. An "international" series of food-and-wine pairings also takes place at Lynmar in summer, when participants can learn from the winery's chef how to match Chardonnay and Pinot Noir to the cuisine of Greece, Morocco, or the Caribbean ($35 per person). Reservations are required for all of these special tastings. Open daily from 11 a.m. to 4 p.m. (to 5 p.m. on weekends).

Merry Edwards Winery, 2959 Gravenstein Hwy., Sebastopol, CA 95476; (707) 823-7466; www.merryedwards.com. Merry Edwards has been a winemaker for 40 years, having launched her foray into fermentation after reading a book on home winemaking. This winery is a testament to her exceptional career as a producer of award-winning Pinot Noir and Sauvignon Blanc. The building was completed in 2008 and is surrounded by rolling vineyards. Open daily from 9:30 a.m. to 4:30 p.m.

Brewpubs & Microbreweries

Hopmonk Tavern, 230 Petaluma Ave., Sebastopol, CA 95472; (707) 829-7300; www.hopmonk.com. Housed in a historic stone building near the intersection with Highway 12, Hopmonk opened several years ago in what was once the "powerhouse" that supplied the electric power for a rail line that ran from Petaluma to Sebastopol and Forestville. The building received Historical Landmark designation in 1990 and is also on the National Register of Historic Places. Beermakers Dan Gordon and Dean Biersch founded the Gordon Biersch Brewery Restaurant Group many years ago before selling their interest in the company and going their separate ways. Dean then put his energy into creating craft beers such as Hopmonk Kellerbier (an unfiltered pilsner), Hopmonk Tavern Ale (a smooth, hoppy brew), and Hopmonk Dunkelweizen (a Bavarian-style drink with hints of chocolate and cloves). The Abbey, where live music takes place, features shows nearly every night. The menu at Hopmonk is almost identical to the options at the company's Sonoma location: burgers, mac and cheese, fish-and-chips, cider braised salmon, and hot beer sausage with mustard mashed potatoes. Open daily for lunch and dinner.

Stumptown Brewery, 15045 River Rd., Guerneville, CA 95446; (707) 869-0705; www.stumptown.com. It's called "stumptown" because that was Guerneville's nickname at one time, when the clear-cutting of giant redwood trees oh-so-many years ago left unfortunate stumps out in the forest (they didn't know any better then). The brewery doesn't knock your socks off as you gaze at it from the street, east of Guerneville proper, but out back is a pleasant patio for sipping suds and digging into a basket of wings as you watch the river drifting by. Stumptown doesn't aspire to clever marketing lingo either (its motto: "because beer is good"), and serves its own beers alongside a few other regional brews. Stumptown's own Rat Bastard Pale Ale, with a hoppy bite, was a blue-ribbon winner at the California State Fair. The malty Boot Legger India Pale Ale was brought to market in 2003 in time for the 70th anniversary of the repeal of Prohibition. The Bushwacker Wheat beer has a subtle essence of orange peel and coriander, a refreshing drink on a hot day. The bar bites can tend toward seafood: gumbo, shrimp, ceviche, crab cakes, and others. Menu options include the Stumptown burger, a couple of chicken sandwiches, hummus, a wedge salad or Caesar salad, and a half-rack of barbecued ribs. Open "most days" from 11 a.m. to midnight (to 2 a.m. on weekends); the kitchen is closed Tues.

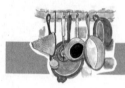

Learn to Cook

VIVA, 7160 Keating Ave., Sebastopol, CA 95472; (707) 824-9913; www.saiprograms.com/viva. VIVA is the northern California outpost for Study Abroad Italy (SAI), an organization that for almost two decades has been giving American students outstanding opportunities to study in the major cities of Italy, including culinary education in Florence. As such, SAI has a pool of experts and chefs to call upon, and their cooking classes in Sebastopol might be either demonstration-style or hands-on instruction. Classes include one for the serious apprentice butcher called "The Whole Hog" ($250 per person). The 4-hour class is kept small and includes approximately 35 pounds of meat to take away for your own use. Goat butchering is also a possibility ($90), as you learn to break down the entire animal, followed by a barbecue and glass of wine for each participant (the freshly butchered goat meat may also be purchased afterward). Vegetarians might appreciate a class that uses various types of squash for each course of a meal: soup, salad, entree, and dessert ($90 per person). Most VIVA classes are limited to 15 students maximum and typically last about 3 hours. Bring your own apron, if it's a favorite or "lucky" garment, or VIVA can supply one for you. Upon completion of a class, you receive the recipes and any pertinent notes gathered about what you just learned. Products offered by VIVA are also available at a 10 percent discount for students.

Recipes

In Sonoma County you can always find fresh ingredients to prepare a great meal. Picked in a nearby garden, pulled from the ocean, or sourced from special purveyors, the basic building blocks for countless delectable dishes are all available here almost any time of the year. The following recipes from Sonoma-based chefs demonstarte how they use the best the region has to offer.

Honey Blackberry Flan

Created by Sheana Davis of The Epicurean Connection, this dessert makes use of fresh blackberries for an elegant end to a meal, perhaps accompanied by a glass of amber ale.

Serves 6

¾ cup fresh honey

6 whole eggs

3 egg yolks

4 cups whipping cream

⅛ teaspoon salt

1 cup fresh blackberries

Preheat oven to 350°F. Prepare six 6- to 8-ounce ramekins by pouring 1 teaspoon of honey into each. Place the ramekins in a 2-inch deep baking pan and add ¼ inch of water to the pan.

In a large bowl, whisk together the whole eggs, yolks, and ½ cup honey. Over low flame in a heavy-bottom pan, heat the cream and salt to 160 degrees, then gently ladle and whisk it into the egg mixture. Pour the mixture into the ramekins and place the baking pan in the oven. Bake for 45 minutes or until custard is set.

Remove the pan from the oven and place on a cooling rack. Arrange blackberries on top of each ramekin while warm, gently pressing into the flan. Allow to rest and cool for 2 to 4 hours until firm. To serve, gently cut around the edges of each flan using a paring knife, and invert onto a serving plate. The flan can also be served in the individual ramekins.

Courtesy of Sheana Davis of The Epicurean Connection (p. 59).

Blue Cheese Stuffed Figs Wrapped in Prosciutto

Want to impress your friends? This is a simple appetizer that looks and tastes great. It's delicious served with a superior Chardonnay wine, such as B.R. Cohn's Sonoma County Chardonnay.

Serves 4

12 Black Mission figs
¼ pound blue cheese, such as Gorgonzola, Oregon Blue, Roquefort, Stilton, or other
4 to 6 slices prosciutto

1 to 2 tablespoons white cane sugar
2 to 4 tablespoons B.R. Cohn Fig Balsamic Vinegar

Preheat oven to 400°F. Cut a slit in each fig, being careful not to cut all the way through it. Stuff each fig with approximately ½ teaspoon blue cheese. Slice each piece of prosciutto in half lengthwise, then slice each strip in half, creating strips long enough to wrap around the cheese-stuffed figs. Place on a large baking sheet, sprinkle with sugar, and bake in the preheated oven for approximately 8 minutes, or until the figs are soft and glistening. Place on a serving platter and drizzle each fig with B.R. Cohn Fig Balsamic Vinegar.

Courtesy of B.R. Cohn Winery & Olive Oil Co. (p. 68).

Zazu Chicken, Cherry, Chocolate, and Chile Tostada

Chefs Duskie Estes and John Stewart came up with this tostada recipe for a barrel-tasting event a few years ago, when wine tasters were given delectable bites to eat as they traveled from one winery to the next. It was such a hit that everyone wanted to know how to make it for themselves.

Serves 4–6

To cook the chicken:

6 chicken legs
Kosher salt to taste
2 carrots, roughly chopped
2 ribs celery, roughly chopped
1 onion, roughly chopped
4 cloves garlic, whole and
  peeled

1 cup of your favorite red wine
2 cups chicken stock
1 cup freshly squeezed orange
  juice
2 cinnamon sticks
1 dried ancho chile

For the tostada filling:

2 dried ancho chiles, seeds and
  stems removed
¼ cup dried sour cherries
1 medium onion, peeled and
  diced
2 tablespoons peanut oil
½ bunch cilantro, chopped

¼ teaspoon ground cinnamon
1 tablespoon grated Mexican
  chocolate, or substitute
  grated bittersweet chocolate
  with a pinch of cinnamon
Kosher salt to taste
Tortilla chips or tortillas

Preheat the oven to 350°F. Season the chicken with the salt. In a large ovenproof pan on medium-high heat, sear the chicken until browned, about 10 minutes. Remove from the pan. In the same pan, sear the carrots, celery, onion, and garlic until browned, about 10 minutes. Deglaze the pan with the wine.

Return the chicken to the pan and cover with the stock and orange juice. Add the cinnamon sticks and ancho chile and cover with foil.

Braise in the oven until the chicken begins to pull back from the bone, about 1½ hours. Remove the chicken from the stock and set aside some of the braising liquid. When cool enough to handle, remove the skin from the chicken and pick the meat from the bones.

While the chicken is cooking, prepare the rest of the filling. In two small bowls, separately place the ancho chiles and the sour cherries. Cover each with boiling water. When the chiles are soft (after about 5 minutes), puree them in a blender with a little bit of the water. Strain the puree through a sieve. When the cherries are plumped and soft (after about 10 minutes), strain them from the water.

In a small sauté pan on medium-high heat, sauté the onion in the peanut oil until translucent, about 3 minutes. In a medium mixing bowl, combine the picked chicken, ancho puree, plumped cherries, sautéed onion, cilantro, cinnamon, and Mexican chocolate. Season to taste with salt. Add some of the braising liquid to moisten.

Serve on tortilla chips or tortillas, and garnish with sour cream, if desired.

Courtesy of Chefs Duskie Estes and John Stewart of Zazu Restaurant + Farm
and Bovolo Restaurant, and the Black Pig Meat Co. (pp. 113, 168, and 188).

Pan-Roasted Chicken with Fig Glaze, Olives & Capers

Carrie Brown, owner of the Jimtown Store, bottles numerous gourmet spreads that can turn a simple chicken into an event. The Jimtown Fig & Olive Spread is perfect for roasted chicken—sweet and salty. This recipe is ideal for a family meal or to make special when company's coming.

Serves 4–6

- 6 tablespoons of Jimtown Fig & Olive Spread
- 6 tablespoons white wine
- 1 ½ tablespoons balsamic vinegar
- 1 ½ tablespoons olive oil
- 1 ½ teaspoons juice from a jar of capers
- ¾ teaspoon herbes de Provence, crumbled, or 2 tablespoons

- mixed fresh oregano and thyme, chopped
- 8 chicken quarters (light meat, dark meat, or assorted), about 3 pounds
- ½ cup drained whole small pitted green olives
- 10 whole garlic cloves, peeled
- 2 tablespoons drained capers
- Freshly ground pepper to taste

Position rack in the middle of the oven and preheat to 350°F. In a medium bowl, stir together the Jimtown Fig & Olive Spread, wine, vinegar, olive oil, caper juice, and herbes de Provence. Arrange chicken quarters in a shallow baking dish just large enough to hold them. Pour the olive spread mixture over the chicken. Scatter the green olives, garlic, and capers over the chicken. Season generously with pepper.

Bake, basting the chicken with the pan juices as they accumulate, until the chicken is just cooked through while remaining juicy, about 50 minutes. Serve hot, warm, or cold.

Courtesy of Carrie Brown of the Jimtown Store (p. 182).

Zuppa de Pesce (Seafood Stew)

Chef Renzo Veronese shops the local farmers' markets to source the freshest ingredients possible for all the cuisine he creates as chef for Hop Kiln Winery. Serve this stew with a good Chardonnay, such as HKG Russian River Valley Estate 2009 Chardonnay.

Serves 4

3 large garlic cloves, minced

2½ cups chopped onions

⅓ cup vegetable oil

1 pound boiling potatoes

3 carrots, cut into ¼-inch slices

1 (28- to-32-ounce) can whole tomatoes, chopped, including juice

1 cup water

2 cups dry white wine

1 large green bell pepper, cut into matchsticks

½ pound clams, fresh Manila

1 pound mussels (preferably cultivated), scrubbed well and beards pulled off

1½ pounds monkfish, cut into 1-inch pieces

½ pound medium shrimp (about 12), shelled and deveined

1 tablespoon fresh tarragon leaves, chopped fine, or 1 teaspoon dried tarragon, crumbled

Salt and pepper to taste

In a 4-quart kettle cook garlic and onions in oil over moderately low heat, stirring, until softened. Peel potatoes and cut into ½-inch cubes. To onion mixture add potatoes, carrots, tomatoes and their juice, water, and wine. Bring mixture to a boil and simmer 40 minutes, or until the carrots and potatoes are tender. Add bell pepper, clams, and mussels and simmer, covered, for 2 minutes or until clams and mussels begin to open. Add monkfish, shrimp, tarragon, and salt and pepper to taste and simmer, covered, for 5 minutes or until fish is cooked through. Discard any unopened clams or mussels. Accompany with garlic toasts, if desired.

Courtesy of Chef Renzo Veronese of Hop Kiln Winery (p. 194).

Portobello Dumplings
with Goat Cheese Sauce

Redwood Hill Farm & Creamery is the first certified humane goat dairy in the United States, owned by the Bice family since 1968. The goat cheeses it produces, which can be ordered online if you can't find them where you live, are consistent award winners and can be used in many recipes. This delicious appetizer calls for the soft and creamy chèvre—ideal for blending into sauces.

Serves 6–8

Ingredients for dumplings:

3 tablespoons balsamic vinegar

¼ cup extra-virgin olive oil

1 tablespoon minced garlic

Salt and pepper to taste

¼ teaspoon crushed red pepper flakes, or to taste

3 large portobello mushroom caps

3 ounces Redwood Hill Farm chèvre (soft, creamy goat cheese) or other high-quality chèvre

5 scallions (green onions), sliced thin

24 wonton skins

1 tablespoon butter

To prepare the dumplings:

Mix together the vinegar, oil, garlic, salt, pepper, and crushed red pepper. Remove stems from the mushrooms and marinate in the oil mixture for about 30 minutes.

Grill the mushrooms over coals or on a grill pan for about 4 minutes on each side. Dice the mushrooms and mix with the cheese and onions.

Place a heaping teaspoon of the mushroom mixture in the center of each wonton skin and wet the edges of the skin with water. Fold each wonton skin into a triangle and wet the tip of the long end to seal together, forming a dumpling.

Steam the dumplings for 5 minutes, then sauté one side of the dumplings in butter to brown.

Goat cheese sauce ingredients:

1 finely chopped shallot
2 teaspoons butter
1 cup white wine

1 cup cream
3 ounces Redwood Hill Farm chèvre (soft, creamy goat cheese)

To prepare the sauce:

Sauté the shallot in butter until just limp. Turn down the heat, add the wine and reduce until thick and syrupy. Add the cream and reduce the mixture slightly. Add the cheese and stir until smooth. Serve immediately with the dumplings.

Courtesy of Redwood Hill Farm & Creamery (p. 247).

Disappearing Chicken

Best prepared on a Weber-style grill using the indirect cooking method, this recipe also works with other poultry—simply adjust cooking times. It can also be prepared in a hot oven. The owners of DaVero named it "disappearing" because there's never any left. It's easy, quick, and delicious.

Serves 2–4

- 1 medium (4 pound) chicken
- Coarse kosher salt
- Fresh ground pepper
- 1 head garlic, coarsely chopped
- ½ medium yellow onion, quartered

- 2 3-inch sprigs of fresh rosemary
- DaVero Meyer Lemon olive oil for drizzling

Start the grill, or preheat the oven to 450°F. Wash and dry the chicken inside and out.

Mix a fistful of salt together with about a tablespoon of pepper and sprinkle about a third of the mixture inside the cavity. Stuff the garlic, onion, and rosemary into the cavity. Rub the skin with a tablespoon or two of olive oil, then rub the remaining salt and pepper mixture into the skin. (Note: You can also add some freshly chopped rosemary into the rub mixture for more flavor.)

If grilling, place the chicken breast down in a V-shaped wire roasting rack and place it in the middle of the grill. Close the cover, leaving the vents open.

After 45 minutes, turn the rack upside down to "dump" the bird onto the grill, so it now faces breast up. After 30 minutes more, or when the drumsticks wiggle easily and the juices run clear, remove the bird from the grill and let it rest for 15 minutes.

If using an oven, set the rack in a roasting pan. Roast the chicken breast down at 450°F for 15 minutes, then reduce heat to 375°F. After 20 to 30 minutes, invert the bird so it is breast up, then roast an additional 10 to 15 minutes, or until done. Allow the bird to rest about 10 minutes before slicing.

Separate the legs and wings, cut the breast meat into quarters, and drizzle olive oil over all the pieces.

Courtesy of Colleen McGlynn of DaVero (p. 188).

Cocoa Cherry Almond Tart with Almond Crumb Crust

Elaine Bell was raised in the Sonoma Valley and trained for her career in food at the Culinary Institute of America. She started her catering company in 1981 (Elaine Bell Catering, 707-603-1400, www.elainebellcatering.com) and has been creating unforgettable wine-and-food pairing events ever since.

Serves 8

For the filling:

- 4 cups dark sweet cherries, pitted, fresh or frozen (thawed)
- ½ cup orange juice
- 1 tablespoon orange rind, chopped
- 1 cup sugar
- ½ teaspoon salt
- 1 tablespoon almond extract
- 1 teaspoon cinnamon
- ½ cup Valrhona brand dark cocoa, or other dark cocoa

Combine the cherries, orange juice, orange rind, sugar, and salt in a heavy saucepan. Bring to a boil and simmer for 5 minutes. Stir in the almond extract, cinnamon, and cocoa. Set aside. The cocoa will thicken the filling.

For the crust:

- 1½ cups all-purpose flour
- ⅓ cup sugar
- 1 teaspoon orange rind, grated
- ¼ teaspoon salt
- ½ cup butter, unsalted
- 1 egg yolk, large
- Butter for parchment paper

Combine the flour, sugar, orange rind, and salt in a food processor, then pulse together for a few seconds. Add the butter and process until it looks like coarse crumbs. Add the egg yolk and process until the dough comes together, about 40 seconds. Wrap and chill for 30 minutes.

Roll the dough out to ⅛-inch thickness. Pat the dough into a 10-inch tart pan, making sure to bring it all the way up the sides. Butter a piece of parchment paper large enough to fit over the bottom of the dough and up the sides, and place the buttered side against the dough. Fill the tart pan with dry beans (chickpeas work well), to prevent the crust from bubbling or puffing as it bakes. Bake for 15 minutes at 375°F. Remove the beans and check the crust for doneness—it should be nearly done but not completely baked. (Save the beans—they can be used again for the same purpose.)

For the almond crumb crust topping:

⅔ cup flour
½ cup almond meal
½ cup brown sugar
½ tablespoon almond extract
1 teaspoon cinnamon

½ teaspoon salt
7 tablespoons butter, unsalted
1 cup almonds, sliced and toasted

Combine the flour, almond meal, brown sugar, almond extract, cinnamon, and salt in a food processor. Process until combined. Add the butter and pulse on and off until it looks like crumbs. Stir in the almonds.

To assemble the tart, spoon the cherry mixture into the tart pan just to the top of the crust. Cover the top with the crumb topping, making sure to spread out to the sides and just thick enough to hide the cherry mixture. Bake for 15 to 20 minutes, until the topping is golden brown.

Courtesy of Elaine Bell Catering.

Apple Prune Cake

Gail Dutton of the Dutton family, wine-grape growers and apple farmers in west Sonoma County since the 1880s, has been baking apple cakes and pies for a long time, using fruit from the ranch's trees that are more than 80 years old. She developed this recipe to combine the flavors of Gravenstein apples and prunes (dried plums), another tree crop that Gail and her husband, Warren Dutton Jr., planted in the mid-1960s. For this recipe, Gail says it's important to cut the apples into chunky cubes, because, "Gravensteins cook down—they're a soft apple." The result is a super moist cake, and no leftovers.

Serves 8

2 large eggs
4 cups peeled, cored, and cubed (2-inch by 2-inch) Gravenstein apples
1 cup brown sugar, lightly packed
1 cup granulated sugar
½ cup vegetable oil

1 teaspoon ground cinnamon
½ cup walnut pieces
½ cup dried and pitted prunes, cut in half
½ teaspoon vanilla extract
2 cups flour
2 teaspoons baking soda
½ teaspoon salt

Preheat oven to 375°F. Grease and flour a 9 x 13-inch cake pan.

Place the eggs in a mixing bowl and beat with a fork. Add the cubed apples and mix well with a large spoon. Add the sugars and the oil and blend well until the apple cubes are coated. Add the cinnamon, walnuts, prunes, and vanilla and blend with a large spoon.

Sift together the flour, baking soda, and salt. Add it to the apple-prune mixture, sifting it over the fruit in batches and blending after each addition. Spoon the batter into the prepared baking pan.

Bake in the middle of the preheated oven for approximately 55 minutes, or until the cake springs back when pressed and a toothpick inserted into the "cakey" part comes out clean.

Courtesy of Gail Dutton of Dutton Ranch (p. 243).

Lisa Hemenway's Crab Cakes

This recipe makes the same phenomenal crab cakes found on the menu at Fresh, Lisa's restaurant and market, and they are also available by the pound in the market's to-go section. Use Dungeness crab, if possible.

Serves 6

For the crab cakes:

- ¼ cup butter, unsalted
- 1 cup minced celery
- ½ cup minced onion
- 1 cup panko bread crumbs (or a gluten-free version)
- 1 teaspoon dry mustard
- 2 cups crabmeat (Dungeness preferred), with excess water squeezed out
- ¼ cup heavy cream
- 2 eggs, blended
- 2 tablespoons chopped parsley
- 2 tablespoons vegetable oil or clarified butter

Melt unsalted butter in a large skillet and sauté the celery and onion over medium heat for about 5 minutes. Remove from heat, add the bread crumbs and the dry mustard into the skillet, and mix well. Stir in the crab, cream, eggs, and the parsley and blend well, being careful not to break up the crab too much.

Form the crab mixture into cakes by using a ¼-cup measuring cup. Tap each cake out of the measuring cup and onto a sheet pan, then chill. When ready to serve, fry the cakes in vegetable oil or clarified butter over medium heat for about 3 to 5 minutes on each side until golden brown, turning the cakes gently. Remove the cakes from the skillet and drain briefly on paper towels. Makes 12 cakes (2 cakes per serving). Serve the cakes on top of the warm salsa cruda (recipe follows).

Salsa Cruda

¼ cup yellow pepper, cored and seeded, then cut into ¼-inch dice

¼ cup red pepper, cored and seeded, then cut into ¼-inch dice

2 plum or Roma tomatoes, seeded and chopped to ¼-inch dice

1 tablespoon capers, or to taste

¼ cup hearts of palm, cut lengthwise or quartered and chopped into ¼-inch pieces

1 teaspoon chopped garlic

2 tablespoons red onion, finely diced

¼ cup zucchini, diced into ¼-inch pieces

1 teaspoon lemon juice

1 teaspoon lime juice

4–6 tablespoons olive oil

Salt and pepper to taste

Blend all ingredients in a mixing bowl and chill for 2 hours to let the flavors marinate. When ready to serve the crab cakes, gently warm the salsa mixture in a saucepan on low heat, then spoon onto individual plates or a single platter. Add the cooked crab cakes on top and serve immediately.

Courtesy of Lisa Hemenway of Fresh (p. 117).

Appendices

Appendix A: Index of Foodie Faves & Landmark Eateries

Appendix B:
Index of Purveyors

Honey Producers

Index